D0068363

NEW
TESTAMENT
WORDS

by

WILLIAM BARCLAY

WESTMINSTER JOHN KNOX PRESS
LOUISVILLE, KENTUCKY

© SCM Press Ltd. 1964

Index © The Westminster Press 1974

Published by Westminster John Knox Press
Louisville, Kentucky

PRINTED IN THE UNITED STATES OF AMERICA

10 12 14 15 13 11 9

Library of Congress Cataloging in Publication Data

Barclay, William, lecturer in the University of
  Glasgow.
  New Testament words.

  Bibliography: p.
  1. Greek language, Biblical—Dictionaries—
English. I. Title.
PA881.B29   487′.4   73-12737
ISBN 0-664-24761-X pbk.

NEW TESTAMENT WORDS

Silence is indeed the friend and help-meet of thought and invention; but, if one aims at readiness of speech and beauty of discourse, he will get at them by no other discipline than the study of words, and their constant practice.

GREGORY THAUMATURGUS
The Panegyric on Origen I

Introduction

"What benefit can we reap from this generous gift if we have not the meaning of the words explained to us."
— Gregory of Nyssa, *Sermons on the Beatitudes*

This quotation was from the original introduction of my father's *A New Testament Workbook,* and went on to say, "William Barclay does what a good teacher ought to do, he illuminates."

I have vivid memories of my father illuminating the meaning of the Greek words in his sermons in Scottish churches thirty years ago. He loved to stress the point that Jesus is described as *tektōn*—a master carpenter. I can still see him, arms outstretched in the pulpit, explaining *hamartia,* one of the Greek words for "sin." "The archer draws his bow, the arrow flies to the target, and the cry goes up '*hamartia*'—'a near miss,'" and the meaning of sin was immediately illuminated for every member of his audience.

The wonder of this book is that it communicates with beginner and expert alike. My father was a wonderful teacher and communicator with people at all stages of their learning, and this book is a perfect example of his skill. Again, the first introduction stated truly: "Perhaps those who talk about the problems of communication can learn something from William Barclay, that to communicate anything, it is necessary to know it and to know equally the people to whom we wish to communicate it."

Ronnie Barclay
Glasgow, Scotland

CONTENTS

ABBREVIATIONS

NT NEW TESTAMENT
OT OLD TESTAMENT
AV AUTHORIZED VERSION
RSV REVISED STANDARD VERSION

PREFACE

IT would be true to say that this book began almost accidentally. Words are always fascinating things. I was asked a few years ago by a parish minister if I would write three short articles on three great NT words for his congregational magazine, and I did so. At that time another series of articles which I was writing for the *British Weekly* was coming to an end, and I had to think of something with which to follow it. I suggested to Mr Shaun Herron, the editor of that weekly, that I might experiment with a series of word articles in his columns. He agreed, and that series of articles has been running ever since. I wish to say that I am deeply grateful to him, first, for allowing me space in the *British Weekly* for these word articles, and second, for giving me permission to republish them in this form. Had it not been for his continual encouragement that series would never have begun and this book would never have been written.

As the series went on it became clear that there were many people who wished to possess the articles in more permanent form. At first I was surprised at this, for these articles might be defined as an attempt to popularize the Greek dictionary, and to teach Greek to people who do not know any Greek. But it seems to me that this interest was simply one facet of the quite extraordinary interest in the Bible which exists today and which is becoming ever stronger. I do not think that there ever was a time when people were more interested in what the Bible has to say and in what the Bible means.

Therein lies the justification for a book like this. Translation from one language into another is in one sense impossible. It is always possible to translate words with accuracy when they refer to *things*. A chair is a chair in any language. But it is a different matter when it is a question of *ideas*. In that case some words need, not another to translate them, but a phrase, or a sentence, or even a paragraph. Further, words have associations. They have associations with people, with history, with ideas, with other words, and these associations give words a certain flavour which cannot be rendered in translation, but which affects their meaning and significance in the most important way. This book is an attempt to take certain great NT words and to find out what these words meant to the writers of the NT and to those who read and heard their message for the first time. To do that means seeking to trace the meaning of these words in classical Greek, in the Septuagint, when they occur there, in Hellenistic Greek and in the papyri.

Since these terms are constantly used in these word studies, it will be well to explain them at the beginning. It may be said that the classical Greek comes to an end in 300 B.C. From then until A.D. 300 may be taken as the age of Hellenistic Greek. During that age Greek became the language of the world. The conquests of Alexander the Great took the Greek language everywhere. A situation arose in which people, in their private and domestic life, spoke their own native tongue, but in business and commercial and public life they spoke Greek. The extent to which this was true can be seen that in those days many people had two names. It might be that one was the name in their own tongue, and the other was a translation of that name into Greek. So *Cephas* is the Hebrew for a 'rock', and *Peter* is the Greek for the same word. *Thomas* is the Hebrew for a 'twin', and *Didymus* is the Greek for the same word. It might be that the Greek name was taken because it was like the native name in sound. So a Jew called *Eliakim* or *Abel* became in Greek society Alcimus or or Apelles. Now this Greek which spread all over the world was not classical Greek. It was a kind of simplified Greek with the irregularities and the dialectic peculiarities and the subtle nuances of Greek moods and tenses ironed out. It was called the *Koinē*, which is short for *hē koinē dialektos*, the common tongue. It would be wrong to think of it as a debased form of Greek; it is still a beautiful, flexible language, but it is a form of Greek simplified to meet the needs of a world and not of a country or nation.

The Septuagint is the Greek version of the OT. The translation was begun in Alexandria about 275 B.C. By that time the Jews of the Dispersion were far more familiar with Greek than they were with the original Hebrew. The Septuagint is of the greatest importance because it was the Bible of the Christian Church before the NT came to be written. Very often when the NT writers quote the OT it is the Septuagint which they use, and not the original Hebrew. The language of the Septuagint therefore became entwined in Christian thought.

Of all sources the papyri throw the most vivid light on the language of the NT. Papyrus was a writing material made from the pith of a bulrush which grew on the banks of the Nile. It was made by cutting the pith into strips and pressing the strips together. So long as it does not become damp it lasts practically for ever. It was the universal writing material of NT times. In Egypt writings on papyrus were thrown on the rubbish heaps; the desert sands drifted over them and buried them; and they can still be dug up and deciphered today. The papyri contain things like census and tax returns, marriage and trade contracts, schoolboys' exercises, petitions to the government, and, above all, private letters. In the papyri we see the Greek language as the ordinary, non-literary person of NT times spoke it. We see how words were used, and what significance they had, not in careful literary prose, but in everyday speech.

He who writes about words is obviously dependent on the labours of others, and the following is a list of the books which I have constantly used.

LEXICONS AND CONCORDANCES

H. G. Liddell and R. Scott, *A Greek-English Lexicon*, revised and augmented by Sir H. S. Jones.

Gerhard Kittel, *Theologisches Wörterbuch zum Neuen Testament*.

Erwin Preuschen, *Handwörterbuch zum Griechischen Neuen Testament*.

J. H. Moulton and G. Milligan, *The Vocabulary of the Greek Testament*, illustrated from the papyri and other non-literary sources.

W. F. Moulton and A. S. Geden, *A Concordance to the Greek Testament*.

J. H. Thayer, *A Greek-English Lexicon of the New Testament*, being Grimm's Wilke's *Clavis Novi Testamenti*, translated and enlarged by J. H. Thayer.

G. Abbott-Smith, *Manual Greek Lexicon of the New Testament*.

Hesychius, *Hesychii Alexandrini Lexicon*, ed. M. Schmidt.

Suidas, *Suidae Lexicon*, ed. I. Bekker.

E. A. Sophocles, *Greek Lexicon of the Roman and Byzantine Periods*.

E. J. Goodspeed, *Index Patristicus*.

E. Hatch and H. A. Redpath, *A Concordance to the Septuagint*.

W. F. Arndt and G. W. Gingrich, *Griechisch-deutsches Wörterbuch zu den Schriften des Neuen Testaments u. der übrigen urchristlichen Literatur* (Preuschen-Bauer, fourth edition 1949-52): English trans.: *A Greek-English Lexicon of the New Testament and other Early Christian Literature* (Cambridge University Press, 1957). This volume is completely indispensable to the student of the language of the New Testament. It has, of course, always been available in German, but this beautifully produced English translation now makes it available to many who otherwise could not have used it.

GENERAL WORKS

M. David and B. A. von Groningen, *Papyrological Primer*.

A. Deissmann, *Light from the Ancient East*, E.T. by
L. R. M. Strachan.

Bible Studies, E.T. by A. Grieve.

F. Field, *Notes on the Translation of the New Testament*.

E. Hatch, *Essays in Biblical Greek*.

H. A. A. Kennedy, *Sources of New Testament Greek*.

A. S. Hunt and G. C. Edgar, *Select Papyri*, two volumes,
Loeb Classical Library.

H. G. Meecham, *Light from Ancient Letters*.

G. Milligan, *Here and There among the Papyri*.

Selections from the Greek Papyri.

J. H. Moulton, *From Egyptian Rubbish Heaps*.

E. K. Simpson, *Words worth weighing in the Greek New
Testament*.

R. C. Trench, *Synonyms of the New Testament*.

J. G. Winter, *Life and Letters in the Papyri*.

S. Witkowski, *Epistulae privatae Graecae quae in papyris
aetatis Lagidarum servantur*.

I should like to think of this book as an attempt to make
the results of linguistic scholarship available for the
ordinary reader of the NT. It is my hope and my prayer
that it may do something to make the NT more meaningful for at least some than it was before.

WILLIAM BARCLAY

Trinity College
Glasgow

Note on the transliteration and
pronunciation of Greek words

For the most part Greek letters are commonly pronounced as in English. But there are certain things which
ought to be noted.

(i) Greek has four letters which represent more than a single letter in English. These four letters are *phi*, *psi*, *chi* and *theta*; they are transliterated respectively, *ph*, *ps*, *ch* and *th*.

(ii) Two of the Greek vowels have a double sound. *Omicron* and *omega* both represent the English letter *o*. But *omicron* represents a short *o* as in the word *hot*, and *omega* represents a long *o* as in the word *go*. In this book *o* represents *omicron*, and *ō* represents *omega*. Similarly *epsilon* represents a short *e* as in the word *get*, and *eta* represents a long *e*, which is pronounced as the *a* in *hate*, or as the *ee* in *feet*. In this book *e* represents *epsilon* and *ē* represents *eta*.

(iii) When two *g*'s come together in Greek they are pronounced *ng*. So *aggelos* (*messenger or angel*) is pronounced *angelos*.

AGAPĒ AND AGAPAN

GREEK is one of the richest of all languages and it has an unrivalled power to express shades of meaning. It therefore often happens that Greek has a whole series of words to express different shades of meaning in one conception, while English has only one. In English we have only one word to express all kinds of *love*; Greek has no fewer than four. *Agapē* means *love*, and *agapan* is the verb which means to *love*. Love is the greatest of all the virtues, the characteristic virtue of the Christian faith. We shall therefore do well to seek to discover its meaning. We shall best begin by comparing these words with the other Greek words for love, so that we can discover their distinctive character and flavour. We begin, then, by looking at the other Greek words for love.

1. The noun *erōs* and the verb *eran* are mainly used for love between the sexes. They can be used for such things as the passion of ambition and the intensity of patriotism; but characteristically they are the words for physical love. Gregory Nazianzen defined *erōs* as 'the hot and unendurable desire'. Xenophon in the *Cyropædia* (5.1.11) has a passage which exactly shows the meaning of *erōs* and *eran*. Araspas and Cyrus are discussing the different kinds of love and Araspas says: 'A brother does not fall in love with his sister, but somebody else falls in love with her; neither does a father fall in love with his daughter, but somebody else does, for fear of God and the law of the land are sufficient to prevent such love' (*erōs*). The predominant connexion of these two words is with sexual love. In the English language the word *lover* can bear a lower sense; and in Greek the meaning of these two words had degenerated so that they stood for lower things. Christianity

could hardly have annexed these words for its own uses; and they do not appear in the NT at all.

2. The noun *storgē* and the verb *stergein* have specially to do with *family affection*. They can be used for the love of a people for their ruler, or for the love of a nation or household for their tutelary god; but their regular use is to describe the love of parents for children and children for parents. Plato writes: 'A child loves (*stergein*) and is loved by those who begat him' (*Laws* 754b). A kindred word occurs very often in wills. A legacy is left to a member of the family *kata philostorgian*, i.e. 'because of the *affection* that I have for you'. These words do not occur in the NT but a kindred adjective does once. The adjective *philostorgos* occurs in Paul's great ethical chapter, in Rom. 12.10, where the AV translates it *kindly-affectioned*. That is suggestive, because it implies that the Christian community is not a *society*, but a *family*.

3. The commonest words for *love* in Greek are the noun *philia* and the verb *philein*. There is a lovely warmth about these words. They mean to look on someone with affectionate regard. They can be used for the love of friendship and for the love of husband and of wife. *Philein* is best translated to *cherish*: it includes physical love, but it includes much else beside. It can sometimes even mean *to kiss*. These words have in them all the warmth of real affection and real love. In the NT *philein* is used of the love of father and mother and son and daughter (Matt. 10.37). It is used of the love of Jesus for Lazarus (John 11.3, 36); and once it is used of the love of Jesus for the beloved disciple (John 20.2). *Philia* and *philein* are beautiful words to express a beautiful relationship.

4. By far the commonest NT words for *love* are the noun *agapē* and the verb *agapan*. We shall deal, first, with the noun. *Agapē* is not a classical word at all; it is doubtful if there is any classical instance of it. In the Septuagint it is used 14 times of sexual love (e.g. Jer. 2.2.) and twice (e.g. Eccles. 9.1) it is used as the opposite of *misos*, which means

hatred. Agapē has not yet become a great word but there are hints of what is to come. The Book of Wisdom uses it for the love of God (Wisdom 3.9) and for the love of wisdom (Wisdom 6.18). The Letter of Aristeas in talking of beauty says (229) that piety is closely connected with beauty, for 'it is the pre-eminent form of beauty, and its power lies in *love (agapē)* which is the gift of God'. Philo uses *agapē* once in its nobler sense. He says that *phobos* (fear) and *agapē* (love) are kindred feelings and that both are characteristic of man's feeling towards God. But we can only find scattered and rare occurrences of this word *agapē*, which is to become the very key word of NT ethics. Now we turn to the verb *agapan*. It occurs oftener in classical Greek than the noun, but it is not very common. It can mean *to greet affectionately*. It can describe the love of money or of precious stones. It can be used for *being content* with some thing or some situation. It is even used once (Plutarch, *Pericles*, 1) to describe a society lady caressing a pet lap-dog. But, the great difference between *philein* and *agapan* in classical Greek is that *agapan* has none of the warmth that characterizes *philein*. There are two good instances of this. Dio Cassius reports Antony's famous speech about Cæsar, and he says (44.48). 'You loved (*philein*) him as a father, and you held him in regard (*agapan*) as a benefactor.' *Philein* describes the warm love for a father; *agapan* describes the affectionate gratitude for a benefactor. In the *Memorabilia* Xenophon describes how Aristarchus took a problem to Socrates. Owing to war conditions he has fourteen female relatives, displaced persons, billeted on him. They have nothing to do and, not unnaturally, there is trouble. Socrates advises him to set them to work, gentlefolk or not. Aristarchus does and the situation is solved. 'There were happy instead of gloomy faces; they loved (*philein*) him as a protector; he regarded them with affection (*agapan*) because they were useful'. (Xenophon, *Memorabilia* 2.7.12). Once again there is a warmth in *philein* which is not in *agapan*.

It would not be true to say that the NT never uses anything else but *agapē* and *agapan* to express the Christian love. Some few times *philein* is used. *Philein* is used for the Father's love for the Son (John 5.20); of God's love for men (John 16.27); of the devotion that men ought to bear to Jesus (I Cor. 16.22); but the occurrences of *philein* in the NT are comparatively few, while *agapē* occurs almost 120 times and *agapan* more than 130 times. Before we go on to examine their use in detail, there are certain things about these words and their meaning we must note. We must ask why Christian language abandoned the other Greek words for love and concentrated on these.

It is true to say that all the other words had acquired certain flavours which made them unsuitable. *Erōs* had quite definite associations with the lower side of love; it had much more to do with passion than with love. *Storgē* was very definitely tied up with family affection; it never had in it the width that the conception of Christian love demands.

Philia was a lovely word, but it was definitely a word of warmth and closeness and affection; it could only properly be used of the near and the dear, and Christianity needed a much more inclusive word than that. Christian thought fastened on this word *agapē* because it was the only word capable of being filled with the content which was required.

The great reason why Christian thought fastened on *agapē* is that *agapē* demands the exercise of the whole man. Christian love must not only extend to our nearest and our dearest, our kith and kin, our friends and those who love us; Christian love must extend to the Christian fellowship, to the neighbour, to the enemy, to all the world.

Now, all the ordinary words for love are words which express an emotion. They are words which have to do with the heart. They express an experience which comes to us unsought, and, in a way, inevitably. We cannot help loving our kith and kin; blood is thicker than water. We speak about *falling in love*. That kind of love is not an achievement; it is something which happens to us and which we cannot help. There is no particular virtue in falling in love. It is something with which we have little or nothing consciously to do; it simply happens. But *agapē* is far more than that.

Agapē has to do with the *mind*: it is not simply an emotion which rises unbidden in our hearts; it is a principle by which we deliberately live. *Agapē* has supremely to do with the *will*. It is a conquest, a victory, and achievement. No one ever naturally loved his enemies. To love one's enemies is a conquest of all our natural inclinations and emotions.

This *agapē*, this Christian love, is not merely an emotional experience which comes to us unbidden and unsought; it is a deliberate principle of the mind, and a deliberate conquest and achievement of the will. It is in fact the power to love the unlovable, to love people whom we do not like. Christianity does not ask us to love our enemies and to love men at large in the same way as we love our nearest and our dearest and those who are closest to us; that would be at one and the same time impossible and wrong. But it does demand that we should have at all times a certain attitude of the mind and a certain direction of the will towards all men, no matter who they are.

What then is the meaning of this *agapē*? The supreme passage for the interpretation of the meaning of *agapē* is Matt. 5.43-48. We are there bidden to love our enemies. Why? *In order that we should be like God.* And what is the typical action of God that is cited? God sends his rain on the just and the unjust and on the evil and the good. That is to say—*no matter what a man is like, God seeks nothing but his highest good.*

Let a man be a saint or let a man be a sinner, God's only desire is for that man's highest good. Now, that is what *agapē* is. *Agapē* is the spirit which says: 'No matter what any man does to me, I will never seek to do harm to him; I will never set out for revenge; I will always seek nothing but his highest good.' That is to say, Christian love, *agapē*, is *unconquerable benevolence, invincible good will.* It is not simply a wave of emotion; it is a deliberate conviction of the mind issuing in a deliberate policy of the life; it is a deliberate achievement and conquest and victory of the will. It takes all of a man to achieve Christian love; it takes not only his heart; it takes his mind and his will as well.

If that is so, two things are to be noted.

(i) Human *agapē*, our love towards our fellow men, is bound to be *a product of the Spirit*. The NT is quite clear about that (Gal. 5.22; Rom. 15.30; Col. 1.8). Christian *agapē* is unnatural in the sense that it is not possible for the natural man. A man can only exercise this universal benevolence, he can only be cleansed from human hatred and human bitterness and the natural human reaction to enmity and injury and dislike, when the Spirit takes possession of him and sheds abroad the love of God in his heart.

Christian *agapē* is impossible for anyone except a Christian man. No man can perform the Christian ethic until he becomes a Christian. He may see quite clearly the desirability of the Christian ethic; he may see that it is the solution to the world's problems; mentally he may accept it; practically he cannot live it, until Christ lives in him.

(ii) When we understand what *agapē* means, it amply meets the objection that a society based in this love would be a paradise for criminals, and that it means simply letting the evil-doer have his own way. If we seek nothing but a man's highest good, we may well have to resist a man; we may well have to punish him; we may well have to do the hardest things to him—for the good of his immortal soul.

But the fact remains that whatever we do to that man will never be purely vindictive; it will never even be merely retributory; it will always be done in that forgiving love which seeks, not the man's punishment, and still less the man's annihilation, but always his highest good. In other words, *agapē* means treating men as God treats them —and that does not mean allowing them unchecked to do as they like.

When we study the NT we find that love is the basis of every perfect relationship in heaven and in earth.

(i) Love is the basis of the relationship between the Father and the Son, between God and Jesus. Jesus can speak of 'the love wherewith thou hast loved me' (John 17.26). He is God's 'dear Son' (Col. 1.13; cf. John 3.35; 10.17; 15.9; 17.23, 24).

(ii) Love is the basis of the relationship between the Son and the Father. The purpose of Jesus' whole life was that 'the world may know that he loves the Father' (John 14.31).

(iii) Love is God's attitude to men (John 3.16; Rom. 8.37; Rom. 5.8; Eph. 2.4; II Cor. 13.14; I John 3.1, 16; I John 4.9, 10). Sometimes Christianity is presented in such a way that it looks as if it was the work of a gentle and a loving Jesus to pacify a stern and an angry God, as if Jesus did something which changed the attitude of God to men. The NT knows nothing of that. The whole process of salvation began because God so loved the world.

(iv) It is man's duty to love God (Matt. 22.37; cp. Mark 12.30 and Luke 10.27; Rom. 8.28; I Cor. 2.9; II Tim. 4.8; I John 4.19). Christianity does not think of a man finally submitting to the power of God; it thinks of him as finally surrendering to the love of God. It is not that man's will is crushed, but that man's heart is broken.

(v) The motive power of Jesus' life was love for men (Gal. 2.20; Eph. 5.2; II Thess. 2.16; Rev. 1.5; John 15.9). Jesus is indeed the lover of the souls of men.

(vi) The essence of the Christian faith is love of Jesus (Eph. 6.24; I Peter 1.8; John 21.15, 16). Just as Jesus is the lover of the souls of men, the Christian is the lover of Christ.

(vii) The mark of the Christian life is the love of Christians for one another (John 13.34; 15.12, 17; I Peter 1.22; I John 3.11, 23; I John 4.7). Christians are people who love Jesus and who love each other.

The basis of every conceivable right relationship in heaven and earth is love. It is on love that all relationships, both human and divine, are founded.

The NT has much to tell us about God's love for men.

(i) Love is the very nature of God. God is love (I John 4.7, 8; II Cor. 13.11).

(ii) God's love is a *universal* love. It was not only a chosen nation, it was the world that God so loved (John 3.16).

(iii) God's love is a *sacrificial* love. The proof of his love is the giving of his Son for men (I John 4.9, 10; John 3.16). The guarantee of Jesus' love is that he loved us and gave himself for us (Gal. 2.20; Eph. 5.2; Rev. 1.5).

(iv) God's love is an *undeserved* love. It was while we were sinners and enemies that God loved us and Jesus died for us (Rom. 5.8; I John 3.1; 4.9, 10).

(v) God's love is a *merciful* love (Eph. 2.4). It is not dictatorial, not domineeringly possessive; it is the yearning love of the merciful heart.

(vi) God's love is a *saving* and a *sanctifying* love (II Thess. 2.13). It rescues from the situation of the past and enables men to meet the situations of the future.

(vii) God's love is a *strengthening* love. In it and through it a man becomes more than a conquerer (Rom. 8.37). It is not the softening and over-protective love which makes a man weak and flabby; it is the love which makes heroes.

(viii) God's love is an *inseparable* love (Rom. 8.39). In the nature of things human love must come to an end, at least for a time, but God's love outlasts all the chances and the changes and the threats of life.

(ix) God's love is a *rewarding* love (James 1.12; 2.5). In this life it is a precious thing, and its promises are still greater for the life to come.

(x) God's love is a *chastening* love (Heb. 12.6). God's love is the love which knows that discipline is an essential part of love.

The NT has much to say about what man's love for God must be.

(i) It must be an *exclusive* love (Matt. 6.24; cp. Luke 16.13). There is only room for one loyalty in the Christian life.

(ii) It is a love which is *founded on gratitude* (Luke 7.42, 47). The gifts of God's love demand in return the whole love of our hearts.

(iii) It is an *obedient* love. Repeatedly the NT lays it down that the only way we can prove that we love God is by giving him our unquestioning obedience (John 14.15, 21, 23, 24; 13.35; 15.10; I John 2.5; 5.2, 3; II John 6). Obedience is the final proof of love.

(iv) It is an *outgoing* love. The fact that we love God is proved by the fact that we love and help our fellow men (I John 4.12, 20; 3.14; 2.10). Failure to help men proves that our love of God is unreal and untrue (I John 3.17).

Obedience to God and loving help to men are the two things which prove our love.

We now turn to the other side of the picture—man's love for man.

(i) Love must be the very atmosphere of the Christian life (I Cor. 16.14; Col. 1.4; I Thess. 1.3; 3.6; II Thess. 1.3; Eph. 5.2; Rev. 2.19). Love is the badge of the Christian society. A church where there is bitterness and strife may call itself a church of men, but it has no right to call itself a church of Christ. It has destroyed the atmosphere of the Christian life and is bound to be suffocated; it has lost the badge of the Christian life and is no longer recognizable as a church.

(ii) Love is that by which the Church is built up (Eph. 4.16). It is the cement which holds the Church together; the climate in which the Church can grow; the food which nourishes the Church.

(iii) The motive power of the Christian leader must be love (II Cor. 11.11; 12.15; 2.4; I Tim. 4.12; II Tim. 3.10; II John 1; III John 1). There ought to be no place in the Church for the man who takes office in the Church for the sake of prestige and prominence and power. The motive of the Christian leader must be solely to love and serve God and his fellow-men.

(iv) At the same time the attitude of the Christian to his leaders must be that of love (I Thess. 5.13). Too often that attitude is an attitude of criticism and discontent and even resentment. The bond of the Christian army is the bond of love between those of all ranks within it.

Christian love expands in ever widening circles.

(i) The Christian love begins in the *family* (Eph. 5.25, 28, 33). It is a fact not to be forgotten that a Christian family is one of the finest witnesses in the world to Christianity. Christian love begins at home. The man who has failed to make his own family a centre of Christian love has little right to exercise authority in the wider family of the Church.

(ii) The Christian love goes out to the *brotherhood* (I Peter 2.17). It was the astonished cry of the heathen in the early days, 'See how these Christians love one another.' One of the severest handicaps of the modern Church is that to the outsider it must often appear to be a company of people squabbling bitterly about nothing. A church completely enveloped in the peace of mutual love is a rare phenomenon. Such a church would not be a church where everyone thought the same and agreed on everything; it would be a church in which men could differ and still love each other.

(iii) The Christian love goes out to our *neighbours* (Matt. 19.19; 22.39; cp. Mark 12.31 and Luke 10.27; Rom. 13.9; Gal. 5.14; James 2.8). And the definition of our neighbour is simply that our neighbour is anyone who happens to be in need. As the Roman poet said: 'I regard no human being as a stranger.' It is the simple fact that more people have been brought into the Church by the kindness of real Christian love than by all the theological arguments in the world; and more people have been driven from the Church by the hardness and the ugliness of so-called Christianity than by all the doubts in the world.

(iv) The Christian love goes out to our *enemies* (Luke 6.27; cp. Matt. 5.44). We have seen that Christian love means unconquerable benevolence and invincible goodwill. No matter what any man does to him, the Christian will never cease to seek that man's highest good. No matter how he is insulted, injured, wronged and slandered, the Christian will never hate and will never let bitterness into his heart. When Lincoln was accused of treating his opponents with too much courtesy and kindness, and when it was pointed out to him that his whole duty was to destroy them, he answered: 'Do I not destroy my enemies when I make them my friends?' The Christian's only method of destroying his enemies is to love them into being his friends.

We must now look at the characteristics of this Christian love.

(i) Love is *sincere* (Rom. 12.9; II Cor. 6.6; 8.8; I Peter 1.22). It has no ulterior motive; it is not cupboard love. It is not a surface pleasantness, which cloaks an inner bitterness. It is the love which loves with open eyes and with open heart.

(ii) Love is *innocent* (Rom. 13.10). The Christian love never injured any man. So-called love can injure in two ways. It can lead into sin. Burns said of the man whom he met when he was learning flax-dressing in Irvine: 'His friendship did me a mischief.' Or it can be over-possessive and over-protective. Mother love can become smother love.

(iii) Love is *generous* (II Cor. 8.24). There are two kinds of love—the love which demands and the love which gives. The Christian love is the giving love, because it is a copy of the love of Jesus (John 13.34), and has its mainspring in the giving love of God (I John 4.11).

(iv) Love is *practical* (Heb. 6.10; I John 3.18). It is not merely a kindly feeling, and it does not limit itself to pious good wishes; it is love which issues in action.

(v) Love is *forbearing* (Eph. 4.2). The Christian love is the love which is proof against the things which so easily turn love to hate.

(vi) Love issues in *forgiveness and restoration* (II Cor. 2.8). Christian love is able to forgive, and, in forgiving, it enables the wrong-doer to return to the right way.

(vii) Love is not *sentimental* (II Cor. 2.4). Christian love does not shut its eyes to the faults of others. Love is not blind. It will use rebuke and discipline when these are needed. The love which shuts its eyes to all faults, and which evades the unpleasantness of all discipline, is not real love at all, for in the end it does nothing but harm to the loved one.

(viii) Love *controls liberty* (Gal. 5.13; Rom. 14.15). It is perfectly true that a Christian man has the right to do anything which is not sin. But there are certain things in which a Christian may see no harm, but which may offend other Christians. There are certain things which may do one man no harm, but which may be the ruination of another man. The Christian never forgets his Christian liberty, but he also never forgets that Christian liberty is controlled by Christian love, and by Christian responsibility for others.

(ix) Love *controls truth* (Eph. 4.15). The Christian loves truth (II Thess. 2.10), but he never cruelly or unsympathetically speaks the truth in order to hurt. It was said of Florence Allshorn, the great teacher, that, when she had occasion to rebuke any of her students, she always did it as if with her arm around the person who had to be rebuked. The Christian is never false to the truth, but he always remembers that love and truth must go hand in hand.

(x) Love is *the bond which holds the Christian fellow-*

ship together (Phil. 2.2; Col. 2.2). Paul speaks of Christians being knit together in love. Our theological views may differ; our views on methods may differ. But across the differences there should come the constant memory that we love Christ, and that therefore we love each other.

(xi) Love is *that which gives the Christian the right to ask a help or favour from another Christian* (Philemon 9). If we were really bound together in love as we ought to be, we would find it easy to ask and natural to give when need arose.

(xii) Love is *the motive power of faith* (Gal. 5.6). More people are won for Christ by the appeal to the heart than to the head. Faith is born, not so much from intellectual search, as from the uplifting of the Cross of Christ. It is true that sooner or later we must think things out for ourselves; but in Christianity the heart must feel before the mind can think.

(xiii) Love is *the perfecting of the Christian life* (Rom. 13.10; Col. 3.14; I Tim. 1.5; 6.11; I John 4.12). There is nothing higher in this world than to love. The great task of any church is not primarily to perfect its buildings or its liturgy or its music or its vestments. Its great task is to perfect its love.

Finally, the NT lays it down that there are certain ways in which love can be misdirected.

(i) *Love of the world* is misdirected love (I John 2.15). It was because Demas loved the world that he forsook Paul (II Tim. 4.10). A man can so love time that he forgets eternity. A man can so love the world's prizes that he forgets the ultimate prizes. A man can so love the world that he accepts the world's standards and abandons the standards of Christ.

(ii) *Love of personal prestige* is misdirected love. The scribes and Pharisees loved the chief seats in the synagogues and the praises of men (Luke 11.43; John 12.43). A man's question must always be, not: How does this look to men? but, How does this look to God?

(iii) *Love of the dark* and fear of the light is the inevitable consequence of sin (John 3.19). As soon as a man sins, he has something to hide; and then he loves the dark. But the dark may conceal him from men; it cannot conceal him from God.

So at the end of things we see beyond a doubt that the Christian life is built on the twin pillars of love of God and love of man.

AGGAREUEIN

THE WORD OF AN OCCUPIED COUNTRY

THERE are some words which carry in their history the story of a nation's triumph or a nation's tragedy. *Aggareuein* is such a word. It is used three times in the NT, with the meaning to *compel*. It is the word used in Matt. 5.41 when Jesus speaks of going two miles when we are *compelled* to go one; and in Matt. 27.32 and Mark 15.21 it is the word that is used of Simon of Cyrene being *compelled* to carry the Cross of Jesus to Calvary.

In origin the word is Persian; it comes from the noun *aggaros*, which means a 'courier'; it became naturalized into Greek, just as the Italian word *estafette* has been to some extent naturalized into English with the same sense of a 'military courier' or an 'express messenger'. The Persians had a remarkably efficient courier system, like an express post. Herodotus has a description of it (Herodotus 8.98). 'Nothing travels so fast as these Persian messengers. The entire plan is a Persian invention; and this is the method of it. Along the whole line of road there are men (they say) stationed with horses, in number equal to the number of days which the journey takes, allowing a man and a horse to each day; and these men will not be hindered from accomplishing at their best speed the distance which they have to go, either by snow, or rain, or heat, or by the darkness of the night. The first rider delivers his despatch to the second, and the second passes it to the third; and so it is borne from hand to hand along the whole line, like the light in the torch race. . . . The Persians give the riding post in this manner the name *aggareion*.' Xenophon has an even more vivid description of it (*Cyropaedia* 8.6.17). He says that Cyrus had to find some way of finding out what was going on in his vast empire. He experimented and found out how far a horse and rider could go in one day without breaking down, and so arranged his stations. At each station there was a permanent official to see to the transference of the letters and to change the horses. Night and day this express service went on. 'It is undeniable,' says Xenophon, 'that this is the fastest overland travelling on earth.' Aeschylus in the *Agamemnon* tells how there came to Greece news of the capture of Troy. The chorus will hardly believe Clytaemnestra that word could have come so quickly. She tells how the news was transmitted by torch from Ida to Lemnos, from Athos to Olympus by what she calls 'the courier fire' (*aggarou puros*). Now it was the law that anyone could be compelled to provide a horse or to act as guide to keep this service going. And therefore *aggareuein* came to mean 'forcibly to impress some one to service', to compel him to serve whether he liked it or not. In an occupied country that was a grave and serious thing. Anyone could be impressed to carry the baggage of the army for a certain distance; anyone could be compelled to perform any service that the occupiers chose to lay upon him. That is what happened to Simon of Cyrene. This business of impressment was one of the bitterest and most constant humiliations that subject nations had to endure. Epictetus (4.1.79) is talking about how a man must submit to whatever the gods lay upon him. He may not even desire health, if the gods wish to take it away. 'You ought to possess your whole body as a paltry ass with a pack-saddle on, as long as may be, as long as it is allowed you. But if there should come an act of impressment (*aggareia*) and a soldier should lay hold on it, let it go. Do not resist or murmur. If you do, you will first be beaten and lose the ass after all.' A man had no appeal when this humiliation came upon him.

How humiliating this could be, and how this *aggareia* was abused can be seen in the regulations that governments had to make to curb the exercise of it. When Demetrius of Syria was wooing the Jews in the times of the Maccabaean Jonathan, Josephus says (*Antiquities*, 13.2.3) that he offered to abolish many taxes, such as the salt tax and the poll tax, and 'I also give order that the beasts of the Jews be not "impressed" (*aggareuein*) into our service'. From the papyri we learn that in Egypt boats for instance, and cattle and labour were regularly 'impressed'. Ptolemy Euergetēs the second and his queen decree that his governors and officials 'shall not impress any of the inhabitants of the country for private services, nor requisition (*aggareuein*) their cattle for any purpose of their own', and that 'No one shall requisition boats (*aggareuein*) for his own use on any pretext whatsoever'. In the Temple of the Great Oasis in Egypt there was an inscription, in which Capito, the prefect of Egypt, admitted that soldiers had made illegal requisition and laid it down that 'no one shall take or requisition (*aggareuein*) anything, unless he has a written authorization from me'. It is quite clear that the local and the military officials requisitioned both things and people, not only for the public services and for the army's purposes, but for their own private convenience and profit.

Now it is even clearer what Jesus is saying in the Sermon on the Mount (Matt. 5.41). He is saying: 'If someone exacts from you the most distasteful and humiliating service, if someone compels you to do something that invades your rights and that he has no right to ask, if you are treated like a defenceless victim in an occupied country, don't resent it. Do what you are asked and do even more, and do it with good will, for such is my way.' A generation which is for ever standing on its rights might well think of that.

AIŌNIOS

THE WORD OF ETERNITY

WE do well to search out the true meaning of the word *aiōnios*, for in the NT this is the word which is usually translated *eternal* or *everlasting*, and it is applied to the eternal life and the eternal glory, which are the Christian's highest reward, and to the eternal judgment and the eternal punishment, which must be the Christian's greatest dread.

Even in classical and in secular Greek *aiōnios* is a strange word, with a sense of mystery in it. Itself it is an adjective formed from the noun *aiōn*. In classical Greek this word *aiōn* has three main meanings.

(i) It means a *life-time*. Herodotus can speak of ending our *aiōn* (Herodotus, 1.32); Aeschylus, of depriving a man of his *aiōn* (Aeschylus, *Prometheus* 862); and Euripides of breathing away one's *aiōn* (Euripides, *fragment* 801).

(ii) Then it comes to mean an *age*, a *generation*, or an *epoch*. So the Greeks could speak of this present *aiōn*, and of the *aiōn* which is to come, this present age and the age which is to come.

(iii) But then the word comes to mean a *very long space of time*. The prepositional phrase *ap'aiōnos* means *from of old*; and *di'aiōnos* means *perpetually* and *for ever*. It is just here that the first mystery begins to enter in. In the papyri we read how at a public meeting the crowd shout 'The Emperor *eis ton aiōna*, The Emperor *for ever*.'

The adjective *aiōnios* becomes in Hellenistic Greek times the standing adjective to describe the Emperor's power.

The royal power of Rome is a power which is to last for ever. And so, as Milligan well puts it, the word *aiōnios* comes to describe 'a state wherein the horizon is not in view'. *Aiōnios* becomes the word of far distances, the word of eternities, the word which transcends time.

But it was Plato who took this word *aiōnios*—he may even have coined it—and gave it its special mysterious meaning. To put it briefly, for Plato *aiōnios* is the word of eternity in contrast with time. Plato uses it, as it has been said, 'to denote that which has neither beginning nor end, and that is subject to neither change nor decay, that which is above time, but of which time is a moving image'.

Plato does not mean by this word simply indefinite continuance—this is a point to which we must later return —but that which is above and beyond time. There are three significant instances of the word in Plato.

In the second book of the *Republic* (363d) Plato is talking of the poets' pictures of heaven. He talks of the rewards Musæus and Eumolpus offer the just men: 'They take them down into the world below, where they have the saints lying on couches at a feast, *everlastingly* drunk, with garlands on their heads; their idea seems to be that an immortality of drunkenness (*aiōnios methē*) is the highest meed of virtue.'

In *The Laws* he speaks of the soul and the body being indestructible, but not *eternal* (904a). There is a difference between simple existence for ever and eternity, for eternity is the possession of gods, not of men.

The most significant of all the Platonic passages is in the *Timæus* 37d. There he speaks about the Creator and the universe which he has created, 'the created glory of the *eternal gods*'—The Creator was glad when he saw his universe, and he wished to make it as nearly like the eternal universe as it could be. But 'to attach eternity to the created was impossible.' So he made time as a moving image of eternity.

The essential point in this picture is that eternity is always the same and always indivisible; in it there is no being created and no becoming; there is no such thing as being older and younger in eternity; there is no past, present or future.

There is no *was* or *will be* but only an eternal *is*. Obviously we cannot have that state in a created world; but none the less the created world is, within its limits, the image of eternity.

Here then is the salient fact. The essence of the word *aiōnios* is that it is the word of the eternal order as contrasted with the order of this world; it is the word of deity as contrasted with humanity; essentially it is the word which can be properly applied to no one other than God. *Aiōnios* is the word which describes nothing less and nothing other than the life of God.

We must now turn to the use of the word *aiōnios* in the NT itself. By far its most important usage there is in connexion with *eternal life*. But that usage is so important that we must retain it for separate treatment. And we must first take a sweeping view of all its usages.

As we do so we must remember that *aiōnios* is distinctively the word of eternity, and that it can properly describe only that which essentially belongs to and befits God.

It is used of the great blessings of the Christian life, blessings which have been brought by Jesus Christ.

It is used of the *eternal covenant* of which Christ is the mediator (Heb. 13.20). A covenant means a relationship with God, and through Jesus Christ men enter into a relationship with God which is as eternal as God himself.

It is used of the *eternal habitations* into which the Christian shall enter (Luke 16.9; II Cor. 5.1.). The ultimate destiny of the Christian is a life which is none other than the life of God himself.

It is used of the *eternal redemption* and the *eternal inheritance* into which the Christian enters through Jesus

Christ (Heb. 9.15). The safety, the liberty, the release which Christ wrought for men is as lasting as God himself.

It is used of the *glory* into which the faithful Christian will enter (I Peter 5.10; II Cor. 4.17; II Tim. 2.10). There awaits God's faithful man God's own glory.

So it is used in connexion with the words *hope* and *salvation* (Titus 3.7; II Tim. 2.10). There is nothing fleeting, impermanent, destructible about the Christian hope and salvation; even another world could not change or alter them; they are as unchangeable as God himself.

It is used of the *Kingdom of Jesus Christ* (II Peter 1.11). Jesus Christ is not surpassable; he is not a stage on the way; his revelation, his value is the revelation and the value of God himself.

It is used of the *Gospel* (Rev. 14.6). The Gospel is not merely one of many revelations; it is not merely a stage on the way of revelation; it is eternity entered into time.

But while *aiōnios* is used to describe the greatest blessings of the Christian life, it is also used to describe the greatest threats of the Christian life.

It is used to describe the *fire of punishment* (Matt. 18.8; 25.41; Jude 7). It is used to describe *punishment* itself (Matt. 25.46). It is used to describe *judgment* (Heb. 6.2). It is used to describe *destruction* (II Thess. 1.9). It is used to describe the sin which finally separates man from God (Mark 3.29).

It is in these passages that we need to be specially careful in our interpretation of the word. Simply to take is as meaning *lasting for ever* is not enough. In all these passages we must remember the essential meaning of *aiōnios*. *Aiōnios* is the word of eternity as opposed to and contrasted with time.

It is the word of deity as opposed to and contrasted with humanity. It is the word which can only really be applied to God. If we remember that, we are left with one tremendous truth—both the blessings which the faithful shall inherit and the punishment which the unfaithful shall receive are *such as befits God to give and to inflict*.

Beyond that we cannot go. Simply to take the word *aiōnios*, when it refers to blessings and punishment, to mean *lasting for ever* is to oversimplify, and indeed to misunderstand, the word altogether. It means far more than that.

It means that that which the faithful will receive and that which the unfaithful will suffer is that which it befits God's nature and character to bestow and to inflict —and beyond that we who are men cannot go, except to remember that that nature and character are holy love.

We must now turn to the greatest of all uses of the word *aiōnios* in the NT, its use in connexion with the phrase *eternal life*. We must begin by reminding ourselves of the fact which we have so often stressed, that the word *aiōnios* is the word of eternity in contrast with time, of deity in contrast with humanity, and that therefore *eternal life is nothing less than the life of God himself*.

(i) The promise of eternal life is the promise that it is open to the Christian to share nothing less than the power and the peace of God himself.

Eternal life is *the promise of God* (Titus 1.2; I John 2.25). God has promised us a share in his own blessedness, and God cannot break a promise.

(ii) But the NT goes further than that—eternal life is not only the promise of God; eternal life is *the gift of God* (Rom. 6.23; I John 5.11). As we shall see, eternal life is not without its conditions; but the fact remains that eternal life is something which God out of his mercy and grace gives to man. It is something which we could neither earn nor deserve; it is the free gift of God to men.

(iii) Eternal life is *bound up with Jesus Christ*. Christ is the living water which is the elixir of eternal life (John 4.14). He is the food which brings to men eternal life (John 6.27, 54). His words are the words of eternal life (John 6.68). He himself not only brings (John 17.2, 3) but *is* eternal life (I John 5.20).

If we wish to put this very simply, we may say that through Jesus there is possible a relationship, an intimacy, a unity with God which are possible in no other way. Through what he is and does men may enter into the very life of God himself.

(iv) This eternal life *comes through what the NT calls belief in Jesus Christ* (John 3.15, 16, 36; 5.24; 6.40, 47; I John 5.13; I Tim. 1.16). What does this *belief* mean? Clearly it is not simply intellectual belief. Belief in Jesus means that we believe absolutely and implicitly that what Jesus says about God is true.

If we really believe that God is Father and that God is love, that God cares enough for men to send his Son into the world to die for them, it literally makes all the difference in the world to life, for it means that life is in the hands of the love of God. But further, this belief means believing that Jesus is who he claims to be.

Obviously the reliance that we can place on any statement depends entirely on the position of the person who makes it. We are bound to ask: How can I believe for sure that what Jesus tells me about God is true? The answer is that we believe what Jesus tells us about God, because we believe that Jesus had a unique right to speak about God, because we believe that Jesus is the Son of God. Therefore we enter into eternal life by believing that Jesus is the Son of God.

But belief goes even further than that. We believe that God is Father and that God is love, because we believe that Jesus, being the Son of God, has told us the truth about God—*and then we act on the belief.* We live life in the certainty that we can do nothing other than render a perfect trust and a perfect obedience to God.

Eternal life is nothing else than the life of God himself. We enter into that life through believing in Jesus Christ. That belief involves three elements.

(i) It involves believing that God is the kind of God Jesus told men about.

(ii) It involves the certainty that Jesus is the Son of God, and therefore has the right to speak about God in a way that no one else ever could or ever will be able to speak.

(iii) It involves living all life on the assumption that these things are true. When we do that, we·share nothing less than the life of God, the power and the peace which God alone can give.

We have already said that eternal life is the gift of God; all God's gifts are freely given, but they are not given away. They are there for the taking, but they must be taken.

Let us use a human analogy. All the beauty and the wealth and the loveliness and the wisdom of classical literature are there for any man to take; but before he can enter into them, he must undergo the work, the study and the discipline which the learning of Latin and Greek demands.

God's offer of eternal life is there; but man must claim it and enter into it before he can receive it.

(i) Eternal life demands *knowledge of God*. Eternal life means 'to know the only true God' (John 17.3). Now man can only know God through three avenues. He must use his mind to think; he must use his eyes to see and his heart to love Jesus Christ; he must use his ears to listen to what God is seeking to say to him.

If we are to enter into life eternal we must never be too busy with the things of time to think about the eternal things, to walk looking unto Jesus, and to be regularly in a listening silence wherein we wait upon God.

(ii) Eternal life demands *obedience to God*. God's commandment is eternal life (John 12.50). Jesus is the author of eternal salvation to all that obey him (Heb. 5.9). Only in doing his will is our peace.

God's pleading is with the rebellious; but God's gifts are for the obedient. We can never enter into complete intimacy and unity with someone from whom we continually differ, and whom we continually grieve by our disobedience. Obedience to God and eternal life from God go hand in hand.

(iii) Eternal life is the reward of *strenuous loyalty* (I Tim. 6.12). It comes to the man who has fought the good fight of faith and who has clung to Christ through thick and thin. Eternal life comes to the man who *hears and follows* (John 10.27, 28).

No man who goes his own way can enter into eternal life; eternal life is for the man who in complete loyalty takes the way of Jesus Christ.

(iv) There is an *ethical demand in eternal life.* Eternal life is the goal of the way of holiness (Rom. 6.22). It comes to those who show patient continuance in well-doing (Rom. 2.7). It cannot come to the man who hates his brother, and who is therefore in his heart a murderer (I John 3.15). It comes to those who keep themselves in the love of God (Jude 21).

There is no escaping the ethical demand of Christianity. Eternal life is not for the man who does as he likes; it is for the man who does as Jesus Christ likes. It is not a case of demanding that we should be perfect; but it is a case of demanding that, however often we fall and fail, we should still fasten our eyes on Jesus Christ.

(v) Eternal life is the reward of *the labourer for Christ* (John 4.36). Eternal life is promised to the man who helps Jesus Christ to reap the harvest of the souls of men. Eternal life is God's offer to the man who is more concerned to save others than selfishly to save his own soul.

(vi) Eternal life is the reward of the *adventurer* of *Christ* (John 12.25). It is for the man who hates his life and who is prepared to throw it away for the sake of Jesus Christ. It is for the man who is ever ready 'to venture for thy name'. It is for the man who accepts the risks of the Christian life, and who is prepared 'to bet his life that there is a God'.

(vii) Eternal life is the result of that *righteousness which comes through the grace of Jesus Christ* (Rom. 5.21). The essential meaning of righteousness is a new relationship with God through that which Jesus Christ has done for us.

And so we end where we began—eternal life is the life of God himself, and into that life we, too, may enter when we accept what Jesus Christ has done for us, and what he tells us about God.

We shall never enter into the full ideas of eternal life until we rid ourselves of the almost instinctive assumption that eternal life means primarily life which goes on for ever. Long ago the Greeks saw that such a life would be by no means necessarily a blessing.

They told the story of Aurora, the goddess of dawn, who fell in love with Tithonus, the mortal youth. Zeus offered her any gift she might choose for her mortal lover. She asked that Tithonus might never die; but she forgot to ask that he might remain for ever young. So Tithonus lived for ever growing older and older and more and more decrepit, till life became a terrible and intolerable curse.

Life is only of value when it is nothing less than the life of God—and that is the meaning of eternal life.

AKOLOUTHEIN

THE DISCIPLE'S WORD

Akolouthein is the common and normal Greek verb which means *to follow*. It is a word with many uses and with many associations and all of them add something to its meaning for the follower of Christ. First, let us look at its usage and its meaning in classical Greek.

(i) It is the common and the usual word for *soldiers following their leader and commander*. Xenophon (*Anabasis* 7.5.3) speaks about the generals and captains who have *followed* the leader for whom they are fighting.

(ii) It is very commonly used of a slave *following* or *attending* his master. Theophrastus, in his character sketch of the Distrustful Man, says that such a man compels his slave to walk before him instead of following behind him, as a slave would normally do, so that he can be sure the slave will not dodge away (Theophrastus, *Characters* 18.8).

(iii) It is commonly used for *following* or *obeying* someone else's advice or opinion. Plato says that it is necessary to find out those who are fitted by nature to be leaders in philosophy and government, and those who are fitted by nature to be followers of the leader (Plato, *Republic* 474c). Some people are fitted to give leadership; others are only fitted to accept it.

(iv) It is commonly used of *obeying* the laws. To *follow* the laws of a city is to accept them as the standard of life and of behaviour.

(v) It is commonly used of *following the thread or argument of a discourse*. When the argument has got into a difficult position Socrates says: 'Come now, try to *follow* me, to see if we can get this matter adequately explained' (Plato, *Republic* 474c).

(vi) In the papyri *akolouthein* is very commonly used for *attaching oneself to someone* in order to extract some favour which is desired. One writes in advice to another: '*stick to* Ptollarion all the time. . . . *Stick to* him so that you may become his friend.' The idea is that of following a person until the favour desired is finally extracted from him.

Every one of these usages has light to throw on the Christian life.

The Christian is in the position of the soldier who follows Jesus Christ, and who must immediately obey his leader's command.

The Christian is in the position of the slave, who must obey as soon as his master speaks.

The Christian must ask for the advice and for the ruling

of Jesus Christ and must have the humility to follow it, whatever it may be.

The Christian is the man who desires citizenship of the Kingdom of Heaven, and, if he is to receive it, he must agree to live according to its laws.

The Christian is the learner and the listener who must listen to the words of Jesus, and who must follow their thread, so that day by day he may learn more of the wisdom which Jesus is ever wishing to teach him.

The Christian is always in the position of one who needs and desires the favour and the grace and the help which Jesus Christ can give to him, and who follows Christ because in Christ alone he finds his need supplied.

We now turn to the use of *akolouthein* in the NT itself It is very frequent there.

(i) It is used of the disciples who left their various trades and occupations and *followed* Jesus. So it is used of Peter and Andrew (Mark 1.18; cp. Matt. 4.20). It is used of the two disciples of John the Baptist who *followed* Jesus when John pointed at Jesus as the Lamb of God (John 1.37). It is used of the reaction of the disciples after the miraculous catch of fishes; they forsook all and *followed* Jesus (Luke 5.11). It is the claim of the disciples towards the end that they have left everything to *follow* Jesus (Matt. 19.27). It is used of the would-be disciples whom Jesus told to think again before they launched out on the adventure of following him (Matt. 8.19; cp. Luke 9.59, 61).

(ii) It is the word which Jesus used to summon men to himself. On Jesus' lips it is the word of challenge. His commandment to Matthew is: *Follow* me (Mark 2.14; cp. Luke 5.27; Matt. 9.9). It is Jesus' command to Philip (John 1.43). It is his final command to Peter (John 21.19, 22). It is his unaccepted command to the Rich Young Ruler (Matt. 19.21; cp. Luke 18.22). His command to all his would-be followers is that they should take up their cross and *follow* him (Mark 8.34; 10.21; Matt. 10.38; 16.24; Luke 9.23).

(iii) Most commonly of all this word is used of the crowds who *followed* Jesus (Matt. 4.25; 8.1; 12.15; 14.13; 19.2; 20.9; 21.9; Mark 3.7; 5.24; 11.9; John 6.2). This use is very closely connected with the usage of the verb in the papyri to describe the act of attaching oneself to someone until a request is granted. Sometimes the crowds followed Jesus to experience his healing power; sometimes they followed him to listen to his words; and sometimes, towards the end, they followed him in wondering admiration to see what was going to happen to him. Another instance of this use of *akolouthein* in the sense of following to receive a favour is Matt. 9.27, when the two blind men are said to follow Jesus in order that he might heal them.

(iv) Sometimes the following is the result of gratitude. In Matt. 20.34 the two blind men are said to *follow* Jesus after they had received their sight; the same is said of the blind man in Luke 18.43; and of Bartimæus in Mark 10.52. They followed because they were drawn with the cords of gratitude for what Jesus had done.

(v) In Mark 2.15 it is said that the sinners *followed* Jesus. That is a most significant usage. There was that about Jesus which they knew would meet their need; they would have avoided a Pharisee, but Jesus they followed, because they knew that he knew and understood their case.

We can distinguish in these uses of *akolouthein* five reasons for following Jesus.

(i) The disciples followed Jesus because of the sheer compelling attraction of his summons.

(ii) The crowds followed Jesus because they desired the things which he alone could give them.

(iii) The sinners followed Jesus because they felt that he alone could enable them to mend their broken lives and to begin again.

(iv) The blind men followed Jesus that they might receive their sight. They desired to experience his wonder-working power.

(v) The blind men whose eyes were opened followed Jesus in sheer gratitude for what he had done for them.

There we see in summary the motives of the approach of the heart to Jesus Christ.

It will repay us still further to study the usages of *akolouthein* in the gospels.

1. We must see what following Jesus *involves*.

(i) Following Jesus involves *counting the cost*. In Luke 9.59, 61, Jesus seems actually to discourage people from following him until he has made quite sure that they know what they are doing. Jesus does not want anyone to follow him on false pretences, nor will he accept an emotional and easily-moved offer of an unconsidered service.

(ii) Following Jesus involves *sacrifice*. Repeatedly it is pointed out what people left to follow him (Luke 5.11; Matt. 4.20, 22; 19.27). The real point for us there is that following Jesus is what in modern language is called a whole-time job. But there is this difference for us—that following Jesus involves for us serving him within our work, and not by leaving it. In many cases it would be far easier to leave it; but our duty is to witness for him where he has sent us.

(iii) Following Jesus involves a *cross* (Matt. 16.24; cp. Mark 8.34 and Luke 9.23). The real reason for that is that no man can follow Jesus and ever again do what he likes. To follow Jesus may well mean the sacrifice of the pleasures, habits, aims, ambitions which have woven themselves into our lives. Following Jesus always involves this act of surrender—and surrender is never easy.

2. We must see what following Jesus *gives*. In this direction there are two great promises from the Fourth Gospel.

(i) To follow Jesus means to walk not in the darkness, but in the light (John 8.12). When a man walks by himself he walks in the darkness of uncertainty, and he may well end in the darkness of sin. To walk with Jesus is to be sure of the way, and in his company to be safe.

(ii) To follow Jesus is to be certain of ultimately arriving at the glory where he himself is (John 12.26). This is the other side of the warning that to follow Jesus means a sacrifice and a cross. The sacrifice and the cross are not pointless. They are the price of the eternal glory. Jesus never promised an easy way, but he did promise a way in the end of which the hardness of the way would be forgotten.

3. We must see that there are *inadequate* ways of following Jesus. These ways are not to be condemned. They are infinitely better than nothing, but they are not the best.

(i) At the end Peter followed Jesus *afar off* (Matt. 26.58; cp. Mark 14.54 and Luke 22.54). The real reason was that Peter did not dare to follow any nearer; and the real tragedy is that if Peter had kept close to Jesus, the disaster of his denial might never have happened, for it was when Peter saw Jesus' face again that he discovered what he had done by his repeated denials.

(ii) On the last journey to Jerusalem the disciples followed *afraid* (Mark 10.32). In a way that was the bravest act of all. They did not understand what was happening; they feared the worst; and yet they followed him. We can take comfort from reminding ourselves that often the man who follows Christ in fear and trembling is showing the highest courage of all.

4. Lastly we must note that a man can *refuse* to follow Jesus. That is what the Rich Young Ruler did (Matt. 19.21; cp. Luke 18.22). The result of his refusal was that he went away sorrowful. The result of refusal is always sorrow; the result of following, however hard and frightening the way, is always joy.

ALAZŌN AND ALAZONEIA

THE WORDS OF THE EMPTY BOAST

THE word *alazōn* occurs twice in the NT, in Rom. 1.30 and II Tim. 3.2. In both places the AV translates it *boasters* and Moffatt *boastful*.

The word *alazoneia* also occurs twice in the NT, in James 4.16 and I John 2.16. In the James passage the AV translates it *boastings*, and Moffatt *proud pretensions*. In the I John passage the AV translates it by the famous phrase *the pride of life*, and Moffatt translates it *the proud glory of life*.

These words have behind them a most interesting picture, which makes them all the more vivid and meaningful. The Greeks derived them from *alē*, which means *a wandering about*; and an *alazōn* was one of these wandering quacks who could be found shouting their wares in every market-place and in every fair-ground, and offering to sell men their patent cure-alls.

Plutarch, for instance, uses it to describe a *quack doctor* (Plutarch, *Moralia* 523). It was the word for these quacks and cheapjacks who travelled the country and set up their stalls wherever crowds gathered, to sell their patent pills and potions, and to boast that they could cure anything.

So in Greek the word came to mean *a pretentious braggart*. The Platonic Definitions define *alazoneia* as 'the claim to good things which a man does not really possess'.

Aristotle defines the *alazōn* as the man 'who pretends to praiseworthy qualities which he does not possess, or possesses in a lesser degree than he makes out' (Aristotle, *Nicomachean Ethics* 1127a 21). Again in the *Rhetoric* (1384a 6) he says that 'it is the sign of *alazoneia* to claim that things it does not possess belong to it'.

Plato uses the word *alazōn* to describe the '*false* and *boastful* words' which can get into a young man's mind and drive out 'the pursuits and true words which are the best guardians and sentinels in the minds of men who are dear to the gods' (Plato, *Republic* 560c).

In the *Gorgias* Plato draws a picture of the souls of men before the judge in the afterworld, souls 'where every act has left its smirch, where all is awry through falsehood and *imposture, alazoneia,* and nothing straight because of a nurture that knew not the truth' (Plato, *Gorgias* 525a).

Xenophon tells how Cyrus the Persian king, who knew men, defined the *alazōn*: 'The name *alazōn* seems to apply to those who pretend that they are richer than they are, or braver than they are, and to those who promise to do what they cannot do, and that, too, when it is evident that they do this only for the sake of getting something or making some gain' (Xenophon, *Cyropaedia* 2.2.12).

In the *Memorabilia* he tells how Socrates utterly condemned such imposters. Socrates said they are found in every walk of life, but they were worst of all in politics. 'Much the greatest rogue of all, is the man who has gulled his city into the belief that he is fit to direct it' (Xenophon, *Memorabilia* 1.7.5).

Theophrastus has a famous character sketch of the *alazōn.* '*Alazoneia*', he begins, 'would seem to be, in fact, pretension to advantages which one does not possess'. The *alazōn* is the man who will stand in the market-place and talk to strangers about the argosies he has at sea and his vast trading enterprises when his bank balance is precisely tenpence! He will tell of the campaigns he served with Alexander the Great, and how he was on terms of personal intimacy with him.

He will talk about the letters which the chiefs of the state write to him for help and advice. When he is living in lodgings he will pretend that the house in which his room is situated is the family mansion, and that he is thinking of selling it because it is not commodious enough for the entertaining which he has to do (Theophrastus, *Characters* 23).

The *alazōn* was the braggart and the boaster out to impress men; the man with all his goods in the shop window; the man given to making extravagant claims which he can never fulfil. But we have still to see the *alazōn* in his most damaging and dangerous form.

It was not so very dangerous for a man to lay claim to a business or a fortune which he did not possess; but in the days of the NT there were men who made claims which were exceedingly dangerous.

These men were the Sophists. The Sophists were Greek wandering teachers who claimed to sell knowledge; and, in effect, the knowledge they claimed to sell was the knowledge of how to be a success in life. The Greeks loved words; and the Sophists claimed to give men subtle skill in words, so that, in the famous phrase 'they could make the worse appear the better reason'. They claimed to give men that magic of words which would make the orator the master of men.

Aristophanes pillories them in *The Clouds*. He says the whole object of their teaching was to teach men to fascinate the jury, to win impunity to cheat, and to find an argument to justify anything. Isocrates, the great Greek teacher, hated them. 'They merely try,' he said, 'to attract pupils by low fees and big promises' (Isocrates, *Sophist* 10. 193a).

He said: 'They make impossible offers, promising to impart to their pupils an exact science of conduct by means of which they will always know what to do. Yet for this science they charge only £15 or £20. . . . They try to attract pupils by the specious titles of the subjects which they claim to teach, such as Justice and Prudence.

'But the Justice and Prudence which they teach are of a very peculiar sort, and they give a meaning to the words quite different from that which ordinary people give; in fact they cannot be sure about the meaning themselves, but can only dispute about it. Although they profess to teach justice, they refuse to trust their pupils, and make them deposit the fees with a third party before the course begins' (Isocrates, *Sophist* 4. 291d).

Plato savagely attacks them in his book called *The Sophist*: 'Hunters after young men of wealth and position, with sham education as their bait, and a fee for their object, making money by a scientific use of quibbles in private conversation, while quite aware that what they are teaching is wrong.'

It is these men, and the like of them, of whom the NT is thinking, and against whom it warns the Christian. The warning is against the false teacher who claims to teach men the truth, and who does not know it himself. The world is still full of these people who offer men a so-called wisdom, who shout their wares wherever men meet, who claim to have the cure and the solution to everything. How can we distinguish these men?

(i) Their characteristic is *pride*. In the *Testament of Joseph*, Joseph tells how he treated his brethren: 'My land was their land, and their counsel my counsel. And I exalted myself not among them in *arrogance* (*alazoneia*) because of my worldly glory, but I was among them as one of the least' (*Testament of Joseph* 17. 8). The *alazōn* is the teacher who struts as he teaches, and who is fascinated by his own cleverness.

(ii) Their stock in trade is *words*. The Sophist defended himself to Epictetus that the young men came to him looking for someone to teach them. 'To teach them to live?' demands Epictetus. And then he answers his own question: 'No, fool; not how to live, but how to talk; which is also the reason why he admires you' (Epictetus, *Discourses* 3.23). The *alazōn* seeks to substitute clever words for fine deeds.

(iii) Their motive is *profit*. The *alazōn* is out for what he can get. Prestige for his reputation and money for his pocket is his aim. The programme he preaches is designed to return his party to power and himself to office.

The *alazōn* is not dead. There are still the teachers who offer worldly cleverness instead of heavenly wisdom; who spin fine words which never end in any lovely action; whose teaching is aimed at self-advancement and whose desire is profit and power.

APECHEIN

PAYMENT IN FULL

In the NT there are certainly three, and perhaps five, extremely interesting technical usages of the word *apechein*. The main part of the word is the verb *echein*, which means 'to have'.

In Matt. 6.2, 6, 16, Jesus says of those who give alms ostentatiously, or those who pray in such a way that everyone will see them, and of those who make a parade of their fasting: 'Verily I say unto you, *they have their reward.*' (*Apechousin* [the present indicative of *apechein*] *ton misthon.*) This word *apechein* is the technical Greek word for 'receiving payment in full'. Sometimes it is used in a general sense. Callimachus (*Epigram* 51) speaks of a certain Miccus, who paid all honour to his aged nurse Aeschra. He 'cared for her in her old age with all good things, and when she died he set up her statue for future generations to see, so that the old woman has received thanks (*apechei charitas*) for her nursing breasts'. She received in full the grateful reward for her tender care. Callimachus (*Epigram* 55) has another epigram in which he speaks of a certain Aceson, who has set up a tablet to Asclepius, the god of healing, in gratitude for his wife's recovery from illness. 'Know, Asclepius, that thou hast received the debt (*chreos apecheis*) which Aceson owed thee by his vow for his wife Demodice. But if thou dost forget and demand payment again, this tablet says it will bear witness.' The tablet is the witness that the debt is paid in full. In his life of Solon (ch. 22) Plutarch tells how Solon, to check immorality, made a law that an illegitimate son need not support his father. Then he goes on to say of the father, 'he has his reward (*misthon echei*) in that he robs himself of all right to upbraid his sons for neglecting him, since he has made their very existence a reproach to them'. The sinning father has received full pay for his sin. In his life of Themistocles (ch. 17) Plutarch tells how Themistocles won the admiration of all. Sparta gave him the prize for wisdom. At the Olympic games the crowds gazed on him rather than on the competitors, and pointed him out to visiting strangers, 'so that Themistocles was delighted and confessed to his friends that he was now reaping in full measure the harvest (*ton karpon apechein*) of his toils for Hellas'. The admiration of the people was payment in full for all his toils.

But *apechein* has a still more technical use. It was the technical word which was used for 'receipting an account' which had been paid in full. It is the equivalent of the English phrase 'received payment of . . .' Deissmann and Moulton and Milligan provide ample examples of this use of the word in every connection. It is used in connection with 'the payment of rent'. Asclepiades, a landowner, writes to Portis, his tenant: 'Asclepiades, the son of Charmagon, to Portis, the son of Permamis, greeting. I have *received* from you the fruit that falls to me (rents were paid in kind) (*apechō*) and the increase of the lot that I have let to you, for the sowing of the year 25, and I have no further claims to make on you.' 'I have *received* from you the rent of the olive-press which you have from me on hire.' It is used in connection with 'the payment of taxes'. A resident alien had to pay a tax and a receipt for such a tax runs as follows: 'Pamaris, the son of Hermodorus, to Abos. I have *received* from you the alien tax for the months of Thouth and Phaophi. In the year 19 of Tiberius Caesar Augustus.' It is used in connection with 'the payment of religious dues'. 'Psenamunis, the son of Pekusis, to the labourer under contract, Pibuchis, the son of Pateesis, greeting. I have *received* from you 4 drachmae and 1 obol (about 3s. 8d.) being the collection of Isis, on behalf of the public works.' It is used in connection with 'the payment of the price for a slave'. So the seller writes: 'I have *received* the whole price.' In all business transactions *apechein* is the normal word for 'receiving payment in full'.

So what Jesus is saying is that those who give alms and pray and fast in such a way that they deliberately seek the admiration of men, receive the admiration of men—*and that is all*. The admiration of men is their payment in full. They have no further claim; they can write their receipt and consider themselves paid in full. The thing may win the admiration of man, but when it is designed to do so, it is of no value to God. If we aim at personal publicity, we get it—but we get nothing more. By getting it we are paid in full, but we miss completely the far greater rewards of God which are given to humble and selfless and self-effacing service.

The two not so certain instances are, first, Philem. 15. Paul there writes to Philemon that perhaps he lost the runaway Onesimus for a short time, that he might receive him (*apechein*) for ever. If Philemon will only take Onesimus back as a Christian brother, he may have lost him in this temporary world as a slave, but he will receive full payment, by receiving him for ever as a brother. The second instance is of great interest. In Mark 14.41 when Jesus has emerged victorious from his agony in the Garden, he says, as the AV has it, '*It is enough*; the hour is come; the Son of Man is betrayed into the hands of sinners.' And then verse 43 goes on to describe the arrival of Judas. Now the phrase which is translated, 'It is enough', is the one Greek word *apechei*. And it may well mean, not 'It is enough', but it may be a reference to Judas. Jesus may have pointed to him and said: '*He has been paid his money in full.* The traitor is here.' Jesus may well have been saying to Judas:

'Is this the payment in full which you have been looking for?' And so Jesus may have been trying to remind Judas that there was an account with himself and with God still to be settled.

APOBLEPEIN, APHORAN AND ATENIZEIN

THE STEADFAST GAZE

Apoblepein is used in the NT only twice, and *aphoran* only once, but they are such vivid words that they repay the closest study. They are to all intents and purposes synonyms and both of them mean the same thing and have much the same history. Both *blepein* and *horan* mean 'to see' or 'to look'; and *apo*, which is the first part of both of these words, means 'away from'; and both words mean 'to look away from everything else in order to focus one's gaze on one thing'; they mean to neglect everything else in order to concentrate one's attention on one thing.

The important instance of *apoblepein* is in Heb. 11.26. There it is said that Moses gave up the pleasure and the ease and the luxury that he might have enjoyed with the Egyptians in order to identify himself with the struggles and the sorrows of his own people; and he is said to have done this because 'he had respect unto the recompense of the reward'. The American RSV puts it, 'For he looked to the reward'; Moffatt puts it, 'for he had an eye to the reward'. The meaning is that he turned away from the rewards of earth to concentrate on the reward of heaven.

The one instance of *aphoran* is in Heb. 12.2, where we are enjoined to run 'looking unto Jesus'. Moffatt translates it, 'our eyes fixed upon Jesus'; the American RSV translates it, 'looking to Jesus'. Moffatt, in his commentary on Hebrews, suggests the translation, 'with no eyes for anyone but Jesus'. The idea is that we are to withdraw our gaze from everyone else to gaze at Jesus.

But to get the full flavour of these words, let us look at their usage in Greek.

First, let us look at *apoblepein*. Suidas, the Greek lexicon, tells us that *apoblepein* is used by Aeschines as a synonym of *thaumazein*, which means 'to wonder'. Philostratus tells us that when Apollonius, the famous sophist, landed in Egypt, as he advanced from the ship the people 'gazed at him' (*apoblepein*) as a god. When Xenophon is telling of a man whose services the country was needing, he says, Your fatherland is 'looking' (*apoblepein*) to you. Philo describes the builder, as building and all the while 'looking' (*apoblepein*) into the pattern of the architect. Xenophon speaks of a person as being so vain that she kept 'gazing' (*apoblepein*) at her own reflection. Plato says that it is the aim of the lover to make the loved one so dependent on him that the lover in all things 'will look' (*apoblepein*) to him in utter love and complete dependence. An Ephesian inscription tells of one who 'looked' (*apoblepein*) to the reverence of the gods and to the honour of the most illustrious city of the Ephesians. Theophrastus in his *Characters* uses *apoblepein* to describe the look of the flatterer who gazes with rapt attention at the person he wishes to impress.

Now let us look at *aphoran*. Lucian uses it for one man looking intently at another as they pursued an argument. Twice Epictetus uses it. He uses it in a description of his aims with his pupils. 'And so now I am your teacher, and you are being taught in my school. And my purpose is this —to make of you a perfect work, secure against restraint, compulsion and hindrance, free, prosperous, happy, looking to (*aphoran*) God in everything both great and small.' He describes the great hero and benefactor Hercules as 'looking to' (*aphoran*) Zeus is everything he did. Josephus, describing the death of Aaron, tells how, as he died, the crowd 'looked wonderingly' (*aphoran*) upon him.

From all this there emerges a wonderful picture of the way in which the true Christian looks at the blessedness of God and the wonder of Jesus Christ. He looks with an utter fixity of concentration; he looks with wondering amazement; he looks as one who looks to a champion and a saviour; he looks as one who looks at the master plan and pattern of life; he looks as a loved one looks with adoration at his lover; he looks as a man looks at his familiar friend; he looks as a man looks to God when God has become for him the only reality in the world.

Aphoran and *apoblepein* describe the look of the soul which is 'lost in wonder, love and praise'.

There is another NT word which implies a fixity of gaze. It is the word *atenizein*, which means 'to gaze intently at'. It is a favourite word of Luke. It occurs fourteen times in the NT; of these fourteen instances two are in II Cor. (3.7, 13), two are in the Gospel according to St Luke, and the remaining ten are in Acts.

It is used of the people in the Synagogue of Nazareth gazing with intent bewilderment at Jesus (Luke 4.20). It is used of the close scrutiny of the servant in the courtyard of the High Priest's house when Peter was recognized (Luke 22.56). It is used of the disciples gazing after Jesus when the ascension had taken place (Acts 1.10). It is used of Peter's and John's gaze at the lame man at the Temple gate (Acts 3.4), and of the astonished gaze of the people at them after the miracle had taken place (Acts 3.12). It is used of the Sanhedrin gazing at Stephen as he spoke with eloquence and debated with power (Acts 6.15) and of Stephen's own gaze up into heaven as he died beneath the stones of the mob (Acts 7.55). It is used of Peter's astonished gaze at the angel who warned him of the coming of Cornelius (Acts 10.4), and of his gaze at the vision of the creatures on the sheet (Acts 11.6). It is used of Paul's penetrating look at Elymas, the hostile sorcerer (Acts 13.9). It is used of the look of dawning hope in the eyes of the lame man at Lystra (Acts 14.9). It is used of Paul's piercing look at the San-hedrin (Acts 23.1). And it is used of the way in which the people looked at Moses when he came down from the mount, or rather of the way in which it was impossible for them to look at him because of the divine glory that shone from him (II Cor. 3.7, 13).

It can, therefore, be seen that this word *atenizein* expresses a look of astonishment and amazement, a look of scrutiny ending in recognition, a look of wonder, a look of expectation and hope, and a look of sheer, piercing authority. Now the interesting thing is that when we come to the writings of Clement of Rome, who wrote towards the very end of the first Christian century, and who was the first of the apostolic fathers and one of the great leaders of the Church, we find that he does not use *apoblepein* or *aphoran*, but that he is notably fond of this word *atenizein*. We find that he uses it in three notable connections.

(i) First of all in his first letter to the Corinthians, chapter 36, he urges the Christian to gaze steadfastly (*atenizein*) at the heights of the heavens. In a tempting and a hostile world the Christian's gaze must be fixed on heaven.

(ii) Second, he uses it of God. In the same letter in chapter 19, he says, 'Let us fix our gaze (*atenizein*) on the Father and Creator of the whole universe.' God must be the object of the Christian's thought and contemplation.

(iii) Third, he uses it of Jesus Christ. In the same letter in chapter 7, he says, 'Let us fix our gaze (*atenizein*) upon the blood of Christ, and let us know how costly it is to his Father, because it was poured out for our salvation.' The Christian must fix his eyes upon the wounded and the crucified Christ.

The word is different from *apoblepein* and *aphoran*, but the thought is precisely the same. In a word where it was hard to be a Christian, a world where the tainting pollu-tions sought to infect the Christians on every side, a world where Christians had already died terribly for their faith, the one thing necessary was the steadfast gaze upon heaven and God and Jesus Christ. That alone could enable a Christian man to remain a Christian—and it is still so.

ARRABŌN

THE FORETASTE OF WHAT IS TO COME

THE word *arrabōn* has one of the most human and interesting backgrounds of all NT words. It is used only by Paul, and it was a favourite word of his because he uses it three times, always in the same connexion. In II Cor. 1.22 he says that God has given us the *arrabōn* of the Holy Spirit in our hearts. In II Cor. 5.5 he again talks about the *arrabōn* of the Holy Spirit. And in Eph. 1.14 he speaks about the Holy Spirit being the *arrabōn* of our inheritance. In each of these cases the AV translates the word *arrabōn* by the English word 'earnest'. Moffatt translates it 'pledge' and 'instalment'. The American RSV translates it 'guarantee'.

In classical Greek the word *arrabōn* regularly means the caution money that a purchaser had to deposit and pay down when a bargain was struck and which was forfeited if the purchase was not carried out. It was the first instalment which was the pledge and guarantee that the rest would follow in due time.

The word is very common in the papyri in business documents and agreements. Milligan quotes some very interesting usages of it. We take three of them as examples. A woman was selling a cow and she received one thousand drachmae as an *arrabōn* that the remainder of the price would be paid. Certain dancing girls were being hired for a village festival and they are paid so many drachmae in advance as an *arrabōn*, with proviso that this already paid sum will be taken into account when the final payment is made after the performance has been given. And—a rather amusing instance—a man writes, 'Regarding Lampōn, the mouse-catcher, I paid him for you as *arrabōn* eight drachmae in order that he may catch the mice while they are with young.' The advance payment is made, as a guarantee of full payment, so that Lampōn will get on with the job of catching mice while the going is good! So then in secular Greek contemporary with the NT *arrabōn* is regularly a part payment which is an assurance and a guarantee that full payment will follow; it is an instalment paid down in advance which is the proof and the pledge that the whole sum will in due course be forthcoming.

Now Paul's use of the word is always as a description of the Holy Spirit. So what Paul is saying is that God's gift to us of the Holy Spirit here and now is an instalment, a guarantee, an advance foretaste of the life which the Christian will some day live when he lives in the presence of God.

Paul spoke out of a Jewish background. To a Jew the Holy Spirit of God had two great functions. (i) It was through his Holy Spirit that God spoke to man. The prophet spoke because the Spirit of the Lord was on him. It was God's Holy Spirit who revealed to Simeon that he would see God's Anointed One before he died (Luke 2.25). (ii) But also, it was God's Holy Spirit in his heart which enabled a man to recognize God's truth when he heard it. The Jews believed that the Holy Spirit of God operated from *without* to bring men truth; and from *within* to enable them to recognize truth. The Holy Spirit was at once, to them, the revealer and the touchstone of truth.

So when Paul uses the word *arrabōn* of the Holy Spirit the thought in his mind is that the imperfect knowledge that men now possess is the first instalment of the full knowledge they will one day possess; that which God has told them now is the pledge and guarantee that he will some day tell them all; that the joy that comes to a man now in the Spirit is the pledge of the perfect joy of heaven. The Holy Spirit to Paul is the guarantee of God that, though now we see through a glass darkly, we shall some day see face to face; and that, though now we only know in part, we shall some day know even as we are known (I Cor. 13.12).

ASELGEIA

THE UTTER SHAMELESSNESS

IN many ways *aselgeia* is the ugliest word in the list of NT sins. It occurs quite frequently (Mark 7.22; II Cor. 12.21; Gal. 5.19; Eph. 4.19; I Pet. 4.3; Jude 4; Rom. 13.13; II Pet. 2.2, 7, 18). The AV varies between 'lasciviousness' and 'wantonness'. The RSV consistently prefers 'licentiousness'. Moffatt regularly translates it 'sensuality'. To some extent all these translations fail to give the one essential characteristic of *aselgeia*.

Let us look first at some of the classical and Christian definitions of it. It is used by Plato in the sense of 'impudence'. It is defined by a late writer as 'preparedness for every pleasure'. It is defined as 'violence coupled with insult and audacity'. It is defined by Basil as 'a disposition of the soul which does not possess and cannot bear the pain of discipline'. It is described as 'the spirit which knows no restraints and which dares whatever caprice and wanton insolence suggest'. It is Lightfoot who seizes on the essential quality in *aselgeia*. He says that a man may be 'unclean' (*akathartos*) and hide his sin, but the man who is *aselgēs* (the adjective) shocks public decency. Here is the very essence of *aselgeia*; the man in whose soul *aselgeia* dwells is so much in the grip of sin, so much under its domination, that he does not care what people say or think so long as he can gratify his evil desire. He is the man who is lost to shame. Most men have enough decency left to seek to hide their sin, but the *aselgēs* is long past that. He will be guilty of any outrageous conduct, and care for nothing except to satisfy his desires. He is like a drug-taker. At first the drug-taker will indulge secretly and will try to conceal the fact that he takes drugs at all. In the end he will whine and grovel and beg and beseech and implore completely without restraint and completely without shame, because the drug has so mastered him.

Now it so happens that, in the NT, *aselgeia* usually occurs, not alone, but either in lists of sins or in conjunction with other sins. It is instructive to see with what other sins it is most closely connected.

(i) Three times (Mark 7.22; Eph. 4.19; II Pet. 2.2) it occurs close to *pleonexia*. *Pleonexia* is the unbridled longing to possess more, the uncontrollable desire to possess things which are forbidden and which should not be desired at all. Therefore there is in *aselgeia* the idea of 'sheer, shameless greed'. It is the vice of the man who will submit to demean himself and to shame himself in any way in order to possess that which he has set his heart upon.

(ii) In four cases (Mark 7.22; II Cor. 12.21; Gal. 5.19; II Pet. 2.18) it is connected with adultery and lust and sexual sin. Therefore in *aselgeia* there is involved the idea of 'sheer animal lust'. One has only to walk the streets of any great city to see that kind of *aselgeia* in terrible action. It is the vice of a man who has no more shame than an animal in the gratification of his physical desires.

(iii) In three cases (Gal. 5.19; I Pet. 4.3; Rom. 13.13) it is connected with drunkenness. In particular it is connected with the word *kōmoi*. Originally a *kōmos* was a band of friends who accompanied a victor in the games on his way home. They sang their rejoicings and his praises. But the word degenerated until it came to mean a 'carousal', a band of drunken revellers, swaying and singing their way through the streets. Therefore *aselgeia* has in it that 'sheer self-indulgence', which is such a slave to its so-called pleasures that it is lost to shame.

It is perhaps Josephus who gives us the flavour of the meaning of *aselgeia* best of all. He couples it with *mania*, 'madness', and he declares that that was the sin of Jezebel when she erected a shrine of Baal in the Holy City, the very city of God. Such an act was a shocking outrage which defied all decency and flaunted all public opinion. *Aselgeia* is a grim word. It is the wanton insolence that is lost to shame. It is a grim commentary on human nature that a man can be so mastered by sin that in the end he loses even shame.

CHARISMA

THE GIFT OF GOD

Charisma basically means 'a gift'. Outside the NT it is not at all a common word. In classical Greek it is rare. It is not common in the papyri, but there is one suggestive occurrence where a man classifies his property as that which he acquired *apo agorasias*, 'by purchase', and that which he acquired *apo charismatos*, 'by gift'. In the NT *charisma* is a characteristically Pauline word. Altogether it occurs seventeen times, fourteen times in the undoubted Pauline letters, twice in the Pastoral Epistles, and once in I Peter.

(i) It is used of what we might call 'gifts of grace'. Paul longs to visit Rome in order to impart to the Romans some *charisma* (Rom. 1.11). The Corinthians are deficient in no *charisma* (I Cor. 1.7). He bids them covet the best *charismata* (I Cor. 12.31) and then goes on to sing his hymn to love. *Charismata* are the graces of the Christian life.

(ii) It is used of God's 'grace and forgiveness' in that situation where judgment and condemnation would have been only just. In Rom. 5.15, 16, man's sin and God's *charisma* of gracious forgiveness are contrasted. In Rom. 6.23—a verse to which we shall return—the wages of sin is death, but the *charisma* of God is eternal life.

(iii) It is used of the 'natural endowments' which a man possesses. Every man, says Paul, has his own *charisma* from God (I Cor. 7.7). Peter exhorts every man to serve others as he has received his *charisma* (I Pet. 4.10).

(iv) It is used of 'the gift which is implanted in a man when he is ordained to the ministry'. Timothy must never neglect the gift that came to him by the laying on of hands by the Presbytery (I Tim. 4.14; cp. II Tim. 1.6). The gift of God comes to men through the hands of men, but it remains a gift of God.

(v) It is specially used for all 'the special gifts which can be exercised in the service of the Church'. There are two great lists of these gifts. Rom. 12.6-8 lists prophecy, ministry, teaching, exhortation, giving, ruling, showing mercy. I Cor. 12.8-10 is a longer list. I Cor. 12.28-30 points out how different *charismata* are given to different people.

(vi) It is used for 'God's rescue in a difficult situation' (II Cor. 1.11).

The whole basic idea of the word is that of a free and undeserved gift, of something given to a man unearned and unmerited, something which comes from God's grace and which could never have been achieved or attained or possessed by a man's own effort.

It is Rom. 6.23 which gives the essential meaning of the word. There two words are contrasted with each other. The 'wages' of sin is death. The word used is *opsōnia*, which literally means 'money to buy cooked meat' and which is the regular word for 'a soldier's pay'. That is to say, if we had got the pay we earned it would have been death. The 'gift' of God is eternal life. The word is *charisma*. Now *charisma* also is a military word. When an emperor came to the throne, or when he was celebrating his birthday, he gave his troops a *donativum* or *charisma*, which was a free grant of money, a free gift. They had not earned it as they had their *opsōnia*; they got it unearned out of the goodness of the emperor's heart.

So then what we have earned, our *opsōnia*, would be death. All that we have is *charisma*, God's free gift. All is from God. Every grace with which life is adorned, the grace which covers every sin, every natural endowment we possess, every gift which we can lay at the service of the Church, any office we may hold, every time we have been through something which threatened our bodies or our souls—God gave it, God did it, it is God's *charisma*, all is of God.

> 'And every virtue we possess,
>   And every victory won,
>   And every thought of holiness
>   Are His alone.'

DIATHĒKĒ

MAN AND GOD

THE word *diathēkē* is the word which is translated 'covenant'. It is one of the commonest of all words in the Greek translation of the OT, and it is also a great NT word. It is a word which has a certain problem attached to it, and the solution to that problem will show us that in the word there is a whole theology and a complete view of the relationship between God and man.

In its ordinary, non-theological usage a 'covenant' means 'an agreement entered into between two people'. It is occasionally so used in the OT, e.g. of the 'league' the Gibeonites wished to make with Joshua (Josh. 9.6), of the 'league' with the inhabitants of Canaan which is forbidden (Judg. 2.2), of the 'covenant' between David and Jonathan (I Sam. 23.18).

But far more commonly it is used of the relationship entered into between God and man. It is so used of God's new agreement with man after the flood (Gen. 9.12-17). It is specially used of God's agreement with Abraham (Gen. 17.4-9). And it is used everywhere of the relationship and the agreement between the people of Israel and God (Deut. 4.13, 23). It is uniquely the word which is used to describe 'the relationship, the agreement' between God and the people of God.

In the NT the old usages survive. The covenant with Abraham is still remembered (Acts 7.8). The covenant with the people of Israel is still stressed (Acts 3.25; Rom. 9.4). But very specially it is used of that new relationship between man and God which was made possible by the life and death of Jesus (Matt. 26.28; Mark 14.24; Luke 22.20; II Cor. 3.6). In the NT it is a characteristic word of the letter to the Hebrews to describe this new and better relationship between God and man (Heb. 7.22; 8.6, 9, 10; 12.24; 13.20).

So far everything is straightforward, but the real problem is this—the normal Greek word for a covenant between two people is *sunthēkē*, which is the word everywhere used for a marriage covenant, or an agreement between persons or states. In all normal Greek in all ages *diathēkē* means, not a 'covenant', but a 'will'. *Kata diathēkēn* is the regular term for 'according to the terms of the will'. In a papyrus a testator leaves houses and gardens in accordance with the dispositions (*diathēkas*) which are deposited in the temple of Aphrodite, with Eunomides the governor, and with Ctesiphon the lawyer. Why should the NT never use *sunthēkē* and always *diathēkē*?

The reason is this. *Sunthēkē* always describes 'an agreement made on equal terms', an agreement which either party can alter. But the word 'covenant' means something different. God and man do not meet on equal terms; it means that God, of his own choice and in his free grace, offered man this relationship, which man cannot alter or change or annul, but which he can only accept or refuse. Now the supreme example of such an agreement is 'a will'.

The conditions of a will are not made on equal terms. They are made by one person and accepted by the other, who cannot alter them and who could not have made them.

Our relationship with God is not something into which we entered in our own right and on our own terms; it is something given to us solely and completely on the initiative and in the grace of God. Philo says, 'A covenant is a symbol of grace which God sets between himself *who extends the boon and man who receives it.*' 'It is fitting for *God to give and for a wise man to receive.*'

The very word 'covenant', *diathēkē*, is a word which in itself sums up our 'debt' and our 'duty' to God. We are in 'debt' because our new relationship to God is due to the approach of God and to nothing that we could ever have done. We have a 'duty' because we have to accept God's conditions of love and faith and obedience, and we cannot alter them. The very word shows that we can never meet God on equal terms, but only on terms of submission and of gratitude.

Samuel Rutherfurd drew up his own catechism and in it he writes, 'What moved God to make the covenant of grace?' And he answers, 'His own free mercy and grace, for when he made it we were like forlorn bastards and half-dead foundlings that were cast out in the open field to die in their own blood (that actually happened to unwanted children in Rutherfurd's day) when our Lord came by and made a covenant with us.' The very word *diathēkē* has in it the inescapable truth that 'all is of God'.

EILIKRINĒS AND EILIKRINEIA

THE PERFECT PURITY

Eilikrinēs and *eilikrineia*—the first is the adjective and the second is the noun—are two most interesting words.

Eilikrinēs occurs in Phil. 1.10, where the AV translates it 'sincere', the American RSV 'pure', and Moffatt 'transparent'; it also occurs in II Pet. 3.1, where both the AV and Moffatt translate it 'pure', and the American RSV 'sincere'. *Eilikrineia*, the noun, occurs in I Cor. 5.8, II Cor. 1.12 and II Cor. 2.17. The regular translation of all the versions is 'sincerity', with the one exception that Moffatt in the first example translates it 'innocence'.

Neither the noun nor the adjective is very common in classical Greek. In classical Greek *eilikrinēs* has two characteristic usages. First it means 'unmixed, without alloy, pure'. For instance, fire, the purest thing of all, is said to be *eilikrinēs*. It is used of a 'total' eclipse of the sun. Second, it is used as we use the words 'pure' and 'sheer'. For instance it is used of 'pure' intellect, or 'sheer', 'unrelieved' evil.

In the papyri neither is common. A suppliant appeals to the *eilikrineia* of an official, where the word must mean 'probity, fairness, justice'.

The etymology and derivation of these words in Greek has always been doubtful. There are two suggestions.

(i) They may be derived from a Greek word *eilein* which means 'to shake to and fro in a sieve' until the last particle of foreign matter is extracted and the substance is left absolutely pure. So then these words describe a purity which is 'sifted'. They describe the character which has been so cleansed and purified by the grace of God that there is no evil admixture left.

(ii) They may be derived from a combination of two Greek words, *heilē*, which means 'the sunlight', and *krinein*, which means 'to judge'. They would, in that case, describe something which can stand the judgment of the sunlight, something which even when it is held up to the clear light of the sun reveals no faults and flaws. There is a vivid picture here. In the eastern bazaars the shops were small and dark and shadowed. An article, say a piece of pottery or glassware or cloth, might look all right in the dim recesses of the trader's booth; but the wiser buyer would take it out into the street and hold it up and submit it to the judgment of the sunlight; and many a time the clear rays of the sun would reveal faults and flaws that would never have been noticed in the shadows of the shop. Theopylact must have been thinking of that when he spoke of '*eilikrineia*, purity of mind and guilelessness which have nothing concealed in the shadows and nothing lurking beneath the surface'.

The question that this word asks is, Could our inmost thoughts stand being brought out into the full light of day? Could our inmost motives stand being dragged out into the full glare of revealing light? To put the matter at its highest, Could the inmost thoughts of our minds and motions of our heart stand the scrutiny of the light of God's eye?

The Christian purity is a purity which is sifted until the last admixture of evil is gone, a purity which has nothing to conceal and whose inmost thoughts and desires will bear the full glare of the light of day.

EKKLĒSIA

THE CHURCH OF GOD

Ekklēsia is the NT word for 'church', and is, therefore, one of the most important of all NT words. Like so many NT words it has a double background.

(i) *Ekklēsia* has a Greek background. In the great classical days in Athens the *ekklēsia* was the convened assembly of the people. It consisted of all the citizens of the city who had not lost their civic rights. Apart from the fact that its decisions must conform to the laws of the State, its powers were to all intents and purposes unlimited. It elected and dismissed magistrates and directed the policy of the city. It declared war, made peace, contracted treaties and arranged alliances. It elected generals and other military officers. It assigned troops to different campaigns and dispatched them from the city. It was ultimately responsible for the conduct of all military operations. It raised and allocated funds. Two things are interesting to note. First, all its meetings began with prayer and sacrifice. Second, it was a true democracy. Its two great watchwords were 'equality' (*isonomia*) and 'freedom' (*eleutheria*). It was an assembly where everyone had an equal right and an equal duty to take part. When a case involving the right of any private citizen was before it—as in the case of ostracism or banishment—at least 6,000 citizens must be present. In the wider Greek world *ekklēsia* came to mean any duly convened assembly of citizens. It is interesting to note that the Roman world did not even try to translate the word *ekklēsia*; it simply transliterated it into *ecclesia* and used it in the same way. There is an interesting bilingual inscription found in Athens (dated A.D. 103-4). It can be read against the background of Acts 18. A certain Caius Vibius Salutaris had presented to the city an image of Diana and other images. The inscription lays it down that they are to be set up on their pedestals at every *ekklēsia* of the city in the theatre. To Greek and Roman alike the word was familiar in the sense of a convened assembly. So, then, when we look at it against this background, as Deissmann puts it, the Church was God's assembly, God's muster, and the convener is God.

(ii) *Ekklēsia* has a Hebrew background. In the Septuagint it translates the Hebrew word *qahal*, which again comes from a root which means 'to summon'. It is regularly used for the 'assembly' or the 'congregation' of the people of Israel. In Deut. 18.16; Judg. 20.2, it is translated 'assembly'; and in I Kings 8.14; Lev. 10.17; Num. 1.16, it is translated 'congregation'. It is very common in the Septuagint, occurring over 70 times. In the Hebrew sense it, therefore, means God's people called together by God, in order to listen to or to act for God. In a certain sense the word 'congregation' loses a certain amount of the essential meaning. A 'congregation' is a company of people 'who have come together'; a *qahal* or an *ekklēsia* is a body of people 'who have been called together'. The two original words, Hebrew and Greek, put all the emphasis on the action of God.

F. J. A. Hort rightly points out that originally the word does not mean, as is so often stated, a body of people who have been 'picked out' from the world. It has not in it that exclusive sense. It means a body of people who have been 'summoned out' of their homes to come and meet with God; and both in its original Greek and Hebrew usages, that sense was not exclusive but inclusive. The summons was not to any selected few; it was a summons from the State to every man to come and to shoulder his responsibilities; it was a summons from God to every man to come and to listen to and to act on the word of God.

In essence, therefore, the Church, the *ekklēsia*, is a body of people, not so much assembling because they have chosen to come together but assembling because God has called them to himself; not so much assembling to share their own thoughts and opinions, but assembling to listen to the voice of God.

In the NT *ekklēsia* can be used in three different ways. (i) It means 'the universal Church' (I Cor. 10.32; 12.28; Phil. 3.6). (ii) It means 'A particular local Church' (Rom. 16.1; I Cor. 1.2; Gal. 1.2). (iii) It means 'the actual assembly' of the believers in any place, met together for worship (I Cor. 11.18; 14.19; 14.23). In this matter it seems that Paul's thought developed. In his very early letters he thought rather of the individual congregations. So, for instance, he speaks of the '*ekklēsia* of the Thessalonians' (I Thess. 1.1; II Thess. 1.2). But later he speaks of the '*ekklēsia* of God which is at Corinth' (I Cor. 1.2). Paul came to think of the Church, not in terms of separate congregations, but in

terms of one great universal Church of which each congregation was a part. Sir William Ramsay saw in the
Roman Empire a foreshadowing of this which may well
have affected the thought of Paul. Any group of Roman
citizens, meeting anywhere throughout the world, was a
conventus civium Romanorum, 'an assembly of Roman
citizens'. Wherever they might be meeting they were part
of the great conception of Rome. They had no meaning
apart from Rome; they were part of a great unity. And any
citizen coming into that town was automatically and
without introduction a member of the group. Such a group
might be separated from Rome in space, but in spirit they
were part of it. That is precisely the Pauline conception of
the Church. A man must be a member of a local congregation, within a certain given communion; but if his thought
stops there he is far away from the true conception of the
Church.

The Church is the universal whole of which his little
congregation forms a part, and the important thing is, not
that he is a member of such and such a congregation, or
even of such and such a communion, but that he is a
member of the Church of God. To take an army parallel—
a man might be proud to be a soldier in the Argyll and
Sutherland Highlanders; but that regiment was part of the
Eighth Army, and that would bring to him an even greater
pride; and that army was part of the army of his native
country, which ought to be his greatest pride of all. It is
good to be proud of a congregation; it is good to remember
the tradition of a denomination. It is best of all to be
conscious of being a member of the Church of God.

In the NT the Church is set before us in three relationships.

(i) It is sometimes—not often—described in human
terms. So, for instance, Paul speaks of the Church of the
Thessalonians (I Thess. 1.1; II Thess. 1.2). In a sense the
Church is composed of men and belongs to men; men are
the bricks out of which the edifice of the Church is built.

It is worth noting that in all the NT the word Church is never used to describe a 'building'. It always describes a body of men and women who have given their hearts to God.

(ii) Far more frequently it is described in divine terms. By far the commonest description is the 'Church of God' (I Cor. 1.2; II Cor. 1.1; Gal. 1.13; I Thess. 2.14; I Tim. 3.5, 15). The Church belongs to God and comes from God. Had there been no such thing as the love of God there would have been no such thing as a Church; and unless God was a self-communicating God there would be no message and no help in the Church.

(iii) Sometimes the Church is described as the Church of Christ. (a) In this connection Christ is the head of the Church (Eph. 5.23, 24). It ought to be according to the mind and thought and will of Christ that the Church lives and moves. (b) The Church is the body of Christ (Col. 1.24). It is through the Church that Jesus Christ acts. It must be hands to work for him, feet to run upon his errands, a voice to speak for him. An Indian described the Church as 'the Church which carries on the life of Christ'.

One last point is to be noted. In NT times the Church had no buildings. Christians met in any house which had a room large enough to accommodate them. These gatherings were called 'house-churches' (Rom. 16.5; I Cor. 16.19; Col. 4.15; Philem. 2). Every home ought to be in a real sense a Church. Jesus is Lord of the dinner table as he is Lord of the Communion table. And it will always be true that they pray best together who first pray alone.

ELPIS AND ELPIZEIN

THE CHRISTIAN HOPE

THE noun *elpis* means *hope*, and the verb *elpizein* means *to hope*. These words are not of any particular linguistic interest. Their great interest lies in the fact that if we examine and analyse their use in the NT we can discover the content and the basis of the Christian hope.

Elpis, *hope*, is one of the three great pillars of the Christian faith. It is on *hope*, along with faith and love, that the whole Christian faith is founded (I Cor. 13.13). *Hope* is characteristically the Christian virtue and it is something which for the non-Christian is impossible (Eph. 2.12). Only the Christian can be an optimist regarding the world. Only the Christian can hope to cope with life. And only the Christian can regard death with serenity and equanimity.

Let us then see in what this Christian hope consists.

(i) It is the *hope of the resurrection of the dead*. That thought runs consistently all through the NT (Acts 23.6; 26.6; I Thess. 4.13; I Peter 1.3; I John 3.3; I Cor. 15.19). The Christian is a man who is on his way, not to death, but to life. For him death is not the abyss of nothingness and annihilation. It is 'the gate on the skyline'.

(ii) It is *the hope of the glory of God* (Rom. 5.2). It is the hope that no longer shall we see the glory of God in the cloud and through a glass darkly. It is the certainty that the day will come when we shall see and be clothed with the glory of God.

(iii) It is *the hope of a new dispensation* (II Cor. 3.12). So long as men regarded themselves as governed by law, there was room for nothing but despair, for there is none who can obey and satisfy the perfect law of God. But when we see that the key-note of religion is not law but love a new hope is born.

(iv) It is *the hope of righteousness* (Gal. 5.5). In Paul *righteousness* or *justification* means *a right relationship with God*. When a man regards religion as law he must be ever in default before God, and therefore ever in terror of God. But the message of Jesus Christ enables a man to enter into a new relationship with God where the terror is gone and where childlike confidence takes its place.

(v) It is *the hope of salvation*. This has two aspects. (a) It is the confidence of safety in this world (II Cor. 1.10), not in the sense of protection from trouble and danger, but in the sense of independence of them. As Rupert Brooke wrote,

> Safe shall be my going,
> Secretly armed against all death's endeavour;
> Safe though all safety's lost; safe where men fall;
> And if these poor limbs die, safest of all.

(b) It is the confidence of safety in the world to come. It is the hope of safety amidst the perils of earth, and rescue from the judgment of God.

(vi) It is *the hope of eternal life* (Titus 1.2; 3.7). In the NT the word *eternal* always stresses, not the *duration*, but the *quality* of life. *Eternal* is the word which describes anything which is *proper to God*. Eternal life is the kind of life God lives. The hope of the Christian is that some day he will share the very life of God.

(vii) It is *the hope of the triumphant Second Coming of Christ* (Titus 2.13; I Peter 1.13; I John 3.3). The Second Coming is not a fashionable doctrine today, but it does conserve this great truth—*that history is going somewhere*, that history is not a knotless thread, and a haphazard collection of meaningless and disconnected events. There is a consummation. The Christian is a man who regards himself and all life as being on the way to a goal.

(viii) It is *a hope which is laid up in heaven* (Col. 1.5). That is to say, it looks forward to something which is already prepared for the Christian, and that something is not something which is at the mercy of the chances and the changes of time. It is in the keeping of God, and therefore it is something which will be the completing of God's design and the fulfilment of all the hopes and dreams of the soul of man.

We may now look at what we may call the sources of hope, or the springs of hope.

(i) Hope is the product of experience (Rom. 5.4). It may be that the experiences and the testings of life drive the non-Christian to despair. The Christian has a hope which sees all things and which grows ever brighter and not dimmer.

(ii) Hope is the product of the Scriptures (Rom. 15.4). If a man will study the record of God's dealings with men and God's intention for men it will leave him full of hope. Oliver Cromwell, in planning his son Richard's education, said, 'I would have him learn a little history.' For the Christian the lesson of history is hope.

(iii) Hope comes from the sense of being called by God (Eph. 1.18). The Christian has not the despairing sense of a salvation into which he must struggle. Such a struggle would be hopeless. He has the sense of a new relationship with God into which he has been invited, not because he deserved it, but by the sheer mercy of God.

(iv) Hope is the product of the gospel (Col. 1.23). The gospel is good news. A message like the message of John the Baptist (Luke 3.7, 17) is a message with a threat that would drive any man to despair. The message of Jesus is an invitation, an offer, a promise, a piece of startling good news which will lift up the heart of any man who is haunted by his sin.

(v) Hope is dependent on Jesus and on his work (Col. 1.27; I Tim. 1.1). The Christian hope is not founded on anything that a man has done, or can do, for himself. It is founded on what Christ has done for him.

Now let us gather together certain great things which happen by hope.

(i) Hope comes through grace (II Thess. 2.16). The very foundation of Christian hope is the free and undeserved offer of forgiveness and fellowship that God offers to men. Hope is born when we discover that we do not *earn* salvation, but *receive* it.

(ii) It is through hope that we rejoice (Rom. 12.12). A gloomy Christian is a contradiction in terms. The man who knows the power of Christ can never again despair about himself or about the world. He has discovered what Cavour called 'the sense of the possible', for he has discovered that all things are possible with God.

(iii) We are saved by hope (Rom. 8.24). The hope that God is as Jesus said he was is the basis of all salvation. It is not until we begin to see God as the God and Father of our Lord Jesus Christ that we can even contemplate salvation as a possibility for sinful man.

(iv) Hope keeps the Christian steadfast. This is one of the great key-notes of the letter to the Hebrews (Heb. 3.6; 6.11, 18). The Christian is the man who can battle and struggle on, who can fight against himself and his temptations, who can endure the hardness of being a Christian, because he has something infinitely precious to look forward to.

Lastly, let us look as what we may call the foundations of hope.

(i) Hope is in Christ (1 Thess. 1.3). We hope, not because of any strength that we can bring to life, but because we are now sure of the help that Christ can bring.

(ii) Hope is grounded in God (I Tim. 4.10), for God is that God of hope (Rom. 15.13). God is the God who gives hope. The character of God as Jesus told it to us is the ultimate ground of all our hope.

(iii) Hope looks to God. It faces God (Acts 24.15; I Peter 1.21; 3.5; I Tim. 5.5). The Christian is the man of hope because he keeps his eyes fixed on God. Augustine told a wretched man who thought of nothing but his sins, 'Look away from yourself and look to God.' The Godward look is the secret of the Christian hope.

The Christian hope is not simply a trembling, hesitant hope that perhaps the promises of God may be true. It is the confident expectation that they cannot be anything else than true.

ENERGEIA, ENERGEIN, ENERGĒMA, ENERGĒS

DIVINE POWER IN ACTION

IT is quite clear to anyone that the Greek words have in them the root of our English word *energy*. In the NT they are never used to describe any human power. Always they describe the action of some power which is beyond the power of man and the power of this world. On certain infrequent occasions they describe the action of a malignant power, demonic, and hostile to God; but far more frequently they describe the action of God himself.

They are therefore very important words, for through them we shall learn something of the power of God in action in Christ, in the world, and in the lives of men.

These words came into Christianity with a long and an important history and their history goes a long way towards helping us to understand their Christian flavour and usage. So then, first of all, let us study their usage in classical Greek.

We may best get at their classical meaning by studying the word *energos*, which does not occur in the NT at all, but which has in it the germs of all the other meanings. *Energos* is an adjective.

In Xenophon's *Memorabilia* (1.4.4) there is a passage where Socrates is discussing the actions of a man who was prepared to reverence the great writers and the great artists, but who was not prepared to reverence the gods. 'Which do you think,' he demands, 'deserve the greater admiration, the creators of phantoms without sense and motion, or the creators of living, intelligent, *active* (*energos*) human beings?' *Energos* describes that which is radiantly and vividly *alive*.

Herodotus (8.26) tells of certain Arcadian deserters who came to the Persians, because they were in need of food and wished *to be employed* (*energos*). *Energos* describes action in opposition to inaction.

Energos is used to describe someone who is *on duty*. Plato in *The Laws* (674b) lays it down: 'Magistrates, during their year of office, and pilots and judges, while *on duty*, should taste no wine at all.' *Energos* describes a man *on duty* in his profession or calling.

Energos frequently has a military connexion. Thucydides speaks on one occasion of the Athenian fleet as having the largest number of ships the Athenians ever had *on active service* (*energos*) (Thucydides, 3.17).

Xenophon tells how Cyrus made an example of certain men, and said that such men must be weeded out, if we are to keep our army *energos, industrious, efficient, fit for active service* (Xenophon, *Cyropædia* 2.2.23). Polybius uses *energos* to describe a *vigorous* attack (4.63.8); an *effective* weapon (1.40.12); a march made *with rapidity* (5.8.34).

Energos is frequently used of land which is *cultivated* and therefore *productive*. Plutarch speaks of a plain *producing enough* to feed tens of thousands (*Caesar* 58). He speaks of the law of Peisistratus against idleness 'in consequence of which the country became more *productive* (*energos*) and the city more tranquil' (*Solon* 31). Xenophon uses *energos* to describe *cultivated* as opposed to uncultivated land.

Energos is used to describe a mine which produces minerals and which is not worked out. It is used of money, capital, which is not lying idle but which is put out to produce interest. In the papyri *energos* is used to describe a mill which is *in working order*. The Septuagint uses *energos* for a *working day* as opposed to the Sabbath when work was forbidden (Ezek. 46.1).

Here then we have a whole series of ideas, all of which have something to contribute to the NT usage of these words. These words have the meaning of vitality as opposed to deadness, activity as opposed to idleness, efficiency as opposed to uselessness, effective activity as opposed to ineffectiveness. All these ideas will light up the conception of the divine activity of God.

But before we go on to study the NT uses of the words, we must look at the other words in their classical usage.

Let us next look at the word *energeia* in its classical usage. *Energeia* is a noun meaning *activity* or *operation*. As we shall go on to see, this activity and operation have a special flavour.

Aristotle (*Rhetoric* 1141b 28) uses *energeia* to describe *vigour of style*. In Greek grammar *energeia* has one technical meaning; it means the *active* mood of the verb in contradistinction to the *passive*. *Energeia* is used of the massive force of a siege engine, a battering-ram (Diodorus Siculus, 20.95). It is used of the actual *performance* of the duties which befit a man (Philodemus, 1.91).

Galen the medical writer has two interesting and significant usages of the word. He describes it as 'the action which is productive of a result' (*On the Natural Faculties* 1.2, 4, 5). And he uses it (*Works*, ed. Kuhn, Vol. 6, p. 647) of the action or the activity of a drug or a medicine, in the same sense as we speak of a drug *acting* or *working*.

Already one thing becomes clear. The whole tone of *energeia* is *effective action*; it is not simply *action*; it is always action which issues in the desired and purposed result.

Aristotle has a very significant usage of *energeia*, a usage which is characteristic of his ethical writings. He uses *energeia* of that which is *actual* in contradistinction to that which is only *potential*. A man may appear to have all the gifts and all the talents, but they may be only potential; they may be there, but they may never emerge in effective action; it is only when these gifts and talents become actual, become manifested in action, that *energeia* exists.

In the *Nicomachean Ethics* he writes (1098b 33): 'It no doubt makes a great difference whether we conceive the Supreme Good to depend on possessing virtue, or displaying it—on disposition, or on the manifestation of a disposition *in action*' (*energeia*).

He writes (1101a 15): 'May we not then confidently pronounce that man happy who realizes complete virtue *in action*?' (*energein*). He writes (1098a 16): 'The good of a man is *the exercise* of his soul's faculties in conformity with virtue and excellence.'

Here is something very suggestive. *Energeia* is not a man's potential action; it is his actual action. *Energeia* is the demonstration of inner character in deeds. It is goodness plus efficiency, which indeed is the most effective force in the world. It is not simply energy; it is not misdirected energy; it is not ineffective energy; it is focussed, purposeful, meaningful, effective, energetic action.

In classical Greek the word *energein* has all the characteristics of its kindred noun *energeia*. It means *to be in action* or *to operate*, but always with the idea of effectiveness behind it. As we have seen, Aristotle uses it of the effective action of virtue in contradistinction to the unrealized potential of virtue. Polybius (1.13.5) uses it of the energetic and effective carrying on of a campaign.

It has two technical medical usages. It is used of *the efficacious action* of a drug; and it is the technical Greek word for *to operate* in surgery. *Energein* has the twin idea of action and of effective action, of action, and of action which achieves its desired result.

The noun *energēma* means *action, activity* or *operation*. It means something actively done, in contradistinction to something merely suffered, endured or experienced. Perhaps its most suggestive use is that it is used of the Labours of Hercules, a series of labours undertaken and brought to a successful conclusion.

Energēs is the NT form of the classical adjective *energos*. In classical Greek it is not common, but when it does occur it means *effective*. It is used of drugs which are effective; and it is used of siege engines which can breach the walls of a city which is attacked.

The more we study this group of words, the more the same idea keeps recurring, the idea of action, strong and powerful, and above all effective. Again and again the idea of power and the idea of purpose achieved meet in these words. And that is most suggestive when we go on to see that in the NT these are the characteristic words for the action of God.

Energeia occurs in the NT nine times, and always in the writings of Paul. In Eph. 1.19 he speaks of the *working of* God's mighty power, which wrought in Christ, when he raised him from the dead. In Eph. 3.7 Paul says that his ministry was given him by the grace of God by the *effectual working* of his power.

In Eph. 4.16 he describes the body of the Church, harmoniously compounded together, according to the *effectual working* in the measure of every part. In Phil. 3.21 Paul speaks of his certainty that Jesus Christ will change the body of our humiliation into the body of his glory, according to the *working* whereby he is able to subdue all things to himself.

In Col. 1.29 Paul speaks of his own preaching in which he strives according to God's *working*, which *worketh* (*energein*) mightily in him. In Col. 2.12 he speaks of the Christian being buried with Christ in baptism, and raised to life anew, through faith in the *operation* of God, which raised Christ from the dead.

In II Thessalonians we find two of the references to the evil, demonic, anti-God power. In 2.9 we read of the *working* of Satan displayed in the signs and wonders which anti-Christ can work; and in 2.11 we read of an *energeia* of delusion, sent by God upon unbelievers.

The word *energein* occurs in the NT about 19 times. It is three times used of the evil and the demonic power. It is used in Rom. 7.5 of the passions of sin *working* in our members to produce death. In Eph. 2.2 it is used of the spirit that *works* in the children of disobedience. In II Thess. 2.7 it is used of the *working* of the mystery of iniquity.

Far oftener it is used of the working of the power of God. It is used of the miraculous power which *worked* in the miracles of Jesus (Matt. 14.2; cp. Mark 6.14), and which still *works* in the miracles of the Church (Gal. 3.5), and in the gifts and graces which are the equipment and adornment of the Christian life.

It is used of the power which works within the Christian life. Eph. 3.20 speaks of the power that *worketh in us*. Phil. 2.13 speaks of God who *works in us* both to know and to do of his good pleasure.

It is used of the working out of the Christian life. Salvation is *worked out*, made *effective*, by endurance (II Cor. 1.6.) It is used of God's power in the ministry of his preachers. The God who *worked* in Paul to make him an apostle to the Gentiles did so in Peter to make him an apostle to the Jews (Gal. 2.8).

It is used of the energizing *power* of love (Gal. 5.6); and of the *power* of prayer (James 5.16). It is used of the *effective working* of the word of God in those who believe (I Thess. 2.13). It is used of the control of God in which he *works* all things according to his will (Eph. 1.11).

It is used of the death which *works* in Paul that the Corinthians may have life (II Cor. 4.12). It is used of the power of God which *wrought* in Christ in the Resurrection (Eph. 1.20).

The word *energēma* occurs twice in the NT; it is used twice in I Cor. 12.6, 10 of the varied gifts of those who make up the Church, gifts which are set in being and in motion by the power of God.

The word *energēs* is used three times in the NT. In I Cor. 16.9 it is used of the effective door of evangelization which has opened to Paul. In Philemon 6 it is used of a fully effective faith. In Heb. 4.12, where it is translated *powerful*, it is used of the effectiveness of the word of God.

We must now go on to bring together the meaning of the uses of this series of words in the NT.

The NT does not shirk or evade the fact that in this world there is a power of evil in action (II Thess. 2.7, 9, 11; Eph. 2.2; Rom. 7.5). The NT is not a speculative book, and it does not stop to discuss and argue and debate the origin and source of that power of evil; that power is there; and the NT offers the greater power with which the evil power can be defeated.

Let us remember that this whole group of words describes, not only power, but *effective power*, power which achieves the aim and end and object which it set out to achieve. Now it is to God that these words are mainly applied; they therefore bear upon them the message of *the effectiveness of the power of God*. Let us then see the directions in which this power of God is effective.

(i) The power of God is *effective in the Resurrection*. It was that power which wrought in Christ to raise him from the dead (Eph. 1.19, 20; Col. 2.12). It is therefore true that the *power of God is effective in the defeat of death*. Not even man's last and final enemy can stand against the power of God.

(ii) The power of God is *effective in the ministry*. God speaks through those who speak for him, and acts through those who act in his name (Eph. 3.7; Col. 1.29; Gal. 2.8). When a man enters the ministry, he not only thinks, he also listens for a voice; he not only brings to the task his own power, he is also clothed with the power of God.

(iii) The power of God is *effective within the Church*. The Church is built up and held together by the power of God (Eph. 4.16). Special gifts like the ministry of healing come from the power of God (Gal. 3.5); and all the differing gifts which are necessary for the administration and stewardship of the Church are supplied by the working of the power of God (I Cor. 12.6, 10, 11).

(iv) God's power is *effective in the defeat of sin*. Through Christ and in Christ there comes that power by which man's being of humiliation can be changed into Christ's being of glory (Phil. 3.21). The humiliations and the frustrations and the defeats of sin are swallowed up in the power of God.

(v) God's power is *effective in the world*. This is not a world which is out of control, but a world where God is working things out (Eph. 1.11). Behind the moving web of things there is design; the kaleidoscope of experience has a pattern, and the designer of the pattern is God.

(vi) God's power is *effective within*. It is not a power which coerces a man from outside; it is a power which floods a man's being from within (Eph. 3.20; Phil. 2.13). It is the power which makes a man most literally powerful.

(vii) There are certain ways and media through which God's power becomes effective.

(a) God's power becomes effective *through his word* (I Thess. 2.13; Heb. 4.12). The word is the source of power. Through God's word to men comes God's power for men. The Bible is not only a history-book; it is also a power-house.

(b) God's power becomes effective *through love* (Gal. 5.6). Love is the energizing power which turns knowledge into devotion and faith into sacrificial service. The power which comes to man is at one and the same time an indwelling and an out-going power.

(c) God's power becomes *effective through prayer* (James 5.16). Prayer is empowering contact with God. Prayer is not only a gateway to God for us; it is a channel for God to us.

(d) God's power becomes effective *through evangelization* (I Cor. 16.9). Man's evangelization of men becomes the channel of God's power to men.

(e) God's power becomes effective *through endurance* (II Cor. 1.6). The power of God does not come to the man who begins and gives up; it comes to the man who endures to the end.

The glory of the Christian life is that it is the life which is clothed with the *energeia*, the energy, the effective power of God himself.

ENTUGCHANEIN AND ENTEUXIS

PETITION TO THE KING

Entugchanein, the verb, and *enteuxis*, the noun, are two of the prayer words of the NT. *Entugchanein* is usually translated *to make intercession for*.

In Rom. 8.26, 27 it is said that the Spirit *makes intercession for us*. In Rom. 8.34 Jesus is said to *make intercession for us*. In Rom. 11.2 Elijah is said *to make intercession* with God against Israel. In Heb. 7.25 it is said that Jesus ever lives *to make intercession for us*.

The noun *enteuxis* occurs twice in the NT. In I Tim. 2.1 it is translated *intercession*; and in I Tim. 4.5 it is translated *prayer*.

It is the idea which lies behind these words, the picture which they contain, which makes them so significant and so important.

Originally *entugchanein* meant quite simply *to meet a person*, to fall in with a person, to come close to a person. When we meet a person we talk to him and he talks to us; and so the word went on to mean *to converse with a person*; even further, it began to mean *to have intimate fellowship and communion with a person*.

For instance, when Socrates was near the end, and when he was preparing to die, he told his friends that he welcomed death because after death he would *have converse with* Palamedes and Ajax and others of the great men of the ancient days who died through unjust judgment (Plato, *Apology* 41b). To Socrates the reward of death was intimate fellowship with the great and good who had gone before.

Here then is the first idea in *entugchanein*. It speaks of the right to approach God; it speaks of the intimate fellowship which the Christian can enjoy with God; it means that we do not make our requests to God from a great distance and across some infinity of space, but that we can talk and converse with him as a man talks with his friend. As we meet our friends, so we can meet God.

But the word develops still another meaning. It begins by meaning simply to meet a person; it goes on to mean to have intimate converse and fellowship with a person; but finally it becomes in the papyri an almost technical word for *presenting a petition to someone* in authority and especially to the king.

Enteuxis, which originally meant simply a *meeting*, comes to be the usual word for a *petition* presented to the king.

There is an interesting papyrus which tells of twins, Thaues and Taous, who served in the Temple of Serapis at Memphis. They felt that they were being unjustly treated and that they were not receiving the treatment which they had been promised. Ptolemy Philometor and his queen, Cleopatra the Second, came on a visit to the temple, and the twins seized the opportunity to present the king with an *enteuxis*, a petition, which set out their grievances and which appealed for justice.

Enteuxis, then, is the technical word for *a petition to a king*; and *entugchanein* is the technical word for presenting such a petition.

Here then is a tremendous picture. When we pray we are in the position of those who have undisputed access that they may bring their petitions to the king. When we pray it is to a king we come. Therein is set forth at once both the tremendous privilege of prayer, and the tremendous power of prayer.

We have the privilege of entry to the presence of the King of kings; and when we enter there we have all his power and greatness on which we may draw. Prayer is nothing less than entering into the presence of the Almighty and receiving the resources of the Eternal.

EPAGGELIA AND EPAGGELLESTHAI

THE WORDS OF PROMISE

In the NT the noun *epaggelia* means a *promise*, and the verb *epaggellesthai* means to *promise*. We must begin by looking at the classical usage of these words, because in the case of these words the classical usages have very definite light to shed on the meaning and the flavour of these words in the NT.

(i) These words in classical Greek are very common—in fact they are almost technical—in connexion with *public announcements*. They are the words which are used of the announcement of the public games, or of the public sacrifices to the gods. They are used of announcements which are everybody's concern.

(ii) In classical Greek there is more than one word for a *promise*, and the most interesting and significant thing about *epaggelia* is that its characteristic meaning is *a promise which is freely offered and volunteered*. It is not a promise which is extracted or coerced or wrung from someone.

It is not even a promise which is made on mutual approach and mutual agreement; that is *hyposchesis*. *Epaggelia* is characteristically a promise freely made and freely given. It has in it far more of a free offer than a conditioned promise.

(iii) In classical Greek *epaggelia* and *epaggellesthai* sometimes bear a meaning which has a tinge of fault in it. Sometimes they imply a profession, and a profession which is not met and carried out in actual practice. The words sometimes have to do with political canvassing.

They describe the manifesto of a candidate for office with all the promises of what he proposes to do, if he is elected to office, promises which are made rather as baits to the electorate than with any honest intention of fulfilling them.

The words sometimes have to do with the offers which the Sophists made. The Sophists were Greek teachers who arose in the fifth century B.C. and who offered to teach anybody anything for pay. The great teachers, like Plato and Isocrates, regarded these Sophists with intense dislike. They believed that all they did was to make people able to argue cleverly, until they could make the worse appear the better reason, and that they were out mainly for money.

They *professed* (*epaggellesthai*) to teach virtue, but it was an empty profession. They competed among themselves, each one *professing* to be able to give a better and more effective curriculum than his rival.

The words sometimes are used to describe a lover's professions. In the first flush of glamour and excitement of love, the lover will promise anything, but when it comes to actual performance, the professions are seen to be empty words. So the words can be used of a promise which is magnificently given, but meanly carried out.

Finally in regard to this usage, the words can be used of claims made for the curative properties of drugs. They are the words which would be used for the claims of patent medicines which profess to be panaceas for all diseases. Sometimes, then, these words can be used in connexion with a profession which is not backed by deeds to fit it.

In the NT the words *epaggelia* and *epaggellesthai* are used uniformly and consistently of God's promises. There are, in fact, only two instances where they are used definitely of human promises.

In Acts 23.21 the Jews await the *promise* of the military commander of Jerusalem to send Paul down to Caesarea, in order that they may take steps to assassinate him on the way. In Mark 14.11 we read of the *promise* of the Jewish authorities to pay Judas the reward for information which will lead to the convenient arrest of Jesus.

But, apart from these two instances the words in the NT are always used of the divine promises and it is to these promises that we must proceed to turn our attention.

When we study the words of promise, we find that the promise did not start with the NT.

(i) God's promise was given specially to *the nation of Israel* (Rom. 9.4; Eph. 2.12). God offered Israel a unique position among the nations; in a special sense Israel was his peculiar people. The tragedy of Israel was that she misunderstood her function. She conceived of herself as having been promised special honour and privilege, when in point of fact she had been offered special duty and responsibility. God's offer is always the offer of a task to do for him.

(ii) God's promise to the nation of Israel derived specially from *Abraham*. The promise to Abraham was threefold. (a) It was the promise of the Promised Land (Acts 7.5; Heb. 11.9, 13). (b) It was the promise to Sara of a son, when the coming of a son seemed impossible (Rom. 9.9; Gal. 4.23, 28). (c) It was the promise that in him all nations of the earth would be blessed (Rom. 4.13; Gal. 3.16; Heb. 6.13).

Abraham was the man who was chosen that through him blessedness might come to the world. God chose Abraham as a man through whom he might act on men. God is always seeking men through whom he may act.

(iii) God's promise was the promise of a *Messiah* of the line of David (Acts 13.23, 32). The word *Messiah* and the word *Christ* are the same word. *Messiah* is the Hebrew and *Christ* is the Greek for *the anointed one*. God's promise was the promise of a King, through whom the kingdoms of the world would become the Kingdom of the Lord.

(iv) All the OT promises of God find their *fulfilment in Jesus Christ* (Rom. 15.8; II Cor. 1.20; Gal. 3.19, 29). When Jesus came, it was as if God said to men: 'Here is the one in whom all my promises come true.' Jesus is the one in whom there meet the dream of God and the dream of men.

(v) In Jesus there comes to men not only the fulfilment

of the old promises; there comes also even *better promises* (Heb. 8.6; 9.15). Jesus is not only the consummation of the hopes and the dreams of the past; he brings to men things more precious and things greater than ever they had dreamed of.

This is important, because it means that Jesus does not only fulfil the OT prophecies and ideals; he surpasses them. He brings into life not only something which grew out of the past, but also something which is completely new.

When we see how far back the promise of God goes, it makes sense of history. We may promise a child some gift or some privilege with the intention of giving it to him when he is fit to use it and enjoy it and to enter into it. For instance, a father might plan and save in order to give a child the benefit of a university education, when the child came of age to benefit from such an education; and during the period of waiting, the father would do everything he could to train the child to reach a stage when he could be fit to enjoy the promise. That is what God did with men.

He chose a man; and chose a nation; that out of that nation there might come his Son in due time. Nor, in the choice of a nation, did God leave the rest of the world alone. Clement of Alexandria saw in pagan philosophy that which prepared the heathen for accepting Christ, just as much as the Law prepared the Jews. When we think of it this way we see the whole of history as a preparation of men to accept the promise and the offer of God.

Let us now see what God did promise to his people in Jesus Christ.

(i) God promised men *the gift of the Holy Spirit* (Luke 24.29; Acts 1.4; 2.23; Eph. 1.15). The Holy Spirit may be taken to be God active in the lives and in the minds of men. The Holy Spirit is the power and the presence and the person who guides men into strength and adequacy of life, power and clarity of thought, lucidity and persuasiveness of speech. The promise of the Spirit is the promise of God to make us live and think with his own power.

(ii) With the gift of the Spirit, God promised the gift of *forgiveness* (Acts 2.39). It is never enough to think of forgiveness as simply the remission of some penalty which should have fallen upon us. Forgiveness is essentially *the restoration of a lost relationship*. It was not that God was estranged from men; it was that men were estranged from God. Through that which Jesus Christ has done men can become friends with God.

(iii) God promises men *eternal life*, life in time and life in eternity (I Tim. 4.8; Titus 1.2; II Tim. 1.1; James 1.12; I John 2.25). Eternal life is not simply life which goes on for ever. It is true that the NT never forgets that God promised men the resurrection from the dead (Acts 26.6). But the essential of eternal life is not simply duration; it is quality.

It is told that once a drooping and depressed soldier came to Julius Caesar with a request to be allowed to commit suicide and so to end his life. Caesar looked at the dispirited figure: 'Man', he said, 'were you ever really alive?'

Eternal life is something which can start here and now. Eternal life is the injection into the realm of time of something of the realm of eternity; it is the coming into human life of something of the life of God himself. It is the promise of God that if a man chooses to live life with Jesus Christ, heaven begins on earth. Into man's trouble and frustration there come the peace and power of God.

(iv) God promises the *Kingdom* to those who love him (James 2.5). It is too often the case that men think of the call of God as a call to a grim life in which all they wish for has to be given up, and all that is stern and hard has to be accepted. It is true that there is submission and discipline in the Christian life; but the end of the submission and the discipline is a kingdom, a royal power in life.

(v) God promises men *the coming again of his Son* (II Peter 3.4, 9). This simply means that God guarantees that there will be a consummation in history. The Stoics, who in NT times were the highest thinkers, conceived of history as circular. They said that, once every so many thousands of years, there was a conflagration which engulfed and destroyed all things, and that then the same old process began all over again. History was a treadmill, not a march to a goal.

When we divest the idea of the Second Coming of all the purely Jewish apparatus, and the purely temporary pictures, we are left with the one significant truth that in history there comes the consummation of the triumph of Christ.

(vi) God promises *rest for his people* (Heb. 4.1). Someone recently was asked what he thought was the greatest mark and characteristic of the modern world. His answer was: 'Tired eyes.'

Life is in any event a struggle; the Christian life takes all a man has to give. The NT describes it as a battle, a campaign, a race, an endurance test; but after it is ended there comes the rest of God; but rest is something which no man can enjoy unless he has done his best.

We must note still further *the nature of this promise* which is offered to the Christian.

(i) It is a *promise of God* (Luke 24.49; Acts 1.4). Here we find something which connects with one of the classical usages of these words. We saw, when we were studying the classical usage, that sometimes these words stood for a profession without a corresponding performance.

That is still so in the NT. I Tim. 2.10 urges Christian women to live a life which befits the faith which they profess. I Tim. 6.20, 21 speaks of the vain and empty knowledge which the intellectualists of the world profess. II Peter 2.19 speaks of those who make an illusory offer of liberty while they themselves are slaves to corruption. The NT more than once goes out of its way to stress the fact that God's promises, God's professions are true and dependable. God's promises are true for two reasons.

(a) They are true because God is *faithful*. 'He is faithful that promised' (Heb. 10.23). God cannot lie (Titus 1.2). God even guaranteed the promises by swearing by himself (Heb. 6.17). The promises of God are guaranteed by the truth of God.

(b) They are true because God is *powerful*. God is able to perform that which he has promised (Rom. 4.21). The promises of God are therefore guaranteed by the power of God. Men's promises may be empty professions, but God's promises are to be utterly relied on because God's truth cannot lie, and God's power cannot fail.

(ii) The promises of God are *founded on grace and not on law*. We already saw that *epaggelia* in classical Greek is a promise and an offer freely and voluntarily made. The promises of God are not dependent on man's merit or man's performance; they are dependent solely on the sheer generosity of God. God's promises were made, not because of man's virtue, but because of God's mercy. Behind them is not man's merit, but God's love.

(iii) The promises of God are therefore *to be appropriated by faith* (Rom. 4.14, 20; Gal. 3.24). They cannot be earned; they must be accepted. Man must rid himself of the pride which seeks to earn God's promises by works; he must have the humility which is ever content to be in God's debt, and which accepts God's promises in faith.

(iv) In spite of that the promises of God are *the motive of man's amendment*. It is because they have the promises that men must cleanse themselves (II Cor. 7.1). No man, who is in love, and whose love is answered, ever believed himself to be worthy of being loved. Any man who is loved well knows that he must spend all his life seeking to deserve the love which he can never deserve. It is so with us and God; we can never earn the promises of God, because they are given to us in the generosity of his love, but nonetheless, we are under the life-long obligation to spend all our lives *trying* to deserve that love.

So this finally brings us to the things we must bring fully to enjoy the promises of God.

(i) We must bring *patience*. It was through patience that Jesus himself earned the promise, and the same must be true of us (Heb. 6.12, 15). We have to run and not be weary; we have to endure to the end; we have to learn to wait. It is patience—the ability to bear things—which in the end inherits and obtains the promise.

(ii) We must bring *loyalty*. It was through their utter fidelity, their unshakable loyalty, that the martyrs obtained the promises (Heb. 11.33). It is the man who is faithful unto death who obtains the crown.

(iii) We must bring *obedience*. It is after we have done the will of God that we receive the promise (Heb. 10.36). As in so many things, so in this, the gifts of God are given, but they are not given away. The promises of God are freely offered in the generosity of God. It is in patience, in loyalty, and in obedience that we shall most fully enter into them.

EPIEIKĒS AND EPIEIKEIA

MORE THAN JUSTICE

WE will not begin with a translation of *epieikēs* for the very good reason that it is extremely difficult to produce one. The adjective *epieikēs* occurs in the NT five times, and the noun *epieikeia* twice. On these seven occasions Moffatt uses six different translations. In Phil. 4.5, where the neuter of the adjective is used as a noun, he translates it 'forbearance'; in I Tim. 3.3, 'lenient'; in Tit. 3.2, 'conciliatory'; in James 3.17, 'forbearing'; and in I Pet. 2.18, 'reasonable'. The two occurrences of the noun are in Acts 24.4, and II Cor. 10.1, which Moffatt respectively translates 'courtesy' and 'consideration'. The American RSV is more consistent. In the occurrences of the adjective, except in the first case, where it also translates 'forbearance', it con-

sistently translates by the word 'gentle'; and in the two
occurrences of the noun it uses 'kindness' in the first and
'gentleness' in the second.

Long before the NT used it, this word had a great record
in Greek ethical writing. Trench sums up the meaning that
is behind it when he says that it expresses that 'modera-
tion which recognizes the impossibility that cleaves to
formal law'. He says that it is the word which recognizes
that there are occasions when a 'legal' right can become a
'moral' wrong. Aristotle discussed *epieikeia* in the *Nicomachean Ethics*. He says that *epieikeia* is that which is just
and sometimes that which is better than justice (*Eth. Nic.*
v. 10.6). He says that *epieikeia* is that which corrects the
law when the law is deficient because of its generality. He
compares the man who is *epieikēs* with the man who is
akribodikaios. The man who is *akribodikaios* is the man
who stands up for the last tittle of his legal rights; but the
man who is *epieikēs* knows that there are times when a
thing may be legally completely justified and yet morally
completely wrong. The man who is *epieikēs* knows when
to relax the law under the compulsion of a force that is
higher and greater than law. He knows the time when to
stand on his rights would unquestionably be legal, and
would just as unquestionably be completely unchristian.

The basic and the fundamental thing about *epieikeia* is
that it goes back to God. If God stood on his rights, if God
applied to us nothing but the rigid standards of law, where
would we be? God is the supreme example of one who is
epieikēs and who deals with others with *epieikeia*.

It may be hard to translate this word, but it is not hard
to see the clamant need of the quality which it describes.
We live in a society where men insist on standing on their
legal rights, where they will do only what they are compelled to do, and where they desire to make others do all
that they can compel them to do. Again and again we have
seen congregations torn by strife and reduced to tragic
unhappiness because men and women, committees and

courts stood on the letter of the law. When a congregation's governing body meets with a copy of its Church's book of laws prominently displayed on the chairman's table trouble is never far away. A new world would arise in society and in the Church if men ceased to base their actions on law and on legal rights and prayed to God to give them *epieikeia*.

EPITAGĒ

THE ROYAL COMMAND

In the NT, the word *epitagē* is peculiar to the writings of Paul, if we include the Pastoral Epistles in the Pauline writings. Paul makes two uses of this word.

(i) There are four passages where he uses it in connexion with the message, the instruction and the advice which he is giving. In I Cor. 7.6, where he is talking about certain problems and customs in the married life, he contrasts that which is by *permission* and that which is by *epitagē*. He contrasts, as it were, that which is a human opinion and that which is a direct, revealed command from God. He contrasts that which is a piece of practical advice and that which is a counsel of God and, therefore, a counsel of perfection.

In I Cor. 7.25 he says that concerning virgins he has no *epitagē*. Again, anything which he says is his own opinion, and is not to be regarded as a definite divine command. He uses the same way of speaking in II Cor. 8.8. When he is writing to Titus, he orders Titus to speak, exhort, and rebuke with all *epitagē*, with the full authority of the divine voice of God.

(ii) There are three passages where he uses it of the direct action of God. In Rom. 16.26 he speaks of the manifestation of Christ to the Gentiles as being in accordance with the *epitagē*, the divine command, of God. In Titus 1.3 he declares that the word which he preaches is committed to him by the *epitagē* of God. In I Tim. 1.1 he declares that he is an apostle by the *epitagē* of God.

In secular Greek, *epitagē* is used of the decrees of the law. Diodorus Siculus (1.70) has an interesting passage on the life of the kings of Egypt; 'The life which the kings of the Egyptians lived was not like that of other men who enjoy autocratic power, and do in all matters exactly as they please without being held to account, but all their acts are regulated by the *prescriptions* (*epitagai*) set forth in the law.' Clearly an *epitagē* is something which comes from and speaks with an authority than which none could be higher.

It is here that we have to add the evidence of the Septuagint. In the Septuagint the word *epitagē* occurs five times. In three instances it is used of a *royal command*. In Esth. 1.8 it is used of the *royal command* of Ahasuerus. In Dan. 3.16 Shadrach, Meshach and Abednego deny that they are answerable to the *epitagē*, *the royal command*, of Nebuchadnezzar which orders them to worship the image of the king.

In Wisdom 14.16, when the time of national degeneration is being described, it is said: 'By *the commandments* (*epitagai*) *of princes* the graven images received worship.' In the other two instances the word is connected with God.

In Wisdom 18.16 the sword of the word is *the unfeigned commandment* (*epitagē*) of God. In Wisdom 19.6 it is said that every part of the new creation will minister to *the several commandments* (*epitagai*) of God.

Clearly, then, this word *epitagē* has in it all the majesty of divine command.

But it is in the Greek of the papyri that the word gains its characteristic sense. There it is used for an order or an injunction, but especially for a divine command. Isias dedicates an altar to the mother of the gods, according to the *epitagē*, *the commandment*, of Cybele, which has come to him direct in a dream. Varius Pollio erects a pillar to the honour of the gods in obedience to the *epitagē, the command*, of God. *Epitagē* becomes the word of the divine command.

Here then are two great truths.

(i) The preacher's message is a divine command. When he is really preaching, he is speaking for God. He is bringing to men, not his own opinions, but the direct commands of God.

(ii) The preacher's commission is from God. Paul was supremely conscious that his task as a missionary to the Gentiles, his office as an apostle to the Church, came to him by the royal command, the *epitagē*, of God.

Paul has another way of saying that. Often he speaks of himself as an apostle by the *thelēma, the will*, of God. (I Cor. 1.1; II Cor. 1.1; Eph. 1.1; Col. 1.1). He speaks of himself as separated by God for his task from his mother's womb (Gal. 1.15). He speaks of necessity being laid upon him to preach (I Cor. 9.16). Paul always felt, not that he had chosen Christ, but that Christ had chosen him. He always thought of himself as a man who held the King's commission. For Paul, the ministry was not a profession; it was a vocation. It was not a trade; it was a calling. He came to it, not because he had chosen it as a career, but because God had chosen and called him to it.

Robert Robinson, the great Cambridge Baptist minister, had an experience of conversion. After it there were many who wished him to enter the ministry of the Church. He said: 'Lord, accomplish Thy will in all I have to say. *But God forbid that I should run before I am sent.*' The word *epitagē* enshrines the fact that no man may dare to contemplate the work of the ministry unless he is truly aware that he has received the King's commission to it.

ERITHEIA

THE WRONG KIND OF AMBITION

Eritheia is a word whose meaning degenerated, and the story of its degeneration is in itself a grim commentary on human nature. In the NT it is used seven times, and always of a fault which ruins Church work. In Rom. 2.8 it is used to describe those who are 'contentious'; in II Cor. 12.20 it occurs amid a list of faults which are ruining the Church at Corinth, and in Gal. 5.20 it is one of the works of the flesh, and in both cases the AV translates it 'strife'; in Phil. 1.16 and 2.3 it is used to describe the wrong motive for preaching and the wrong spirit in which to live; the AV translates it, in the first case, 'contention', and in the second, 'strife'; it is twice used in James (3.14; 3.16), where it is a characteristic of the wisdom which is not from above and where the AV translates it 'envying'.

Now the interesting thing about this word is that, with these cases before us, we would very naturally and almost inevitably derive it from *eris*, which is the word for 'strife'; but that is not its derivation at all. *Erithos* originally meant 'a day labourer'; the word was specially connected with 'spinners' and 'weavers', and the popular derivation was from *erion*, which means 'wool'. *Eritheia* therefore began by being a perfectly respectable word with the meaning 'labour for wages'. It then begins to degenerate. It began to mean that kind of work which is done for motives of pay and for nothing else; that kind of work which has no motive of service whatever and which has only one question—What do I get out of it? It therefore went on to mean 'canvassing and intriguing for public office'. It was the characteristic of the man who sought public office, not for any service he could render the State, but simply and solely for his own honour and glory and for his own profit. It then acquired two other meanings.

First, it came to be used of 'party squabbles', of the jockeying for position and the intriguing for place and power which is so often characteristic of both secular and ecclesiastical politics. Second, it ended up by meaning 'selfish ambition', the ambition which has no conception of service and whose only aims are profit and power.

It is extremely interesting to see how the NT uses it. By far its greater number of uses occur in Paul, and no one knew the inside of the Early Church better than Paul did. It was the fault which could so easily wreck a Church. It was the fault which nearly wrecked the Church of God at Corinth by splitting it into sects and factions who were more concerned with their own supremacy than the supremacy of Christ. In Philippi it had actually become the moving motive of certain preachers. They were eager rather to show their own greatness than the greatness of Christ. Long ago Denney bitingly said that no preacher can show at one and the same time that he is clever and that Christ is wonderful. It was characteristic in Paul of the works of the flesh and in James of the earthly and sensual wisdom. It is the characteristic of the man who applies earthly and human standards to everything, and who assesses things by the measuring rod of personal prestige and personal success.

It is an illuminating light on human nature that the word which began by describing the work that a man does for an honest day's pay came in the end to describe the work which is done for pay and pay alone. It is a warning to our own generation, for most of our troubles today are not basically economic troubles; they spring rather from the spirit which asks, always, What can I get out of life? and, never, What can I put into life?

EUAGGELION

THE GOOD NEWS

THE word *euaggelion* means 'gospel' or 'good news', and
when we come to study it we are of necessity at the very
heart and centre of the Christian faith. The word *euaggelion*
is so specifically and characteristically a Christian word
that it has not a long history outside the NT. In classical
Greek it has three meanings. (i) Originally it meant 'the
reward given to a messenger for bringing good tidings'. It
is so used in the Septuagint in II Sam. 4.10. (ii) It went on to
mean 'the sacrifices made to the gods when such good tidings
were received'. (iii) Not in classical Greek at all, but in late
Hellenistic Greek it comes to mean 'the good tidings themselves'. In the Septuagint it is used for the good tidings of victory' (I Sam. 31.9), the good tidings of 'the birth of a child'
(Jer. 20.15), and sometimes simply of tidings of any kind.

In the Septuagint it has two usages which are faint fore-
tastes of its NT use. (i) In the Psalms the corresponding
verb is used of telling forth the righteousness and the saving
power of God (Ps. 40.10; 96.2). (ii) In Isaiah it is used of
the glad tidings of the coming of God's anointed one to his
people (Isa. 40.9; 52.7). In the papyri both noun and verb
are very rare. The verb (*euaggelizesthai*) is used of a slave
coming with news of a general's victory, and the noun
(*euaggelion*) is used in an inscription which says that the
birthday of the Roman Emperor Augustus was the beginning of good tidings for the world. But it is when we come
to the NT that *euaggelion* becomes a tremendous word.

(i) It is the word which is the summation of the whole
Christian message (Mark 1.1; I Cor. 15.1). The Kingdom
which Jesus preached is 'good news' (Matt. 4.23; 9.35;
24.14). The proof of the centrality of this word in the
Christian message can be seen from the fact that *euaggelion*
occurs 72 times in the NT and of these 72 instances 54 are

in Paul's letters. To the greatest of the Christian mission-aries Christianity was essentially 'good news'. There is an implicit contrast here. The preaching of John the Baptist with its consuming fire, its winnowing fan, its axe laid to the root of the tree is the reverse of good news. It is tidings of disaster, but the whole essence of the message of Jesus is 'good news of God'.

(ii) Sometimes the *euaggelion* is spoken of as the *euaggelion* 'of God' (Mark 1.14; I Thess. 2.2, 8, 9). It is good news of God in two senses. (*a*) It showed to men a God the like of whom they had never dreamed, a God whose heart was love. (*b*) It was good news 'sent by God'. Behind the whole process of salvation is God. It is always wrong to think of an angry God and a gentle Christ, to think that what Jesus did changed the attitude of God to men. It was because God so loved the world that he sent his Son. The good news is *of* God and *from* God.

(iii) Sometimes *euaggelion* is spoken of as the *euaggelion* of 'Jesus Christ' (Mark 1.1; II Cor. 4.4; 9.13; 10.14). It is the good news of Jesus Christ in two senses. (*a*) Jesus 'brought' it to men. Without him they would never have known it. (*b*) Jesus 'embodied' it to men. He did not only *tell* men what God was like, he *showed* them the Father.

(iv) Sometimes Paul uses the expression 'my' or 'our' *euaggelion* (II Cor. 4.3; I Thess. 1.5; II Thess. 2.14). The good news comes from God, and belongs to God. It is brought by Jesus and belongs to Jesus. But, for all that, a man must 'appropriate' it until it belongs to him. He must pass it through his mind and receive it into his heart until it is utterly and inalienably his.

(v) The *euaggelion* is for all men (Mark 13.10; 16.15; Acts 15.7). The Jews had always believed that in God's economy there was a most favoured nation clause. But the gospel of Christ is the gospel without boundaries. The good news is good news for all.

Let us go on to see certain things about this *euaggelion*, this 'good news' in regard to man.

(i) The *euaggelion* is not a human discovery, it is 'a revelation from God'. The fact that God is as Jesus showed him to be is not something which a man could have discovered by intellectual processes. Man does not discover God. God *reveals himself* (Gal. 1.11, 12).

(ii) The *euaggelion* is something in which a man must 'believe' (Mark 1.15). The whole of Christianity consists in living life in the unalterable conviction that the good news that Jesus brought about God is true.

(iii) The *euaggelion* is something which he who knows must 'proclaim to others' (Rom. 15.19; I Cor. 9.14, 18; II Cor. 10.14; 11.7; Gal. 2.2). When a man has found the good news, he has not truly found it until he wishes to share it with others. A missionary tells of an Indian who had been hostile to Christianity and who was converted to it. He got himself a Bible. He got used to reading it, and, as he read, he would come upon a passage which spoke to his heart, and with his finger in the place, he would rush out into the road and stop each passer-by, crying out, 'Have you heard about this?' No Christian can keep the good news to himself. Every Christian is a missionary.

(iv) That task of spreading the *euaggelion* is not something which a man chooses, but something which is 'entrusted' to him and 'laid upon' him (I Thess. 2.4; I Cor. 9.16). It is most literally 'for God's sake' that he must pass on the good news, which he himself has received.

(v) The *euaggelion* is something for which a man must 'risk everything' (Mark 8.35; 10.29; Rom. 1.16; I Cor. 9.23). He must be prepared to stake everything on the certainty that the man who obeys God's commandments will find God's promises true.

(vi) *The euaggelion* is something which a man can 'serve' (Rom. 1.1; 15.16; Phil. 1.12; 2.22; 4.3; I Thess. 3.2). The reception of the good news points at one and the same time 'to privilege and to duty'. A man must give his life to that which gave him life.

(vii) The *euaggelion* is something which a man can

'defend' (Phil. 1.7, 17). By his life and words and conduct and action he must at every moment be 'a defender of the faith'.

(viii) The *euaggelion* is something which a man can 'hinder' (I Cor. 9.12). It is the awe-inspiring responsibility of the Christian life that every one of us can make others think less or more of the Christian faith.

(ix) The *euaggelion* is something which a man can 'miss' or 'refuse' (Rom. 2.16; 10.16; II Thess. 1.7, 8; I Pet. 4.17). To the end of the day a man's will is free. It is the characteristic of love that love can only offer and can never coerce. A man can spurn the offer of God or he can completely disregard it. He can live life as if the good news did not exist, but he does so at the peril of his immortal soul.

(x) The *euaggelion* is something which a man can 'twist' and 'distort' (II Cor. 11.4; Gal. 1.6, 7). There is such a thing as preaching what Paul called 'another gospel'. When a man begins to believe in or to seek to propagate Christianity as he would like it to be instead of as God proclaims it is, he cannot do other than preach 'another gospel'. It is only after we have listened to God that we can speak to men. The danger is that we tell God instead of listening to God telling us.

As we study this word *euaggelion* and as we trace it through the NT we begin to see that it involves and includes certain things.

(i) The *euaggelion* is 'the good news of truth' (Gal. 2.5, 14; Col. 1.5). With the coming of Jesus Christ the time of guesses about God is ended and the time of certainty begun. With his coming the time of groping after the meaning and the method of life is closed and the time of certainty is here. Christianity was never meant to present men with a series of problems but with an armoury of certainties.

(ii) The *euaggelion* is 'the good news of hope' (Col. 2.23). The man who tries to live life with only the materials which human effort can bring to it cannot do other than despair of himself and despair of the world. John Buchan defined an atheist as 'a man with no invisible means of support'. When a man realizes what the good news means he is filled with hope for himself and for the world.

(iii) The *euaggelion* is 'the good news of peace' (Eph. 6.15). So long as a man tries to live life alone he is inevitably a split personality. As Studdert-Kennedy said, 'Part of him comes from heaven, and part of him comes from earth.' The good news tells us that victory comes from surrender, from the death of self and the rising to life of Christ within us. The good news brings to men the possibility of a fully integrated personality where the old unhappy tensions are ended.

(iv) The *euaggelion* is 'the good news of God's promise' (Eph. 3.6). The characteristic of the pagan gods, and even of God as the OT knew him, was that he was a God of threats. Jesus brought the good news which told not of the God of the threat, but the God of the promise. That by no means removes all obligations from life, for a promise brings its obligation just as much as a threat does, but the obligation becomes the obligation to answer to love and not to cower before vengeance.

(v) The *euaggelion* is 'the good news of immortality' (II Tim. 1.10). In face of death the pagan sorrowed and feared as one who had no hope (I Thess. 4.13). One of the saddest of papyrus letters is a letter from a mother to a mother and father whose little child has died. 'Irene to Taonnophris and Philo, good comfort. I was as sorry and wept over the departed one as I wept for Didymus. All things that were fitting I did. . . . But all the same in the face of such things *there is nothing that anyone can do*.' That was the pagan outlook in the face of death. But the good news brings the certainty that death is not the end but the beginning of life, not the departure into annihilation but the departure to be for ever with God.

(vi) The *euaggelion* is 'good news of the risen Christ' (I Cor. 15.1ff.; II Tim. 2.8). The good news which

Christianity brings is that we do not worship a dead hero, but we live with a living presence. We are not left with only a pattern to copy and an example to follow, we are left with a constant companion of our way. Our faith is not a faith in a figure in a book who lived and died, but in one who rose from death and who is alive forever more.

(vii) The *euaggelion* is 'good news of salvation' (Eph. 1.13). It is news of that power which wins us forgiveness for past sin, liberation from present sin, strength for the future to conquer sin. It is good news of victory.

EUSEBEIA

THE WORD OF TRUE RELIGION

THERE is a very great group of Greek words which is characteristic of the language of the Pastoral Epistles. As we shall see, they are not easy to translate, but they all have in them one essential idea.

There is *eusebeia*, the noun, which is usually translated *godliness* in the AV. The RSV usually retains this translation. Moffatt translates it either *piety*, or *religion*, in the sense of *true religion*.

There is *eusebēs*, the adjective, which the AV translates *devout* or *godly*, a translation which the RSV retains; Moffatt translates it *religious, religiously-minded, or pious.*

There is *eusebein*, the verb, which means *to worship, to carry out the duties of true religion.* There is *eusebōs*, the adverb, which the AV translates *godly.*

There is the closely related word *theosebeia*, which the AV translates godliness, and the adjective *theosebēs*, which means *worshipping God.*

It can be seen that all these words come from the same root; and the root meaning of them all is *awe* in the presence of that which is more than human, *reverence* in the presence of that which is majestic and divine; not only do they express that feeling of awe and reverence, but they also imply a *worship* which befits that awe, and a life of active *obedience* which befits that reverence. The fact is that in so far as Greek has a word for *religion* that word is *eusebeia*.

Let us then begin by seeing what the Greeks themselves said about these words. The Platonic Definitions define *eusebeia* as *right conduct in regard to the gods*. The Stoics defined it *as knowledge of how God should be worshipped.*

Lucian (*De Calum.*) said that the man who is *eusebēs*, pious, religious, is a *lover of the gods* (*philotheos*). Xenophon (*Memorabilia* 4.3.2) said that such a man was *wise concerning the gods*.

It was always the Greek custom to define every virtue and every good quality as the mean between two extremes. Virtue was the right point, the happy medium, between some defect and some excess.

So Plutarch says that *eusebeia* is the mean between *atheotēs*, which is *atheism*, and *deisidaimonia*, which is *superstition*; Philo said it was the mean between *asebeia*, which is *impiety*, and *deisidaimonia*.

That is to say, *eusebeia* is the right attitude to God and to things divine, the attitude which does not eliminate God altogether, and which does not degenerate into futile superstition, the attitude which gives God the place he ought to occupy in life and in thought and in devotion.

Josephus sets *eusebeia* over against *eidōlolatreia*, which is *idolatry*. *Eusebeia* gives God *the right place*, and worships God in *the right way*. Plato urges all men to *eusebeia*, that we may avoid evil and obtain good, and so become the friends of God (Plato, *Symposium* 193d).

But not only does *eusebeia* put a man into the right relationship with God; it also puts him into the right relationship with men. Plato speaks of *eusebeia* both to God and to parents (Plato, *Republic* 615c).

In Greek thought the word *eusebeia* has certain uses

which will still further illustrate the idea behind it. Even in pagan religion *eusebeia* was a word of a noble lineage.

(i) Sometimes it can mean that respect for the gods which issues in a careful carrying out of all the ritual which the worship of the gods demands. That is to say, sometimes it can be a word of correct ritual rather than of moral quality. There is an inscription in which the town of Priēnē is praised for its '*reverence for things divine*', that is for the care of the ritual of the temples of the gods. Payments to the temples are said to be *ex eusebeias, in consequence of piety*. This is to some extent the lower and the ritual meaning of the word.

(ii) Sometimes the word can mean *loyalty*, but that loyalty is always to a royal figure. In the papyri there is a letter in which the Emperor Claudius, after a visit to Britain, writes to thank a certain club for a golden crown, which they had presented to him, and which he regards as a token of their *eusebeia*, their *loyalty*. Nero invites the Greeks to meet him at Corinth in order that he may requite them for their good will and *eusebeia, loyalty*, to him. So then *eusebeia* can express a man's loyalty to his king.

(iii) But the word goes higher than that. To Sophocles *eusebeia* was the greatest of all the virtues. Heracles advises Philoctetes '*to have respect for what is due to heaven*' (*eusebein*). He goes on to say that everything else stands second to this in the counsels of Zeus; that *eusebeia* goes beyond death with a man, and is the virtue which can never perish (Sophocles, *Philoctetes* 1440-1444). To him *eusebeia* was the foundation stone of all virtue. Maybe the best of all definitions of *eusebeia* is in the passage of Xenophon's *Memorabilia* (4.8.11) in which he pays his final tribute to the memory of Socrates: 'For myself I have described him as he was; so religious (*eusebēs*) that he did nothing without counsel from the gods; so just that he did no injury, however small, to any man, but conferred the greatest benefits on all who dealt with him; so self-controlled that he never chose the pleasanter rather than the better course. So wise that he was unerring in his judgment of the better and the worse, and needed no counsellor, but relied on himself for his knowledge of them; masterly in expounding and defining such things; no less masterly in putting others to the test, and convincing them of error and exhorting them to follow virtue and gentleness. To me then he seemed to be all that a truly good and happy man must be.' That is the description of what the Greek regarded as *eusebeia*, true religion, and none can say that it is not a noble conception.

From the Greek point of view, we may note one final fact. The Greeks used *eusebeia* to translate the equally noble Latin word *pietas*. *Pietas* was *the spirit of devotion to goodness, to honour, to honesty and to duty.*

Warde Fowler has written: 'The quality known to the Romans as *pietas* rises, in spite of trial and danger, superior to the enticements of individual passion and selfish ease. Aeneas's *pietas* became a sense of duty to the will of the gods, as well as to his father, his son, his people; and this duty never leaves him.'

All the nobility of pagan ethics at their best was in this word *eusebeia* before the Christian faith annexed it and made it even greater.

Now we must turn to the biblical use of *eusebeia*. In the Septuagint *eusebeia* is not common; but there are two occurrences of it which are very illuminating. In Isa. 11.2 *eusebeia* is used for *the fear of the Lord*, which is one of the gifts of the Spirit; and in Prov. 1.7 it is used for that *fear of the Lord* which is the beginning of wisdom. Here again we see that basically *eusebeia* is the right attitude to God, the attitude of awe, of reverence, of worship and of obedience.

But there is one book written between the Old and New Testaments which is dominated through and through by the idea of *eusebeia*; that is Fourth Maccabees.

That book was written sometime in the first century B.C. It was written in a time of trouble for the Jews, and it was written by a Pharisee who above all things loved the Law. He saw that the one necessity of life was to master the passions, and the one way to master the passions was to obey the Law; and to him that mastery and that obedience were *eusebeia*. Those who with their whole heart give heed to *piety* (*eusebeia*) alone are able to overcome the passions of the flesh, in the faith that like our patriarchs, Abraham, Isaac and Jacob, we are not dead to God, but live to God. For is it actually possible that anyone who philosophizes *piously* (*eusebōs*) according to the complete rule of philosophy (i.e. the Law), who believes also in God, and who knows that it is blessedness to endure any affliction on behalf of virtue, will not get mastery over his passions by his *piety* (*eusebeia*)? (IV Mac. 7.18-22).

The writer of that book says that the Jewish philosophy, that is, the Law, 'instructs us in *godliness* (*eusebeia*) so that we may worship the only living God in a manner befitting his majesty' (IV Mac. 5.24). Still again we have this basic conception that *eusebeia* essentially means to give God the place he ought to possess in our minds, in our hearts and in our lives.

Now we turn to the NT itself. *Eusebeia* occurs once in Acts. In Acts 3.12 Peter and John protest that they have not healed the lame man at the Temple gate by their own power or *eusebeia* (AV, *holiness*; Moffatt and RSV, *piety*).

Eusebeia occurs ten times in the Pastorals. In I Tim. 2.2 it is the aim of the Christian life that we should live in all *godliness* (Moffatt, *piety*) and honesty. In I Tim. 3.16 it is said: Great is the mystery of *eusebeia* (AV, godliness; Moffatt: Great is the divine truth of our *religion*; RSV: Great is the mystery of our *religion*).

In I Tim 4.7 the Christian is bidden to exercise himself unto *godliness* (RSV retains *godliness*; Moffatt translates: Train for the *religious life*). In I Tim. 4.8 *eusebeia* is said to be profitable for all things (AV and RSV, *godliness*; Moffatt, *religion*).

In I Tim. 6.3 there is the doctrine which is according to

eusebeia (AV and RSV, *godliness*; Moffatt, *piety*). In I Tim. 6.5, 6, those who seek to make money out of *eusebeia* are condemned, but it is pointed out that *eusebeia* with contentment is great gain (AV and RSV, *godliness*; Moffatt, *religion*).

In I Tim. 6.11 the Christian is bidden to follow after *eusebeia* (AV and RSV, *godliness*; Moffatt, *piety*). II Tim. 3.5 speaks of those who have only an outward form of *eusebeia* (AV, *godliness*; Moffatt and RSV, *religion*). Titus 1.1 speaks of truth which is according to *eusebeia* (AV and RSV, *godliness*; Moffatt, *the religious life*).

Outside the Pastorals *eusebeia* occurs four times in Second Peter. II Peter 1.3 speaks of life according to *eusebeia* (AV and RSV, *godliness*; Moffatt, *piety*). II Peter 1.6, 7 bids the Christian to add *eusebeia* to patience, and brotherly love to *eusebeia* (AV and RSV, *godliness*; Moffatt, *piety*).

In II Peter 3.11 there is the phrase, All holy conversation and *eusebeia* (AV and RSV, *godliness*; Moffatt, What holy and *pious* men you ought to be).

Before we can make a pattern of the meaning of *eusebeia* we must look at the use of its kindred words in the NT. But we can already see that *eusebeia* means true *godliness*, true *piety*. We can see that in fact *eusebeia* is the word for true *religion*. There is therefore no word whose meaning it is more necessary fully to understand.

In the NT the adjective *eusebēs* occurs four times. In Acts 10.2 Cornelius is *eusebēs* and one who fears the Lord (AV and RSV, *devout*; Moffatt, *religious*). In Acts 10.7 we read that Cornelius sent a soldier who was *eusebēs* as his messenger to Peter (AV and RSV, *devout*; Moffatt, *religiously minded*). In II Peter 2.9 it is said that God delivers those who are *eusebēs* out of temptation (AV and RSV, *godly*; Moffatt, *pious folk*). This word does not occur often but once again we see that the basic idea is a right and reverent attitude to God.

The adverb *eusebōs* occurs twice. In II Tim. 3.12 the

warning is given that all who live *eusebōs* will be perse-
cuted (AV, *godly*). The AV uses *godly* both as an adjective
and as an adverb. (As an adverb, as here, more correctly,
but unpronounceably, it would be *godlily*. RSV, all who
live a godly life; Moffatt, all who *live the religious life*.)
Titus 2.12 uses the same phrase, to live *eusebōs* (AV, to live
godly; RSV, *to live godly lives*; Moffatt, to live a *life of
piety*).

The verb *eusebein* occurs twice. In Acts 17.23 Paul uses
it when he speaks to the Athenians of that which they
ignorantly *worship*. In I Tim. 5.4 the children of widows
are told that they must *show piety* at home, by paying their
debt to their parents. The RSV translates this: Let
them first learn *their religious duty* to their own family.
Moffatt translates it: Let them learn that *the first duty of
religion* is to their own household. When we come to make
the Christian pattern of true religion we shall see that this
saying must be given a very prominent place in it.

To complete this study we must take in two kindred
words. In the NT the word *theosebeia* occurs twice. The
difference between *eusebeia* and *theosebeia* is this. It is the
seb- part of the word which means *reverence* or *worship*.
Eu is the Greek word for *well*; therefore, *eusebeia* is worship, reverence well and rightly given. *Eusebeia* stresses
the rightness of the reverence, its freedom from supersti-
tions and imperfections and improprieties.

Theos is the Greek word for *God*; therefore, *theosebeia*
means literally *the worship of God. Theosebeia* is therefore
the wider word, but in effect the two words mean almost
the same, except that *eusebeia* emphasizes the rightness of
the worship.

The one instance of *theosebeia* is in I Tim. 2.10 where
advice is given to women who profess *theosebeia* (AV,
professing *godliness*; RSV, who profess *religion*; Moffatt,
who *make a religious profession*).

In the NT the adjective *theosebēs* occurs once, in John
9.31. God hears the prayers of the man who is *theosebēs*

(AV and RSV, *a worshipper of God*; Moffatt, anyone who is *devout*).

We have now studied in full the occurrences of these great words in the NT. We have seen that the basic meaning which lies behind them is the right attitude to God and to the holiness, the majesty and the love of God. It now remains to work out what that right attitude is.

(i) *Eusebeia*, true religion, comes through the divine power of Jesus Christ (II Peter 1.3). Without the vision of Jesus, without the help of Jesus, without the presence of Jesus true religion is impossible. I Tim. 3.16 speaks, as the AV has it, about 'the mystery of godliness'. In the NT and in the ancient world a *mystery* was not something which was mysterious in the sense of being hard to understand. A mystery was something which was unintelligible to the uninitiated, but crystal clear to those who had been initiated and who had learned to understand. A mystery was a divine secret, unintelligible to the outsider, but open and precious to the true worshipper. So Jesus brought to men the secret of true religion. In him men both see God and learn how to worship God.

(ii) But although *eusebeia*, true religion, is the gift of the power of Jesus Christ, it is none the less something which a man must struggle and battle to attain. We must *train* ourselves to religion (I Tim. 4.7). We must *follow after religion* (I Tim. 6.11).

The first word that Paul uses (*gumnazein*) is an *athlete's* word; and the second passage comes exactly and immediately before he bids Timothy fight the good fight; it is the *soldier's* word. The Christian is at once the *athlete* and the *soldier*. As the athlete trains himself for the contest so the Christian must train himself to be the follower of Christ. As the soldier must battle towards final victory, so the Christian must dauntlessly and tirelessly face the struggle of goodness.

(iii) This gift and this struggle combined bring three things. (a) *Eusebeia* brings *trouble*. The man who will live for Christ must expect to receive persecution (II Tim. 3.12). To be different from the world, to have a different set of standards and a different set of aims, is always a perilous thing. It is not peace but glory that Christ offers us.

(b) *Eusebeia* brings *power*. It was *holiness* and *power* combined that the Jerusalem crowds saw in Peter and John (Acts 3.12). Christ never sends a man a task without also sending him the power to do it. In a world of collapse the Christian alone has the power to stand foursquare against the assaults of all that time can do.

(c) *Eusebeia* brings *God*. For the true worshipper of God the way is ever open to God (John 9.31). In every time of trial the Christian can retire to the presence of God to emerge with a power that is not his own power. The Christian has continual access to and contact with the power of the Eternal.

(iv) *Eusebeia* is the mark of the Christian life. The aim of the Christian, and the duty of the Christian, is to live with godliness and honesty (I Tim. 2.2). 'A saint', as someone has said, 'is someone who makes it easier to believe in God.' Even within the world something of heaven's grace and glory cling to the life of the Christian. He too brings God to men.

(v) *Eusebeia* is the origin of all true theology and of all true thinking (I Tim. 6.3; Titus 1.1). One of the great neglected truths of the Christian life is that inspiration and revelation are morally conditioned. God can only tell a man what that man is capable of receiving and understanding. The closer a man lives to God, the more God can say to him. The great thinker must first of all be a good man. To learn about God we must first of all obey God. It may well be true that the man who says that he cannot understand the Christian faith does not want to understand it, and may even be afraid to understand it.

(vi) *Eusebeia* must never be confounded with material prosperity. The man who sees in his religion, or who uses his religion as, the way to material success has a debased view of what religion is (I Tim. 6.5). But true religion is the way to the real profit and the real joy in this world and in the world to come (I Tim. 4.8). The essence of this matter lies in the basic truth that true happiness never results from the possession of things. It is not in things to give either satisfaction or peace. True happiness lies entirely in personal relationships. If a man has love he has everything. And the greatest of all personal relationships is the relationship with God. If that relationship is right, then life is true happiness.

(vii) *Eusebeia* is the product of the life which is lived in the light of eternity. In II Peter 3.11, holy conversation and godliness are urged upon men, because Christ comes again. It may be that today, after the long slow centuries have passed, we have not so keen an expectation of the Second Coming as the early Church had. But, at the same time, it remains true for every man that no man knows when he must leave time to begin on eternity. And true religion is characteristic of the man whose life is such that he is ever in readiness for the summons of God.

(viii) For all that, true *eusebeia* does not separate a man from his fellow men. To his *eusebeia*, as an essential part of it, he must add *brotherly love* (II Peter 1.6, 7). True religion looks both to God and to man.

There is a religion which separates a man from his fellow men. It may make him, as it made the monks and the hermits, decide to leave the life of the world for the life of contemplation and meditation and prayer. But prayer and contemplation and meditation, great and essential as they are, are imperfect and truncated and even unchristian, if they do not result in action. It is true that there are times when a Christian must retire from the world, but he only retires that he may return better able to face the world, to help the world, and to live with his fellow men. The Christian does not live with God to avoid his fellow men, but rather to be able better to solve the problem of living together.

(ix) *Eusebeia*, true religion, is not confined to the pre-cincts of the church, and is not limited to the worship and the liturgy and the ritual of the church. True religion begins at home. Those who would be real servants of Christ and of his Church must remember that *the first duty of religion is to their own household* (I Tim. 5.4). If a man or a woman's church work involves the neglect of his or her own family then it is irreligion, not religion.

There can never be a Christian church which is not founded on the Christian home; and the most important religious works is not the work that is done in public, but the work that is done in the privacy of the home, and amidst what ought to be the circle of those most dear.

Jesus said that where two or three are gathered together he is there in the midst of them (Matt. 18.20); and it has been suggested that the two or three are father, mother and child. Whether or not that be so, it is certainly true that true Christianity, like true charity, must begin at home, even if it is also true that it cannot stay there but must go out to the wider sphere of the Church and of the world.

When the Christian thinkers took over the word *eusebeia* it was already a great word, but they filled it with a content which made it far greater than ever it could be on the lips of any pagan thinker.

EXALEIPHEIN

THE MERCY WHICH WIPES OUT SIN

THE word *exaleiphein* occurs only five times in the NT, but one, at least, of its uses is of the greatest interest and importance. In classical Greek the word begins by meaning 'to wash over'. It is used, for instance, of 'whitewashing'

the wall of a house. It is used of warriors 'painting' their
bodies with war paint. Herodotus (7.39) tells us that the
Ethiopians painted (*exaleiphein*) their bodies, half with
chalk and half with vermilion, before they went into battle.
It is used of 'anointing' with oil. It goes on to mean 'to
wipe out or to obliterate'. It is so used of 'wiping out' a
memory of an experience from one's remembrance or one's
mind; of 'cancelling' a vote or 'annulling' a law; of 'cancelling' a charge or a debt or of 'striking a man's name off
a roll' or list; of 'wiping a family completely out of
existence'.

In the contemporary papyri it retains all its meanings. A
man writes to his friend, 'I could not read your letter
because it had been obliterated (*exaleiphein*).' Always it has
this meaning of wiping something out as you would with
a sponge.

In the NT it is twice used literally. In Rev. 7.17 and
21.4 it is used of 'wiping away' the tear from every eye. In
Rev. 3.5 it is used for 'wiping out' a man's name from a
roll. In Acts 3.19 it is used of wiping out sin. Repent, the
AV translates it, that your sins may be 'blotted out'. But
the remaining instance is the one which is of supreme
interest. In Col. 2.14 Paul speaks of Jesus 'blotting out the
handwriting of ordinances that was against us'. Now the
word that Paul uses for handwriting is *cheirographos*.
Literally it means a 'holograph'. It goes on to mean a
'signature' and then a 'written agreement'. But it came
to mean technically 'a written agreement acknowledging
a debt', a 'certificate of debt', a 'bond'. In the papyri, a
man writes to his friend, 'If you can, please get on to
Dioscurus and exact from him his *bond*.' A *cheirographos*
was a document which acknowledged a debt that had to
be paid. It was that that Jesus wiped out for us. Let us
remember the literal meaning of *exaleiphein*. Literally it
means 'to wipe out'. In NT times documents were
written on papyrus. The ink was made of soot, mixed with
gum and diluted with water. The characteristic of this ink

is that it has no acid in it and therefore does not bite into the paper. It will last a very long time and will retain its colour, but if, soon after it is written, a wet sponge was passed over the surface of the papyrus, the writing could be sponged off as completely as writing might be sponged from a slate. Now the interesting thing is this—a commoner word for cancelling a certificate of debt was *chiazein*. *Chiazein* means to write the Greek letter *chi*, which was the same shape as a capital X, right across the document. So, after a trial in Egypt, the governor gives orders that a bond should be cancelled (*chiazesthai*), that is, 'crossed out'. But Paul does not say that Jesus Christ 'crossed out' (*chiazein*) the record of our debt; he says that he 'wiped it out' (*exaleiphein*). If you 'cross a thing out', beneath the cross the record still remains visible for anyone to read, but if you 'wipe it out' the record is gone, obliterated for ever. It is as if God, for Jesus' sake, not only 'crossed out' our debt, but 'wiped it out'. There is many a man who can forgive, but who never really forgets the injury that was done to him; but God not only forgives but wipes out the very memory of the debt. There is a kind of forgiveness which forgives but still holds the memory against the sinner; but God's forgiveness is that supreme forgiveness which can forgive and forget.

HAMARTIA AND HAMARTANEIN

THE FAILURE WHICH IS SIN

Hamartia is the commonest NT noun for 'sin'; it occurs in Paul's letters 60 times; and *hamartanein* is the usual verb for 'to sin'. In classical Greek these words had not nearly so serious a meaning as in NT Greek. In classical Greek *hamartia* has as its basic meaning the idea of 'failure'. *Hamartanein* began by meaning 'to miss the mark' as when a spear is thrown at a target. It can be used for missing a road, for failure in one's plan or hope or purpose. In classical Greek these words are always connected with some kind of negative failure rather than with some kind of positive transgression, but in the NT they come to describe something which is very much more serious.

It is to be noted that in the NT *hamartia* does not describe a definite act of sin; it describes the state of sin, from which acts of sin come. In fact in Paul sin becomes almost personalized until sin could be spelled with a capital letter, and could be thought of as malignant, personal power which has man in its grasp.

Let us then see what the NT teaches about *hamartia*.

(i) *Hamartia*, 'sin', is 'universal' (Rom. 3.23; 7.14; Gal. 3.22; I John 1.8). Sin is not like a disease which some men contract and some escape. It is something in which every single human being is involved and of which every human being is guilty. Sin is not simply a sporadic and spasmodic outbreak; it is the universal state of man.

(ii) *Hamartia*, 'sin', is 'a power which has man in its grasp'. Here the words which are used are very interesting and significant. Man is *huph' hamartian*. Literally that means 'under sin'. But this preposition *hupo* with the accusative case, as here, is used to mean 'in dependence on, in subjection to, under the control of'. A minor, for instance, is 'under his father'; an army is 'under its commander'; so we are 'under, in the power of, in the control of sin' (Gal. 3.22; Rom. 3.9). So certain words are used of sin. Sin is said 'to rule over (*basileuein*) men' (Rom. 5.21). *Basileus* is the Greek for 'a king'. Sin is the ruler of men. Sin is said 'to lord it over us' (*kurieuein*) (Rom. 6.14). *Kurios* is the Greek for 'lord', and the word has the flavour of absolute 'possession' and 'domination'. Sin is said 'to take us captive (*aichmalōtizein*) (Rom. 7.23). The word is the word which is used for taking a prisoner in war. Sin is said 'to dwell within man' (*oikein, enoikein*) (Rom. 7.17, 20). So basic is the hold of sin over man that sin is not merely an external power which exercises sway over a man; it has got into the very fibre and centre and heart of his being until it occupies him, as an enemy occupies an occupied country. The result is that we can be said 'to be the slaves of sin' (*doulos, douleuein*) (John 8.34; Rom. 6.17, 20; Rom. 6.6). It is to be remembered that the power of the master over the slave was absolute. There was no part of life, no moment of time, no activity which was the personal property of the slave. He belonged to his master in the most total way. So man is totally under the domination of sin.

In Paul there is the closest connexion between 'law' and 'sin', between *nomos* and *hamartia*.

(i) The law 'teaches what sin is' (Rom. 3.20). It may be said in one sense that the law creates sin (Rom. 5.13). Sin is not sin until it is defined. Until sin is defined a man cannot know what sin is; and until there is a law of sin a man cannot be guilty of sin. To take an analogy—a city street may be for long unrestricted and a motorist may be able to drive his car along it in either direction; then a law is made which makes that street a one-way street. It then becomes a breach of the law to drive along that street in the wrong direction. The laying down of the law has created a new breach of the law. The law has both defined and created sin. If there were no law there would be no sin.

(ii) But 'the law creates sin', as Paul sees it, in another sense. Once a thing is forbidden it somehow or other acquires a new and a fatal fascination, and the law actually produces the desire to sin (Rom. 7.8-11). There is something in human nature which gives the forbidden thing a double attraction. C. H. Dodd quotes the classic example of that from the *Confessions* of Augustine (2.4-6). 'There was a pear-tree near our vineyard, laden with fruit. One stormy night we rascally youths set out to rob it and to carry our spoils away. We took a huge load of pears—not to feast upon them ourselves, but to throw them to the pigs —though we ate just enough to have the pleasure of forbidden fruit. They were nice pears, but it was not the pears that my wretched soul coveted, for I had plenty better at home. I picked them simply in order to be a thief. The only feast I got was a feast of iniquity, and that I enjoyed to the full. What was it I loved in that theft? Was it the pleasure of acting against the law, in order that I, a prisoner under rules, might have a maimed counterfeit of freedom, by doing with impunity what was forbidden, with a dim similitude of omnipotence?' And then Dr Dodd comments: 'That is to say that the desire to steal was aroused simply by the prohibition of stealing.' It is precisely here that the weakness of the law in regard to sin emerges. Law has two defects. First, it can define sin but it cannot cure it. It is like a doctor who can diagnose a disease but who is helpless to eradicate or even arrest it. Second, it is the odd and fatal fact that simply by forbidding a thing the law makes that thing attractive. There is an inextricable connexion between *hamartia* and *nomos*, 'sin' and 'law'.

There are certain inevitable consequences of sin.

(i) Sin results in a certain 'hardening' of the heart. The word used for hardening is *sklērunein* (Heb. 3.13). The adjective *sklēros* can be used, for instance, of a stone which is specially hard for masons to work; it can be used metaphorically of a king who is inhuman and hard in his treatment of his subjects. Sin hardens the heart. In Phil. 1.9 Paul prays that the Philippians may abound in what he calls *aisthēsis*, which is 'sensitive perception'. It is the quality of heart and mind which is sensitive to that which is wrong. It is the experience of life that the first time a man commits a wrong action he does so with a kind of shuddering reluctance; if he does it twice he does it more easily; if he goes on doing it he will end by doing it without thinking at all. His sensitiveness to sin is gone; his heart is hardened. It is indeed true that the most awful thing about sin is exactly its power to beget sin.

(ii) Sin results in 'death' (Rom. 5.12, 21; 6.16; 6.23; James

1.15). This is doubly so. It was Paul's belief that it was because of Adam's sin that death entered into the world. Sin is that which wrecked and ruined the life that God had planned for man. But it is also true that death results in the death of the soul. Physical death and spiritual death are to Paul both the result of sin.

One of the best ways of discovering the real meaning of any word is to examine the company it keeps. A word's meaning, and its inward flavour, will best be found by examining the words in whose company it is usually found. Let us, then, examine the words with which *hamartia* is found in the NT.

(i) *Hamartia* is connected with *blasphēmia* (Matt. 12.31). The basic meaning of *blasphēmia* is insult. Sin is then 'an insult' to God. It insults God by flouting his commandments, by putting self in the place which he ought to occupy, and above all, by grieving his love.

(ii) *Hamartia* is connected with *apatē* (Heb. 3.13). *Apatē* is 'deceit'. Sin is always a deceitful thing, in that it promises to do that which it cannot do. Sin is always a lie. Any man who sins, who does the forbidden thing or who takes the forbidden thing, does so because he thinks that he will be happier for doing or taking that thing. Sin deceives him into thinking so. But the plain fact of experience is that an act or a possession which is the result of sin never brought happiness to any man. Long ago, Epicurus, with his strictly utilitarian morality, pointed out that sin can never bring happiness, because, apart from anything else, it leaves a man with the constant fear of being found out.

(iii) *Hamartia* is connected with *epithumia* (James 1.15). *Epithumia* is desire. *Epithumia* was defined by Aristotle as 'reaching after pleasure'. The Stoics added to that definition by saying that it was a reaching after pleasure 'beyond the bounds of reason'. Clement of Alexandria defined *epithumia* as the spirit which 'aims at and reaches after that which will gratify itself'. *Epithumia* always has the notion of desiring that which should not be desired.

Epithumein is in fact the verb which is used in the Greek version of the tenth commandment, 'Thou shalt not *covet*.' If a man's heart was so cleansed that he never desired the wrong thing he would never sin.

(iv) *Hamartia* is equated with *anomia* (I John 3.4). *Anomia* is 'lawlessness'. Sin is that which every now and then makes a man desire to kick over the traces, to have done with restraints and controls, to do exactly as he likes. *Anomia* is the spirit which makes a man desire to erect his own wishes above his duty to man and his obedience to God. *Anomia* springs basically from the desire to install self and not God at the centre of life.

(v) *Hamartia* is equated with *adikia* (I John 5.17). *Adikia* is 'injustice, unrighteousness, evil'. It is the opposite of *dikaiosunē*, which means 'justice'. Now *dikaiosunē* may be defined as 'giving both to God and to men that which is their due'. *Adikia*, then, is the spirit which at one and the same time refuses its duty to God and its duty to men. Sin is that which makes a man so worship self that he forgets or refuses to serve God and to serve his fellow-men. It is that which makes him act as if he were the most important person in the universe.

(vi) *Hamartia* is connected with *prosōpolēpsia* (James 2.9). *Prosōpolēpsia* is 'respect of person'. Now respect of persons is the result of applying man's standards instead of God's standards to the world and to life and to people in general. Sin is to accept the world's standards instead of the standards of God, to judge things as men see them instead of as God sees them.

It is time now to turn to the cure of *hamartia*. Let us now look at certain of the words which describe what Jesus Christ does for us in relation to sin.

(i) Jesus 'saves' us from sin (*sōzein*) (Matt. 1.21). We are in the position of people who need to be rescued and that rescue is carried out by Jesus at the cost of his life.

(ii) Our sins are 'wiped out' (*exaleiphein*) (Acts 3.19). Ancient ink had no acid in it. It could be sponged off the surface of vellum or of papyrus when the scribe wanted to use the vellum or the papyrus again. Because of the work of Jesus the record of our sin is obliterated, sponged away.

(iii) Through Jesus we are 'washed from sin' (*apolouein*) (Acts 22.16). There comes a 'cleansing from sin' (*katharismos*) (Heb. 1.3; II Pet. 1.9; I John 1.7). It is as if life was soiled and mired and stained and muddied by sin; and Jesus Christ has the power to cleanse it, as the rain washes clean the city pavements.

(iv) In the mercy of God 'a veil is drawn across our sin' (*epikaluptein*) (Rom. 4.7). The verb *epikaluptein* is used of snow obliterating a pathway; it is used of someone covering his eyes so that he cannot see; it is used of drawing a veil over something. It is as if God in his mercy drew a veil over the sorry record of the past and never looked at it again.

(v) In the mercy of God our sins 'are not reckoned against us' (*logizesthai*) (Rom. 4.8). *Logizesthai* is an accountant's word. It means 'to set down to someone's account'. The idea is that our sins have put us completely and unpayably in God's debt. The balance of the ledger of life is infinitely against us. But God in his mercy wipes out the debit balance which we ourselves could never pay.

(vi) By the work of Jesus we are 'liberated from sin' (*eleutheroun*) (Rom. 6.18, 22; 8.2). We are 'released from sin' (*luein*) (Rev. 1.5). *Eleutheroun* means 'to give someone his freedom'. *Luein* means 'to loose someone from his bonds'. We have already seen how man has become the slave of sin, has got himself into the control of sin. Jesus is the supreme liberator and emancipator. At one and the same time he pays the ransom price which liberates from the past and gives the power which gives freedom for the future.

(vii) The coming of Jesus 'cancelled our sin' (*athetēsis*) (Heb. 9.26). *Athetēsis* is technical, legal Greek for 'the cancellation of a contract or agreement'. Were the strict letter of the law carried out there could be for man nothing but condemnation. Through Jesus there is a cancellation of the debt we owe.

(viii) Through Jesus 'we are forgiven' (*aphiesthai*). This is the word which is by far the commonest for the forgiveness of sins. It occurs in every stratum of the NT (Matt. 9.2; Mark 2.10; Luke 7.47; Acts 2.38; 10.43; Col. 1.14; I John 2.12). The word *aphiesthai* has a wide variety of meanings, all of which have some suggestion to make. It can be used for releasing a man from some sentence that has already been passed, as, for instance, from exile. It can be used for remitting a charge that has justly been made. It can be used for acquitting a man from a verdict that might have been carried out or for releasing him from an engagement that might have been insisted upon. It can be used of absolving a man from duty that he could have been compelled to carry out. The whole essence of the word is the undeserved release of a man from something that might justly have been inflicted upon him or exacted from him. Through Jesus Christ man is released from the punishment and penalty that God had every right to inflict upon him. It is the word which tells us that God deals with us, not in justice, but in love; that we are dealt with, not according to our deserts, but according to his mercy and his grace in Jesus Christ.

There is no book which has so great a sense of the horror and the awfulness of sin as the NT has, but equally there is no book which is so sure that the cure and the remedy have been found.

HUBRIS, HUBRIZEIN, HUBRISTĒS

THE WORDS OF IMPIOUS PRIDE

THE words *hubris*, *hubrizein* and *hubristēs* do not occur often in the NT, but they are words which are well worth studying, because to the Greeks these were the words which were concerned with the supreme sin, which could not do anything else but breed destruction and total ruin.

They are words which are not easy to translate. *Hubris* is a noun which means *wanton insolence*: *hubristēs* is also a noun which means *one who acts with wanton insolence*: *hubrizein* is a verb which means *to treat with wanton insolence*. But the basic idea in all these words is *the pride which erects itself against God and man alike*.

W. G. de Burgh writes of *hubris*: 'Its root meaning is the violent over-stepping of the mark, the insolence of triumph, and the pride of life that tramples underfoot the unwritten laws of gods and men. *Hubris* is the closest Greek equivalent for "sin". Its most characteristic application was to the insatiable thirst for power which drives a man or a nation headlong, as though possessed by a demon, on the path of unbridled self-assertion. This blinding passion, outraging alike personal liberty and public law, lures the victim in a frenzy of self-confidence towards destruction. It provokes *nemesis*, the feeling of righteous indignation, in the gods and in his fellow men.'

Ernest Myers speaks of 'the sin of *hubris*, of insolence, ready to trample in violence over law and liberty to gratify selfish lust and pride'.

The basic evil of *hubris* is that when *hubris* enters into a man's heart that man forgets that he is a creature and that God is the Creator. *Hubris* is the sin whereby a man forgets his humanity and makes himself equal with God. *Hubris* is that insolent arrogance which forgets the essential creatureliness of the condition of being a man.

This was accentuated by the strange Greek conception of *the envy of the gods* (*phthonos theōn*). It was the strange conception of the Greeks that the gods grudged man all happiness, all prosperity and all success. That goes as far back as Homer. Even a fair reputation for kindliness and honour was a thing which the gods might grudge and envy men, for was not Poseidon, the sea god, jealous of the Phaeacians because 'they gave safe escort to all men' (Homer, *Odyssey* 8.566)?

The same conception of this envy of the gods is there in Pindar. When he sings in praise of Corinth, he adds the prayer to the sovereign Lord of Olympia not to allow his envy to be awakened by such words of praise (Pindar, *Olymp.* 13.24). In the *Pythians* he prays that the family of the Aleuadae may continue to fare well. 'Of the happy things of Hellas they have received no small portion; I pray that they meet with no reverses from the envious gods' (Pindar, *Pyth.* 10.19). It is the same in the *Isthmians*: 'I will set a garland upon my hair and sing. But let not the envy of the immortal gods bring confusion on me' (Pindar, *Isth.* 7.39). The Greek was haunted by the idea of the envy of the gods.

It may be said that all early Greek history is written on the theme of the envy of the gods. Herodotus draws the picture of Xerxes planning to invade Greece, and of Artabanus seeking to restrain him from an ambition which is bound to awaken the envy of the gods: 'You see how God smites with his thunderbolts the tallest animals, and does not allow them to exalt themselves, whereas the smaller animals in no way provoke his wrath; you see how he ever hurls his shafts at the highest buildings and trees, for it is God's custom to cut down whatever exceeds in point of greatness. Thus a mighty host may be destroyed by a small one, when God, becoming envious, smites them with panic or with lightning, so that they perish in a manner unworthy of themselves. For God will not suffer any but himself to think high thoughts' (Herodotus, 7.10). In the same way Amasis addresses his warning letter to Polycrates: 'Your great successes do not please me, knowing as I do that the divine nature is jealous. I would prefer that I myself and those I care for should be successful in some things and unsuccessful in others, experiencing through life alternate good and evil fortune, rather than that they should invariably succeed. For I have never yet heard of anyone who was successful in everything, without perishing miserably, root and branch, at the last' (Herodotus, 3.40).

At the back of life for the Greek there was the terror of success, for success was bound to awaken the envy of the gods.

To be too successful, to have too much good fortune, to triumph too much, was to court disaster, for it was to incur the inevitable envy of the gods. 'Seek not to become Zeus' said Pindar. 'Mortal things befit a mortal' (Pindar, *Isth.* 5.14). 'If anyone shall possess wealth and shall excel others in beauty, and have won distinction by display of strength in the games, let him not forget that his raiment is on mortal limbs, and that the earth shall be his garment at the last' (Pindar, *Nem.* 11.13).

Even man's voyaging throughout the world must be circumscribed. At the end of the Mediterranean Sea there stood the Pillars of Hercules. Better for a man not to venture beyond. 'By their manly prowess they have touched the Pillars of Hercules, at the boundaries of the world. Beyond that I bid them seek for no further excellence' (Pindar, *Isth.* 4.11).

The same refrain runs through Aeschylus. The man upon a too prosperous voyage, in the midst of a calm sea, strikes a hidden reef, and the end is shipwreck (Aeschylus, *Agamemnon* 993). Xerxes is defeated with all his might and the defeat is due to 'the envy of the gods' (Aeschylus, *Persae* 365).

From beginning to end, classical literature is permeated with this fear of the envy of the gods; and this conception that the supreme sin is the failure of a man to remember that he is a man.

Now if all that be true—and to the Greek it was the truest thing in the universe—then if success is dangerous, pride in success is fatal. And *hubris* is this arrogant and insolent pride which forgets the gods. 'Very certainly', said

Aeschylus, 'insolence, *hubris*, is the child of godlessness' (Aeschylus, *Eumenides* 533). 'Zeus,' he says, 'of a truth is a chastiser of overweening pride and corrects with a heavy hand. Therefore, now that my son has been warned to prudence by the voice of God, do ye instruct him by admonitions of reason, to cease from drawing on himself the punishment of heaven by his vaunting rashness' (Aeschylus, *Persae* 827-831). Darius says of his son Xerxes and his disastrous expedition against Greece: 'Mortal though he was, he thought in his folly that he would gain the mastery over all the gods' (*ibid.* 794).

The trouble about this pride is that it grows ever greater as a man's life goes on: 'An ancient *hubris* ever breeds a fresh and living *hubris* to add to human woes' (Aeschylus, *Agamemnon* 760); and that is the very reason why 'from good fortune there sprouts forth for posterity insatiate calamity'.

Sophocles has it: '*Hubris* begets a tyrant' (Sophocles, *Oedipus Tyrannus* 873). It is this overweening pride which makes a tyrant and men and gods hate a tyrant. Euripides has it: 'If you have more of good than evil, being a man, you will do right well. But, dear child, refrain from evil thoughts; cease from *hubris*, presumptuous pride; for to wish to be greater than God is nothing other than *hubris*' (Euripides, *Hippolytus* 472-474). To try to take one's own way, to resist the will of the gods, to think one knows better than the gods, is *hubris*, insolent, arrogant, overweening pride.

This innate terror of *hubris* was burned into the consciousness of the Greek. For a man to be drunk with success, for a man to get the idea that he can direct life and that he can cope with life and that he can forge out unbroken success, for a man to forget God is *hubris*. For a nation to seek for world power and world domination, and to map out vast schemes of conquest, leaving the gods entirely out of the reckoning, is *hubris*. For a philosopher to grasp a few natural laws and then to think that he can explain the universe and eliminate God is *hubris*. *Hubris* is there whenever a man forgets that he is a man, and forgets that God has the last word, and for the Greek that *hubris* was rendered doubly disastrous because of the envy of the gods.

So far we have been thinking of *hubris* in what might be called its theological sense in Greek thought. But these words have also an *ethical* sense. To put it in another way, if a man has *hubris* in his heart, that *hubris* will come out in a certain attitude to his fellow men, and a certain treatment of them. Just as there is a certain overweening pride in a man's attitude to God, so there can be a certain insolent arrogance in his attitude to his fellow men.

The Greek ethical writers regarded *hubris* as the greatest of sins towards one's fellow men; and in it they identified two basic elements.

(i) *Hubris* is the outcome of allowing the passions to rule. Plato has it: 'When opinion conquers, and by the help of reason, leads us to the best, the conquering principle is called temperance (*sōphrosunē*); but when desire, which is devoid of reason, rules in us, and drags us to pleasure, that power of misrule is called *hubris*' (Plato, *Protagoras* 238a). The man who is governed by *hubris* is governed by passion and not reason. Aristotle draws a distinction between the temperate man (*sōphrōn*), whose conduct is governed by law, and the man who commits outrage (*hubrizein*). Such a man obeys the dictates of passion and not of law and reason.

(ii) But to the Greeks the really terrible thing about *hubris* was that it was partly the product of sheer contemptuous insolence, and partly the product of the sheer desire to hurt other people. *Hubris* is committed in contempt of others (Aristotle, *Nicomachean Ethics* 1149b 22). Speaking with deliberate attempt to insult and to give offence is *hubris* (*ibid*. 1125a 9). *Hubris* is that completely deliberate way of slighting a man, which is bound to beget anger (*ibid*. 1149a 32). *Hubris* is fundamentally a perverted and morbid thing (*ibid.* 1148b 30). But the most terrible thing about *hubris* was the pleasure it takes in inflicting injury. It is wanton insolence done simply for the pleasure it gives to see someone else suffer (*ibid.* 1149b 22).

The Greeks drew a clear distinction between three things. *Anger* is not deliberate; a man blazes into anger because he cannot help it. *Revenge* is taken with the clear intention of getting something back; vengeance is for the sake of retaliation. But *hubris*, wanton insolence, is the spirit which hurts someone in a cold, detached way, and then stands back to see the other person wince. It is hurting for hurting's sake, and it always involves deliberate humiliation of the person injured.

Aristotle describes it fully (*Rhetoric* 2.2.3); 'Insolence (*hubris*) is another form of slight, as being an act of injury or annoyance involving the disgrace of the sufferer, not for the sake of any benefit to the agent beyond the mere fact of its having been done, but only for his personal gratification; for the requital of injuries is not insolence (*hubris*), but revenge. The source of the pleasure found in insolent action is the feeling that in injuring others we are claiming an exceptional superiority to them.'

It can easily be seen that to the Greek *hubris* was the cruellest of all sins. It came from allowing the passions to overthrow the reason, as Plato saw it. Aristotle saw it in an even worse light. For him it came from sheer contempt. The insolent man treated his fellow men as some one might squash, or tear the wings from, a fly. It came from the sheer delight in inflicting needless and useless pain. It came from sheer pleasure in seeing people wince, and knowing that their hearts had been wounded. It always aimed at the public humiliation of the person injured. It is wickedness at its most cruel.

These words acquired a certain almost standard usage in colloquial Greek contemporary with the NT, and that usage we must now go on to investigate.

In the contemporary colloquial Greek in the time of the

NT, in the papyri, this group of words has a special flavour and a special connexion. They are consistently used in connexion with insulting, outrageous and humiliating conduct.

A man complains that he was *grossly insulted* (*hubrizein*) by a certain Apollodorus. A wife lays a complaint against her husband that he has consistently ill-treated and *insulted* her, and he has had recourse even to physical violence. A man complains he has been bound, stripped naked and *maltreated*. A man appeals to the emperor, who writes back: 'Your citizenship will in nowise be injured, nor will you be *subjected to corporal punishment*' (*hubrizein*).

The words consistently express insulting and outrageous treatment, and especially treatment which is calculated publicly to insult and openly to humiliate the person who suffers from it. One of the usages which best illustrates the whole flavour and tone of these words is the use in the Septuagint of II Sam. 10. The chapter tells how Hanun, king of Ammon, cut short the garments of King David's ambassadors, and shaved off half their beards, and then sent them back to their master. That treatment was *hubris*. It was insult, outrage, public humiliation all combined.

Now we turn to the NT usages of these words.

(i) In one case *hubris* is used simply of the disaster which will follow a sea voyage taken against the advice of Paul (Acts 27.10, 21). In one case one of the scribes complains that Jesus has treated the scribes with insolence (*hubrizein*) in his denunciation of them (Luke 11.45).

(ii) The word *hubristēs*, a man of arrogant insolence, is once used to describe one of the characteristic sins of the pagan world (Rom. 1.30). There it describes the pride of godlessness.

(iii) Once Paul uses *hubristēs* to describe his own conduct towards the Church in the days when he was a persecutor (I Tim. 1.13). In those days Paul had taken a savage delight in seeing the Christians hurt and humiliated.

Nothing could better show how savage a persecutor Paul once was.

(iv) *Hubrizein* is twice used of the treatment which Paul received at the hands of his persecutors on his missionary journeys. It is used of what happened to him at Iconium (Acts 14.5), and at Philippi (I Thess. 2.2). In the list of his sufferings in II Cor. 12.10 Paul includes the things he suffered from *hubris*. The Christian had to suffer not only cruelty but also public humiliation.

(v) Jesus uses the word *hubrizein* of the treatment which he himself knew he would suffer at Jerusalem (Luke 18.32). Jesus knew that the cruelty of men would leave nothing undone to hurt and to wound and to insult and to humiliate him.

(vi) But the most suggestive usage of all, the usage which gathers up the whole meaning of the words, is in Matt. 22.6. There the word *hubrizein* is used of the conduct of the people who ill-treated and killed the messengers of the king who brought the king's invitation to the king's feast. There we have the very essence of sin. God sends his invitation into the world, and men reject it; that is *hubris*. That is man erecting himself against God, man in his pride defying God, man forgetting that he is a creature and that God is creator, man in arrogance turning his back on God. That is man deliberately hurting God, for sin is always the breaking of God's heart more than it is the breaking of God's law. That is man publicly humiliating God, for it is the most hurting and humiliating thing in the world to offer love only to have that love spurned and contemptuously refused.

Hubris is mingled pride and cruelty. *Hubris* is the pride which makes a man defy God, and the arrogant contempt which makes him trample on the hearts of his fellow men.

HUPERĒPHANIA
AND HUPERĒPHANOS

THE WORDS OF CONTEMPT

THE words *huperēphania* and *huperēphanos* are not very common in the NT, but they describe one of the gravest and most basic sins in human nature. *Huperēphania* is a noun, and is usually translated *pride*. *Pride* is one of those sins which Jesus says proceeds out of a man's heart (Mark 7.22).

Huperēphanos is an adjective which means *proud, arrogant, overweening*. In the Magnificat it is said that God has scattered the *proud* in the imagination of their hearts (Luke 1.51). The *proud* are included by Paul in his terrible list of the sinners of this world (Rom. 1.30). The *proud* are included among the sinners of the last days in II Tim. 3.2. Both James and Peter quote the saying of Prov. 3.34 that God gives grace to the humble but resists the *proud* (James 4.6; I Peter 5.5).

The sin of *huperēphania* was a sin which the ancient world knew well and about which its ethical teachers had much to say. They derived *huperēphanos* from two Greek words, *huper* which means *above*, and *phainesthai*, which means to *show oneself*. The man who was *huperēphanos* was *the man who showed himself above*.

It does not so much mean the man who is conspicuous and to whom others look up, as the man who stands on his own little self-created pedestal and looks down. The characteristic of the man who is *huperēphanos* is that he looks down on everyone else, secure in his own arrogant self-conceit.

First of all let us look at the usage of these words in classical Greek. Xenophon uses the word to describe *the cruel insolence* of the character of a young king who does not know how to rule his people (Xenophon, *Cyropædia*

5.2.27). The enemies of Socrates accused him of showing *lofty disdain* for his fellow men (Plato, *Symposium* 219c). Plato accuses Homer of depicting Achilles as displaying *overwhelming contempt* for gods and men (Plato, *Republic* 391c). The Greeks told how the new gods headed by Zeus drove the older gods from power, and Aeschylus speaks of the *overweening spirit* of Zeus towards the older gods (Aeschylus, *Prometheus* 405).

Theophrastus has one of his character studies which draws the picture of the man who is *huperēphanos*. He begins by defining *huperēphania* as the spirit of the man who has contempt for everyone except himself. The man who is *huperēphanos* will never pay the first visit to someone else. When he walks on the streets, he never talks to anyone whom he meets, but stalks by with bent head and averted eyes, too proud even to look at other people. When he is elected to office, he declines it, on the grounds that he is too busy to serve. If he gives an entertainment, he never sits down with the guests, but orders some underling to look after them. When he writes a letter, he never says: 'Would you do me the favour of doing such and such a thing?' He says: 'I want this done as quickly as possible.' (Theophrastus, *Characters* 24). The man who is *huperēphanos* has a contempt for everyone else.

As F. J. Hort has it: '*Huperēphania* is shown in overweening treatment of others. . . . It springs from a false view of what our relations with other persons are.' It flaunts its greatness in the face of men.

Plutarch, in his life of Pompey, describes how the pirates haunted the Mediterranean Sea, and made voyaging perilous for merchantmen, and how Pompey exterminated them. He says that in the days when the pirates held sway, they sailed in ships with gilded sails and purple awnings and silver oars, so that 'more annoying than the fear they inspired was the *flaunting extravagance* of their equipment'. Their very pride was an insult to men.

We can see already that *huperēphania* is an ugly sin; we

must go on to look at it in two of its most characteristic manifestations.

(i) *Huperēphania* and wealth were apt to go hand in hand. Riches and possessions have a way of begetting arrogance and pride. Stobaeus preserves a fragment of a writer called Callicratides: 'It is inevitable that those who have great possessions should become inflated with pride; then that being inflated with pride they should become boastful (*alazōn*); then that being boastful they should become *arrogant* (*huperēphanos*), and think that there is no one like themselves' (Stobaeus, 85.15).

Aristotle, in his *Constitution of Athens* (5.3), quotes a saying of Solon, the great Greek lawgiver: 'Commonly the blame for trouble in a state attaches to the rich.' So at the very beginning of his elegy he said that he feared above all covetousness and *arrogance*, because enmity always arose because of them.

In his *Art of Rhetoric* (1390b 33) Aristotle returns to the same point: 'The characters which accompany wealth are plain for all to see. The wealthy are insolent and *arrogant*, being mentally affected by the acquisition of wealth, for they seem to think that they possess all good things; for wealth is a kind of standard of value of everything else, so that everything seems purchasable by it.'

In the papyri a letter speaks of a man who has come to *despise* his friends because he has grown wealthy. Another writer, writing to a former friend who has dropped him, says: 'You doubtless had better things to do; that was why you *neglected* us.' *Huperēphania* is the pride which comes from possessions; the arrogance of the man who is rich and who believes that his money can buy him anything; the insolent pride of the man who believes that every thing and every man has a price, and that he can pay it.

(ii) But *huperēphania* can go even further than that. *Huperēphania* can become the pride and arrogance which in the end despise God. The literature of the Jews between the Old and the New Testaments has much to say of this word and this characteristic. *'Huperēphania* is hateful before God and men. . . . The beginning of *huperēphania* is when a man departs from the Lord, and when his heart forsakes him who made him' (Ecclus. 10.7, 12).

It is the very opposite of that humble spirit which alone can learn true wisdom. We read that 'wisdom is far from *huperēphania*' (Ecclus. 15.8). *Huperēphania* was the characteristic of the proud men who so lifted themselves up that God sent the flood upon the earth (Wisdom 14.6).

Of two men especially did the Jews use this word, for both these men had been guilty of the most terrible sacrilege, the sacrilege of entering the Holy of Holies, where none but the High Priest might go. They used the word of Antiochus Epiphanes who in insolence and *arrogance* tried to obliterate Jewish religion, and who entered the Holy Place and defiled the Temple (II Mac. 9.7). 'In his *huperēphania* he entered into the sanctuary' (I Mac. 1.21, 24).

And they used the words of Pompey, who, when he conquered Jerusalem, was guilty of the same sacrilege. 'When the sinful man *waxed proud* (*huperēphaneuesthai*, the corresponding verb), he cast down fenced walls with a battering-ram, and thou didst not prevent him. The heathen went up against thine altar; they trampled it down with their sandals in their *pride*' (Psalms of Solomon 2.1, 2). 'The adversary *wrought insolence* and his heart was alien from God' (Psalms of Solomon 17.15). 'Let God destroy all those who work iniquity with *insolence*' (Psalms of Solomon 4.28).

Huperēphania is the spirit which despises men and lifts itself arrogantly against God. No wonder Theophylact called *huperēphania* the *acropolis kakōn*, the peak of evils.

This pride can come from pride in birth, from pride in wealth, from pride in knowledge, from aristocratic pride, from intellectual pride, from spiritual pride. It is described by Trench as 'human nature in battle array against God'.

There remains one thing to note. We have already studied the word *alazōn* which describes the *boaster*, the man who shouts his claims and pretensions so that all can hear. But *huperēphania* is worse that that, for the seat of *huperēphania* is in the heart.

The blustering, boasting *alazōn* is plain for all to see; but the *huperēphanos* is the man who might well go about the world with downcast eyes and folded hands and with outward quietness, but with a silent contempt within his heart for his fellow-men; the *huperēphanos* is the man who might walk in outward humility, but in inward pride.

His basic sin is that he has forgotten that he is a creature and that God is the Creator; for the *huperēphanos* has erected an altar to himself within his own heart, and worships there.

HUPOGRAMMOS

THE PERFECT PATTERN

THERE is only one example of the word *hupogrammos* in the NT, but it is an example with a vivid picture behind it. Peter says of Jesus that 'He left us an example (*hupogrammos*) that we should follow in his steps' (I Pet. 2.21).

The word *hupogrammos* is a word which comes from Greek primary education. It is a word which has to do with the way in which Greek boys were taught to write. The common writing material in NT times was *papyrus*, which was a kind of paper made of the pith of the bulrush which grew mainly on the banks of the Nile. It was by no means a cheap material. It was usually manufactured in sheets which measured ten by eight inches. The sheets varied in quality and in price. The cheapest sheets were about fourpence; and the dearest slightly more than a shilling. Obviously papyrus was far too expensive a sub-

stance for boys to practise writing on. So, then, the schoolboy's exercise book was usually the wax tablet. The wax
tablet was like a very shallow box filled with soft wax.
The writing was done with a *stylus* which was pointed at
one end and flat at the other. The pointed end was used to
write with, and the flat end was used to smooth over the
wax, so that it could be used again.

The method by which boys were taught to write is out-
lined for us in two places. Plato in the *Protagoras* (326 D)
tells us that in teaching to write the writing master first
drew lines (*hupographein*, which is the verb corresponding
to the noun *hupogrammos*) with a stylus for the use of the
learner, and then gave him the tablet and made him write
as the lines directed. In practice this meant two things.
The writing master drew parallel lines to keep the boy's
writing straight; and he also wrote at the top of the tablet
a line of writing which the boy had to copy. That line was
the *hupogrammos*, the pattern which the boy must follow.
Sometimes the writing was a moral maxim; more often it
was a nonsense sentence which contained all the letters of
the alphabet. Clement of Alexandria (*Stromateis* 5.8) gives
an example of such a sentence: *marpte sphigx klōps
zbuchthēdon.* (In Greek *ph*, *ps*, *ch* and *th* are all single
letters, respectively *phi*, *psi*, *chi* and *theta*.) That was the
perfect line of writing which the master wrote at the top
of the page and which the schoolboy had to copy. So Peter
is saying: 'Just as the schoolboy learns to write by copying
the perfect copper-plate example, so we are scholars in the
school of life, and we can only learn to live by copying the
perfect pattern of life which Jesus gave to us.'

But there was another way of using the *hupogrammos*
which has something to contribute to Peter's meaning.
Quintilian in his *Education of an Orator* (1.1.27) tells us
that sometimes the schoolmaster traced the letters in the
wax of the tablet; and then the hand of the boy 'is guided
along the grooves, for then he will make no mistakes'. At
first the master helped the boy by placing his hand over

the scholar's, but then he let him try it by himself and the edges of the grooves kept him from 'straying beyond the boundary'. That, too, must have been in Peter's mind. Simply to have to copy the *hupogrammos* all by oneself must often have been difficult and discouraging; but for the scholar to have had the master's hand over his hand, and to have had the grooves to follow, so that his pen could not stray, must have made things much easier. Jesus does not give us an example and leave it at that; an example can be the most discouraging thing on earth. For centuries men watched the birds flying and got no nearer to being able to do the same. A man may watch a champion golfer and be left with nothing but the desire to burn his own clubs! A pianist may hear and see a master executant and be left with nothing but the resolution never to touch a piano again! But Jesus does more than give us an example. As the master's hand guided the scholar's first fumbling efforts, so he guides us; as the groove kept the scholar's pen within the boundary, so his grace directs us. He left us not only a dauntingly perfect *hupogrammos*; he constantly helps us to follow it.

HUPOKRISIS AND HUPOKRITĒS

ACTING A PART

Hupokrisis and *hupokritēs* are the words which, in the NT, are translated 'hypocrisy' and 'hypocrite'. In the NT there is no sin more strongly condemned than hypocrisy, and in popular opinion there is no sin more universally detested.

The curious thing is that in classical Greek these words have no ill flavour and no bad meaning whatsoever; they are words which have definitely come down in the world; and yet we shall see that they had the seeds of their degradation in them. In classical Greek the basic meaning of *hupokritēs* is 'one who answers'. The verb *hupokrinesthai* is the standard word for 'to answer'. From that basic meaning *hupokritēs* develop the following regular meanings. (*a*) An interpreter or expounder of oracles or dreams. When Lucian tells his audience of the dream which made him into a writer, he says that they must be saying to themselves, 'Surely he does not take us for *oneirōn hupokritai*, interpreters, of dreams' (*Somnium* 17). (*b*) An orator. Demosthenes can be called by one of the critics an exceptional and many-talented *hupokritēs*. (*c*) A reciter or declaimer of poetry. In an age where there were no books the 'rhapsodists' recited the poems and the epics and they were *hupokritai*. (*d*) An actor. A play is a work which is made up of question and answer; and an actor can be described as a *hupokritēs*, an answerer. Now it is from this last meaning that *hupokritēs* develops its bad sense, and comes to mean a 'dissembler, one who is playing a part, putting on an act'.

In the Septuagint *hupokritēs* is definitely a bad word (Job 34.30; 36.13). By this time it has acquired a definitely unpleasant meaning; but it is essential to note that by the time the Septuagint was being revised *hupokritēs* has become, not only a bad word, but an *actively evil* word. One of the famous revisions of the Septuagint was made by a man called Aquila. In Job. 15.34; Prov. 11.9; Isa. 33.14, Aquila has *hupokritēs* and the Septuagint has *asebēs*, which means nothing less than 'impious'. In Job 20.5 Aquila has *hupokritēs* and the Septuagint has *paranomos*, which means a 'transgressor', a 'law-breaker'. In Isa. 32.6 Aquila has *hupokrisis*, and the Septuagint has *anoma*, which means 'lawless things'. Clearly this word does not mean simply 'hypocrisy'; it has begun to stand for something evil, lawless, godless, actively malign. In the *Epistle of Barnabas* (2nd century A.D.) there is a description of 'The Two Ways' and in it it is said: 'You must not join yourself with those who walk in the way of death; you must hate everything that is not pleasing to God; you must hate all *hupokrisis*, and you must not abandon the commands of the Lord.' Obviously *hupokrisis* is active and evil sin.

In the NT *hupokrisis* and *hupokritēs* have certain definite lines of thought.

(i) The *hupokritēs* is the man who goes in for play-acting goodness, for what has been called 'theatrical goodness'. He is the man who wants everyone to see him give alms (Matt. 6.2), to see him pray (Matt. 6.5), to know that he is fasting (Matt. 6.16). He is the man whose goodness is designed, not to please God, but to please men, the man who says not 'To *God* be the glory' but, 'To *me* be the credit'.

(ii) The *hupokritēs* is the man who, in the very name of religion, breaks God's laws. He is the man who says that he cannot help his parents because he had dedicated his belongings to the service of God (Matt. 15.7; Mark 7.5); the man who refuses to help a sick person on the Sabbath, because it would be to break the Sabbath Law, although he will see to the comfort of his beasts on the Sabbath day (Luke 13.15). He is the man who prefers his idea of religion to God's idea.

(iii) The *hupokritēs* is the man who conceals his true motives under a cloak of pretence. The true motives of the people who asked Jesus the question about paying tribute were not to get information and guidance but to entangle Jesus in his words. They are *hupokritai* (Mark 12.15; Matt. 22.18). The *hupokritēs* is the subtle schemer with deceptive words.

(iv) The *hupokritēs* is the man who hides an evil heart under a cloak of piety. The Pharisees were like that (Matt. 23.28). He goes through the outward motions of religion while in his heart there is pride and arrogance, bitterness and hate. He is the kind of man who never fails to go to church and never fails to condemn a sinner. His is the pride that apes humility.

(v) The *hupokritēs* in the end becomes blind. He can

read the weather signs but cannot read the signs of God (Luke 12.56). He has deceived others so often that in the end he has deceived himself.

(vi) The *hupokritēs* is the man, who in the cause of religion, seduces others from the right way (Gal. 2.13; I Tim. 4.2; I Pet. 2.1). He persuades others to listen to him instead of to God.

(vii) In the end the *hupokritēs* is the man who is under the condemnation of God (Matt. 24.51).

There is warning here. Of all sins 'hypocrisy' is the easiest to fall into, and of all sins it is most sternly condemned.

HUPOMONĒ

THE MANLY VIRTUE

Hupomonē is one of the noblest of NT words. Normally it is translated 'patience' or 'endurance', but, as we shall see, there is no single English word which transmits all the fullness of its meaning. In classical Greek it is not a very common word, it is used of the endurance of toil that has come upon a man all against his will, of endurance of the sting of grief, the shock of battle and the coming of death. It has one very interesting use—it is used of the ability of a plant to live under hard and unfavourable circumstances. In later Greek, in the later Jewish literature, it is especially common, for instance in Fourth Maccabees, of that quality of 'spiritual staying power' which enabled men to die for their God.

In the NT the noun *hupomonē* is used 30 times, and the corresponding verb *hupomenein* is used in this sense about 15 times. As we have said the normal translation of the noun is 'patience', and of the verb 'to endure', but when we examine its use in detail certain great truths, which are inspirations, begin to emerge.

(i) *Hupomonē* is very commonly used in connexion with 'tribulation'. Tribulation worketh patience (Rom. 5.3). The Christian must approve himself in much 'patience' and in 'afflictions' (II Cor. 6.4). The Thessalonians are commended for their 'patience' and faith in 'persecutions' and 'tribulations' (II Thess. 1.4). The Christian must be patient (*hupomenein*) in 'tribulation'. This use is specially common in the Revelation, which is characteristically the martyr's book (cp. Rev. 1.9; 3.10; 13.10).

(ii) *Hupomonē* is used in connexion with 'faith'. The testing of faith produces 'patience' (James 1.3). It is *hupomonē* which perfects faith.

(iii) *Hupomonē* is used in connexion with 'hope'. Tribulation begets 'patience' and patience begets experience and experience begets 'hope' (Rom. 5.3). It is 'patience' and comfort which produce 'hope' (Rom. 15.4, 5). The 'patience' of the 'hope' of the Thessalonians is praised (I Thess. 1.3).

(iv) *Hupomonē* is connected with 'joy'. The Christian life is marked with 'patience' and long-suffering with joyfulness (Col. 1.11).

(v) Oftenest of all *hupomonē* is connected with some goal of glory, some greatness which shall be. The references are too many to cite in full (Luke 21.19; Rom. 2.7; Heb. 10.36; 12.1; II Tim. 2.10, 12; James 1.12; 5.11).

And now we can see the essence and the characteristic of this great virtue *hupomonē*. It is not the patience which can sit down and bow its head and let things descend upon it and passively endure until the storm is past. It is not, in the Scots word, merely 'tholing' things. It is the spirit which can bear things, not simply with resignation, but with blazing hope; it is not the spirit which sits statically enduring in the one place, but the spirit which bears things because it knows that these things are leading to a goal of glory; it is not the patience which grimly waits for the end, but the patience which radiantly hopes for the dawn. It has been called 'a masculine constancy under trial'. It has been said that always it has a background of *andreia*, which is courage. Chrysostom calls *hupomonē* 'a root of all the goods, mother of piety, fruit that never withers, a fortress that is never taken, a harbour that knows no storms'. He calls it 'the queen of virtues, the foundation of right actions, peace in war, calm in tempest, security in plots', and neither the violence of man nor the powers of the evil one can injure it. It is the quality which keeps a man on his feet with his face to the wind. It is the virtue which can transmute the hardest trial into glory because beyond the pain it sees the goal. George Matheson, who was stricken in blindness and disappointed in love, wrote a prayer in which he pleads that he might accept God's will, 'not with dumb resignation, but with holy joy; not only with the absence of murmur, but with a song of praise'. Only *hupomonē* can enable a man to do that.

KALEIN, KLĒTOS AND KLĒSIS

THE CALLING OF GOD

ONE of the most basic and fundamental of all NT conceptions is the conception of God's calling of men; and it is with that conception that these three words have to do. *Kalein* is the verb which means 'to call'; *klēsis* is the noun which means 'a call'; *klētos* is the adjective which means 'called'.

In classical Greek the verb *kalein* has four main usages, all of which have something to offer for our better understanding of the NT use of the term.

(i) *Kalein* is the regular verb for 'calling' a person or a place by a name. So in Matt. 1.21, 23, 25, Jesus is 'called' by the name 'Jesus'. In Matt. 5.9 the peacemakers are 'called' the sons or God. In Matt. 23.7 the scribes love to be 'called' Rabbi. This is the commonest of all the uses of *kalein*.

(ii) *Kalein* is the regular verb for 'summoning' or 'calling' a person. It may be that the person is 'summoned' to an office and an honour. Paul is 'called' to be an apostle (*klētos*) (Rom. 1.1; I Cor. 1.1). It may be that the person is 'summoned' to be given a task. In Matt. 25.14 the servants are 'called' to take over the estate when the master is away (cp. Luke 19.13). It may be that the person is summoned to be given a reward for his work and to give an account of it (Matt. 20.8). *Kalein* is regularly used for summoning a person to an office, a task, a responsibility, a reward, and an account.

(iii) *Kalein* is the regular verb for 'inviting a person to a meal or a banquet or into a house as a guest'. So much so is this the case that the past participle passive *ho keklēmenos* and the adjective *ho klētos* can both by themselves mean 'the guest' (for this use in the Septuagint cp. I Kings 1.41). So *kalein* is the word used for 'inviting' the guests to the wedding feast (Matt. 22.3). It is used of Simon the Pharisee 'inviting' Jesus to a meal in his house (Luke 7.39). It is the word that Luke uses of the humble and the conceited guests who are 'bidden' to a feast (Luke 14.8). It is the word that is used of those who are 'called' to the marriage supper of the Lamb (Rev. 19.9). *Kalein* is the regular word which is used for a hospitable invitation.

(iv) *Kalein* is the regular word for 'summoning into the law-courts'. It is the word that is used for 'citing' a witness or a defendant to appear before a judge. In the NT it is so used of Peter and John being brought before the Sanhedrin (Acts 4.18); and of Paul being summoned before Felix to face his Jewish prosecutors (Acts 24.2). It is the word which is used when a man is summoned to stand his trial and to give account.

Even if we were to stop here and go no further we would

have a flood of light on what the call of the Christian means. We could say four things at least.

(i) The Christian is a man who hears the summons of God. Now the very essence of a summons is that it is either a challenge or an appeal. A man can either accept it or reject it; he can heed it or disregard it; he can listen to it or be deaf to it. The very word lays upon us the tremendous responsibility of answering—or not answering—the voice of God.

(ii) The Christian life is a summons to duty. Always the Christian is summoned to a task. God is always offering the Christian man a task to do. In Cicero's *Republic* (1.20, 33) Laelius is asked: 'What then do you think we ought to teach the people we have to educate?' And the answer is: 'We ought to teach those arts which will make us of use to the state.' The call of God is a call to the Christian to be of use in this world.

(iii) The call of God is a call to privilege. *Kalein* and *klēsis* are intimately associated with the invitation to a feast, a banquet, the welcome to a table and a home. The call of God to the Christian is the call to come and to enjoy his fellowship, his hospitality, the joy and the fullness of being a guest of God.

(iv) The call of God is a call to judgment. Equally *kalein* and *klēsis* are intimately associated with being cited to appear before a judge and a court. The Christian life is not going nowhere; it is going to the judgment seat of God. And if a man disregards the call of God, if he is deaf to the summons to duty, if he is heedless to the invitation of God, there comes the final call, the call which will call him to account.

The supreme interest and illumination of these words is the connexions in which they are used.

(i) The 'call' which comes to the Christian is the call of God and God alone. It does not come to him because he deserved it, but simply because God knew him and called him. Jacob is not chosen because of any superior achievement to Esau, but simply because God called him (Rom. 9.11). Our own calling goes back directly to the will of God (Rom. 8.30).

(ii) Another way to put it is that the call of God is associated with *charis*, with 'grace' (Gal. 1.6; 1.15). It is not as if God chose us because we stood out because of special goodness or special attainment. It is out of the goodness of his heart that God calls us who never deserved to be called. God's invitation is an invitation to which we have no claim at all. Not our merit, but God's love, is the moving force of this call.

(iii) The 'call' is associated with *eirēnē*, with 'peace' (I Cor. 7.15; Col. 3.15). Now in the NT sense 'peace' is not just the absence of trouble; it is everything that makes for our highest good. It was said of Robert Burns that he was *haunted* and not *helped* by his religion. God's call is to help us to be what we ought to be to him and to our fellow men.

(iv) The 'call' is associated with *koinōnia*, with 'fellowship' (I Cor. 1.9). That fellowship is a double fellowship; it is a fellowship with Christ and with our fellow men. The man who hears and answers the call of God is on the way to being in a new relationship with Christ and with his fellow men.

(v) The 'call' is associated with *eleutheria*, with 'freedom' (Gal. 5.13). To answer God's call is to find, not slavery, but liberation. The man who responds to the invitation of God is freed from self, and sin and Satan.

(vi) The 'call' is associated with *elpis*, with 'hope' (Eph. 4.4). When a man hears and answers the call of God it is the end of pessimism and the end of despair. He is no longer an inevitably defeated man; he is a potentially victorious man. He no longer lives a life encircled by endless frustrations; he lives a life enlarged with endless possibilities.

(vii) The 'call' is associated with 'duty'. Again and again we are urged to walk in a way that is worthy of our calling (Eph. 4.1; I Cor. 7.17). It is a call to follow in the footsteps of Jesus Christ (I Pet. 2.21). It is a call, not to *akatharsia*, which is 'uncleanness', but to *hagiasmos*, which is 'sanctification' (I Thess. 4.7). The man who hears and answers this call sets out on the road to holiness. The one who calls us is *hagios*, 'holy', and we who are called must also be *hagios*, 'holy' (I Pet. 1.15). We must be counted 'worthy of this calling' (II Thess. 1.11). For that very reason it is something which, by our lives, we must for ever strive to make secure (II Pet. 1.10). Think of it this way. A man might receive a gift which he well knew he did not deserve; he might be given something of such a munificent generosity that he knew that he could never repay it; he might be treated with a kindness that he knew that he had not even remotely earned. For that very reason he will be bound to spend all his strength and all his life in one passionate effort to show how grateful he is for the gift that he never deserved. His effort is not the result of fear; it is not the product of the desire for credit; it is simply the inevitable result of an amazed and wondering love. So then we well know that nothing that we have done or can do can make us deserve to be called by God. That is all the more reason why all life should be spent in the effort to be worthy of the love which so honoured us against all our deserving.

There are certain further things that we must still note about this idea of 'the calling of God'.

(i) The 'call' is associated with salvation (*sōzein*) (II Tim. 1.9). To hear and answer the call is at one and the same time to be saved from the penalty of sin and armed with strength for life for the future. It is a call which rescues from penalty and which clothes with power. Now 'salvation' is something which is eschatological. That is to say, it begins on this earth, but it goes beyond this earth. It has its beginning in time, but it has its consummation in eternity; and there are a number of associations of this group of words with conceptions and ideas which embrace both this world and the next.

(ii) The Christians are people who are 'called to be saints' (*klētoi hagioi*). Now *hagios* literally means 'separated'; a person who is *hagios* in the Christian sense of the term is a person who has separated himself from the world in order to consecrate himself to God. Sainthood, in the NT sense of the term, is concerned, not so much with where a man is, but with the direction in which he is facing. The Christian is called to be a man the direction of whose life is towards God, who lives with God now, and who will see God face to face hereafter.

(iii) The Christian is called 'out of darkness into light' (I Pet. 2.9). He is called out of the shadows of the world's sin and frustration and death into the light of the knowledge and the life of God. The Christian is the man who is living, not in the twilight of the gathering dark, but in the light of the breaking dawn.

(iv) The Christian is called 'to eternal life and to an eternal inheritance' (I Tim. 6.12; Heb. 9.15). In the NT the word 'eternal' (*aiōnios*) has much more to do with *quality* than *duration* of life. We may put it this way. *Aiōnios*, 'eternal', is the word which properly and uniquely belongs to God; therefore 'eternal life' is the kind of life which belongs to God. The Christian is 'called' out of his troubled, soiled, frustrated, dying life into the blessedness of the life of God himself.

(v) Sometimes this is put in other ways. The Christian is 'called' by God to 'honour' (Heb. 9.15). He is 'called' to obtain 'the glory of our Lord Jesus Christ' (II Thess. 2.14). He is 'called' to obtain 'the eternal glory of God' (I Pet. 5.10). The Christian is a man who is called to glory. The calling of God makes great demands, but equally it makes tremendous promises. 'Glory' is everything that heaven offers. The Christian is invited to share nothing less than the splendour of the life of God. The NT thinks not so much of the punishment that a man will suffer if he refuses the call, but far more of the splendour he will miss.

(vi) Sometimes this call will come to men through men.

Paul tells the Thessalonians that 'their call' came through 'his gospel' (II Thess. 2.14). It is the great glory of the Christian that he can, if he will, transmit to others the call that he has himself heard. The Christian—and that does not mean only the preacher—can be the bearer of God's invitation to glory to his fellow-men.

We may finally note that twice this word *kalein* is used of Jesus.

(i) It is used of 'the call of the disciples' (Matt. 4.21).
(ii) It is used of 'the call to repentance' (Luke 5.32). Jesus calls men to fellowship with himself and to a life which is a new life. The Christian is called to be Christ's friend and is therefore called to be a new man. The two things go together. The Christian life is at one and the same time an invitation to privilege, to responsibility and to glory. And at the back of it there remains the haunting thought that the tragedy of life is to refuse the invitation of God.

KALOS

THE WORD OF WINSOMENESS

Kalos is a characteristic NT word to describe a characteristic quality of the Christian life. In the NT *kalos* occurs no fewer than 100 times. Usually in the AV it is simply translated *good*, although occasionally it is translated *honest* (e.g., Rom. 12.17; II Cor. 8.21).

Honest in this connexion does not primarily mean *telling the truth*; it is used in the Latin sense of *honestus*, which means, *handsome, gracious, fair to look upon.*

In classical Greek *kalos* is one of the noblest of words; and all through its history it never loses a certain splendour.

Originally it referred to *beauty of form*. It could be applied to any person who was lovely or to any thing that was beautiful. Candaules believed his queen to be the *fairest* (*kallistē*, the superlative) of all women (Herodotus, 1.8).

In Homer Nireus is the *comeliest* (*kallistos*) man of all the Greeks who came to Troy (*Iliad* 2.673). Athene the goddess appeared to Odysseus in the form of a woman *beautiful* and tall (*Odyssey* 13.289). When *kalos* describes persons in Homer it very often appears in company with *megas*, which means *tall*. There is stateliness in the beauty which *kalos* describes.

Xenophon describes Cyrus as *most handsome* (*kallistos*) in person, most generous in heart (Xenophon, *Cyropædia* 1.2.1). In the *Memorabilia* Xenophon tells how Critobulus tells Socrates that he desires the skill to win a good soul and a *fair* (*kalos*) face (Xenophon, *Memorabilia* 2.6.30).

Kalos is used of any part of the body which is *fair* and *shapely*. Homer describes Menelaus with his *shapely* (*kalos*) legs and ankles stained with blood in the battle (*Iliad* 4.147); he speaks of the fair (*kalos*) flesh of Aphrodite the goddess of love (*Iliad* 5.354).

Kalos is used not only of persons; it can describe any thing which is *handsome* and *fair*. Homer uses it of a great and *goodly* court in a splendid house (*Odyssey* 14.7). He uses it of a beautifully wrought shield (*Iliad* 11.33); of the *fair* cloak and tunic which Circe brought to Odysseus (*Odyssey* 10.365); or a robe made for the goddess Athene, *fairest* in its broiderings (*Iliad* 6.224); of a *fair* tract of orchard land (*Iliad* 12.314).

Wherever this word is found there is the idea of loveliness, of attractiveness, of graciousness, of that which delights the heart and gives pleasure to the eyes.

Further, *kalos* is the adjective which implies love and admiration. Her citizens who loved her called Athens *the Beautiful* (*kalos*). Aristophanes tells how Sitalces, as a lover would, writes on the walls of the city: 'Athens is *beautiful*' (*Acharnians* 144).

Pindar speaks of 'inglorious old age reft of all share of *blessings*' (*Olymp.* 1.84). Xenophon tells how Croesus promised the Lydians, when he became king, that whatever *fair possession* man or woman had would come to them (Xenophon, *Cyropædia* 7.2.13).

Herodotus uses *kalos* in an interesting way. Speaking of the essential modesty which should characterize life, he says: 'Men have long ago made *wise* (*kalos*) rules for our learning' (Herodotus, 1.8). He says that, compared with the Persians, the barbarous Massagetae have no experience of the *gracious* (*kalos*) things of life (Herodotus, 1.207). *Kalos* describes the things which make life gracious and lovely and good to live.

Still further, although *kalos* has this essential idea of beauty, it also has the idea of *usefulness*. The beauty which *kalos* describes is not merely decorative; it is also useful to men. So Homer, describing Phæacia, says: 'A *fair* (*kalos*) harbour lies on each side of the city' (*Odyssey* 6.263). He uses it of a *favourable* wind. 'They embarked and set sail from broad Crete with the North wind blowing fresh and *fair* (*kalos*)' (*Odyssey* 14.299).

Thucydides uses *kalos* to describe a well situated camp (Thucydides, 5.60). Xenophon uses *kalos* to describe coins which are made of genuine silver and which are not counterfeit, debased, worn or clipped (*Memorabilia* 3.1.9.). The Greeks often spoke of a *kalos chronos*, a *good time*, a *fitting* time to do something.

Kalos in Greek also means *beautiful* and *honourable* in the *moral* sense. Homer, speaking of rapacious men, says: 'It is not *honourable* (*kalos*) or just to rob the guests of Telemachus' (*Odyssey* 20.294).

When Antigone desires to bury the body of her brother Polyneices, although the giving of the last rites of love has been forbidden, and when she is warned that she will suffer for what she desires to do, her answer is: "Tis *sweet* (*kalos*) to me to die in such employ' (Sophocles, *Antigone* 72).

Pindar speaks of 'the light of *noble* (*kalos*) deeds unquenchable for ever' (*Isthm.* 4.42). Xenophon speaks of

Socrates as a pattern of *nobleness* (*kalos*) (Xenophon, *Symposium* 8.17). Virtue, he says, brings *honour* (*kalos*) to you, and good to the state (Xenophon, *Memorabilia* 3.5.28).

Plato uses it to describe the good conduct in a boy which is a credit to the city of Athens where he is brought up (Plato, *Symposium* 183d). Socrates, Xenophon says, discussed what is godly, what is ungodly; what is *beautiful* (*kalos*), and what is ugly (Xenophon, *Memorabilia* 1.1.16).

Chrysippus the Stoic held that all that is good is beautiful (Diogenes Laertius, 7.101). *Kalos* describes the beauty which lies in the deed which is honourable and fine.

We may best of all see the meaning of *kalos*, if we contrast it with *agathos* which is the common Greek word for *good*. *Agathos* is that which is practically and morally good; *kalos* is that which is not only practically and morally good, but that which is also aesthetically good, which is lovely and pleasing to the eye.

Hort, commenting on James 2.7, says: '*Kalos* is what is good as seen, as making a direct impression on those who come in contact with it—not only good in result, which would be *agathos*.' In the creation story when God looked at the world which he had made, he saw that it was *good* (Gen. 1.8), and *kalos* is the word which is used.

When a thing or a person is *agathos*, it or he is good in the moral and practical sense of the term, and in the result of its or his activity; but *kalos* adds to the idea of goodness the idea of beauty, of loveliness, of graciousness, of winsomeness. *Agathos* appeals to the moral sense; but *kalos* appeals also to the eye.

Aristotle defines nobility (*to kalon*) as that which is agreeable or desirable in itself (*Rhetoric* 1364b 27). He describes it as being at one and the same time agreeable in itself and worthy of praise, as being good and pleasant (*ibid*. 1366a 33).

Latin translates this word *kalos* by the word *honestus*; and Cicero defines that which is *honestus* as being 'such that, even if its utility is taken away, and even if any rewards and fruits which come from it are removed, it can still be praised for its own sake' (*De Fin.* 2.45).

Tacitus describes the quality in *honestus* as 'that quality which makes a man worthy of praise, even if you strip him of everything else' (*Histories* 4.5). In anything that is *kalos* or *honestus* there is an innate and indestructible loveliness and attraction.

We may very briefly look at the use of this word in the papyri. It is used to describe animals which are in good condition and of gentle nature; it is used to describe drugs which are in good condition and efficient in contrast with drugs which have lost their efficacy. It is used to describe grapes which are fully ripe, sweet to the taste and beautiful to look upon. It is used to describe wine which has been left to settle and to mature until it is mellow and at its best.

It is used to describe a *favourable* sale, a *well-cut* tunic. In describing people it is joined with *pistos*, which means *dependable* and *reliable*. It is used of *honourable* men whose word and pledge and oath can be unquestionably accepted. In discussing *kalos* in the papyri Milligan speaks of the *self-evidencing* power which is in *kalos*. That which is *kalos* bears its goodness on its face.

Clearly *kalos* is a noble word. It describes that which is beautiful, that which commands love and admiration, that which is useful, that which is honourable. *Kalos* is the word of the goodness which is a lovely thing, the goodness which not only satisfies the conscience, but which also delights the heart, and gives pleasure to the eyes.

Having studied the word *kalos* in classical Greek and in the papyri, we now turn to its usage in the NT.

(i) *Kalos* is used in the NT as it is in secular Greek, to describe things which are useful for all the purposes of life and which are pleasant to see. It describes the stones of which the Temple is built (Luke 21.5). It describes the fruit which the fruitful and the good tree produces (Matt. 3.10; cp. Luke 3.9; Matt. 7.17-19; 12.33; Luke 6.43). It describes the *good* ground which is clean and rich and fertile (Matt. 13.8, 23; cp. Mark 4.8, 20 and Luke 8.15). It describes the *good* seed which is sown into the ground (Matt. 13.24, 27, 37, 38). It describes the *good* and *useful* fish which are caught in the assortment which the dragnet brings in (Matt. 13.48). Salt is said to be *kalos* (Mark 9.50). It describes *good* wine (John 2.10). It describes the *good* measure which is generously given (Luke 6.38). The Law is *kalos* (Rom. 7.16; I Tim. 1.8). The name of Christ is *kalos* (James 2.7). The word of God is *kalos* (Heb. 5.14). *Kalos* is the word which characteristically describes the good and useful and pleasant things of life.

(ii) One of the most interesting and significant uses of *kalos* is that it is repeatedly and consistently used to describe the *good deeds* which should characterize the life of the Christian. Our light is so to shine before men that they may see our *good deeds* (Matt. 5.16). Jesus has shown his enemies many *good works* (John 10.32, 33).

Paul can will, but cannot do *to kalon*, that which is *good* (Rom. 7.16). The Corinthians must do that which is *kalos* (II Cor. 13.7). The Galatians must not grow weary in doing what is *kalos* (Gal. 6.9). The Thessalonians must test all things, and hold fast to that which is *kalos* (I Thess. 5.21).

The Christian must be an example of, and zealous for, *good works* (Titus 2.7, 14). He must be anxious to produce *good works*, by which his life must be marked (Titus 3.8, 14). Christians must incite each other to love and *good works* (Heb. 10.24); and they must have a *good* conscience (Heb. 13.18).

Here is a use of the word *kalos* which sheds a flood of light on the Christian life. Clearly it is not enough that the Christian life should be good; it must also be attractive. A grim and unlovely goodness is certainly goodness, but it is not *Christian* goodness; for Christian goodness must have a certain loveliness on it. On Christian good works there must be the bloom of charm. Real Christianity must always attract and never repel. There is such a thing as a hard, austere, unlovely and unlovable goodness, but such a goodness falls far short of the Christian standard. In all his efforts to be good, in all his strivings towards moral holiness, the Christian must never forget the *beauty of holiness*.

(iii) From this basic idea of the word *kalos* there follows an appeal which runs through the whole NT. The NT, if we may use an ugly phrase, stresses again and again the propaganda value of the truly Christian life. It stresses the fact that the best advocate of Christianity to the outsider is the sheer attractive loveliness of the life of the true Christian.

It is Paul's advice to the Romans that they should provide things *honest* (*kalos*) in the sense of the Latin *honestus*, i.e., handsome, fair to look upon, in the sight of all men (Rom. 12.17). He urges the Corinthians to provide things that are *honest* (*kalos*), not only in the sight of God, but also in the sight of men (II Cor. 8.21).

The Pastoral Epistles insist that the office-bearers of the Church must have a *good* report from those who are *outside* the Church (I Tim. 3.7). The widows must have a public reputation for *good* works (I Tim. 5.10). A Christian's only wealth and foundation must lie in *good* works (I Tim. 6.18).

James urges men to live a way of life which proves and demonstrates their faith (James 3.13). Peter urges his converts to make their way of life *kalos* among the Gentiles (I Peter 2.12).

The NT holds that the best missionary weapon which the Church possesses is the truly Christian life. It holds that men are to be *attracted*, far more than argued, into the Christian life. There should be in the life of the Christian not only a goodness, but also a loveliness, which will make all men who see it desire the secret which is his.

It is one of the most suggestive and the most illuminating facts about the word *kalos* that, out of its 100 appearances in the NT, 24 are in the Pastoral Epistles.

These letters to Timothy and to Titus were written at a crucial time in the history of the Church. They were written when the Church was a little island of Christianity surrounded by a sea of paganism. They were written at a time when the Church's missionary task was at its most demanding and its most difficult. To meet that situation every person in the Church, and every action of every person in the Church had to be *kalos*. The world had to be presented with the loveliness, the winsomeness, the attractiveness of the Christian faith. We might almost say that men had to be charmed into Christianity.

(i) Office in the Church must be *kalos* (I Tim. 3.1; 3.13). Too often office in the Church is characterized by criticism, obstructiveness, self-righteousness and self-importance; it ought to be characterized by the loveliness of service, encouragement, support and love.

(ii) The Christian is to be a *good* soldier and he is to fight a *good* campaign, which indeed Paul was able to claim that he himself had done (I Tim. 1.18; 6.12; II Tim. 2.3; 4.7). There must be a quality of chivalrous gallantry about the Christian life. The Christian must not serve like a conscript, press-ganged into the service of Christ; he must be the adventurer of Christ. He must make it clear to all by his vital happiness that he finds the service of Christ a thrilling thing, even when it is hard and difficult. The Christian must be the laughing cavalier of Christ.

(iii) The Christian must be the *good* servant of Jesus Christ (I Tim. 4.6). The service of the Christian both to Christ and to his fellow men must be service with a smile, the service of the extra mile, the service given always without a grudge, the service in which the servant obviously finds pleasure and delight. It is not enough to serve Christ efficiently; to the efficiency there must be added the charm and the loveliness which *kalos* always includes.

(iv) The Christian teaching must be *kalos* (I Tim. 4.6). In all Christian teaching, even at its sternest, there must be charm and attractiveness. Robert Louis Stevenson notes in his diary; as if it was a most unusual event: 'Went to church today and was not depressed.' Clovis G. Chappell says: 'No man has a right so to preach as to send his hearers away on flat tyres. . . . Every discouraging sermon is a wicked sermon. . . . A discouraged man is not an asset but a liability.' The Christian teaching must be *kalos*; it must woo men, not bludgeon or threaten men, to Christ.

(v) The Christian witness and profession must be *kalos*, as indeed was the witness of Jesus Christ himself (I Tim. 6.12, 13). A man can witness for Christ in such a way that he attracts his fellow men; and he can witness for Christ in such a way that he repels his fellow men. True Christian witness is not a grim, austere thing, full of protests and prohibitions, a thing which emasculates the vitality and obliterates the colour of life. True Christian witness attracts by its radiance, its vitality, its vividness. One of her pupils said of Alice Freeman Palmer, the great teacher: 'She made me feel as if I were bathed in sunshine.' That is the effect that true Christian witness ought to have.

(vi) To the material of the Pastoral Epistles, I Peter has one thing to add: the steward of the grace of God must be *kalos* (I Peter 4.10). It is the duty of the Christian to bring to his fellow men the grace of God; and especially that is the duty of the minister of Christ and of his Church. He must do so with charm and attractiveness. His first instinct must be, not to shut the door, but to open the door, not to condemn, but always to sympathize. There are preachers who preach with such threats and such denunciation that when we listen to them we almost feel that they hate us; no preacher will ever win men for Christ unless he first makes it clear that he loves them. There must be a certain graciousness in him who would be the steward of the grace of God, if he is to merit the title of *kalos*, which ought to belong to him.

Every Christian should be *kalos*; and every activity of the Christian life should be *kalos*. The Christian should be clad with a mantle of graciousness, and his every action should radiate winsomeness; only so will he serve Christ and win his fellow men.

We have studied the meaning and usage of the word *kalos* in classical Greek and in the NT in some detail; but we have deliberately left to the end the two usages of it in the NT which illustrates its meaning best of all.

One of the loveliest stories in the NT is the story of the anointing of Jesus' head by the woman in the house of Simon the leper at Bethany. The woman loved Jesus, and this was the only way in which she could show her love. The dull, insensitive, unimaginative spectators criticized her for the reckless extravagance of what she had done. Jesus' answer was: 'She hath wrought a *good*, *kalos*, work upon me' (Matt. 26.10; cp. Mark 14.6).

That incident is the perfect illustration of all that *kalos* means. It was a demonstration of love; it was the act of a love which knew that only the best it had to give was good enough; it was the act of a love which refused to count the cost. It was the act of a love which set beauty far above mere utility; of a love which knew that giving can never be dictated by the cautious prudentialities of common sense. A deed which is *kalos* is a deed in which there is enshrined the beauty of love's extravagance.

The second usage in the NT which demonstrates the meaning of *kalos* is that it is the word which is used of Jesus in that title which is for many the most precious title of Jesus—the *Good* Shepherd (John 10.11, 14).

The shepherd does not look after his sheep with only a cold efficiency. He looks after them with a sacrificial love. When the sheep are in trouble, he does not nicely calculate the risk of helping them; he gives his life for the sheep. He does not give so many hours' service to the sheep per day, and carefully calculate that he must work so many hours a week. All through the day he watches over them, and all through the night he lies across the opening in the sheepfold so that he is literally the door. Here we have the same idea again. The *good* shepherd is the shepherd whose service is a lovely and a heroic thing because it is a service, not rendered for pay, but rendered for love.

The basic idea in the word *kalos* is the idea of winsome beauty; and we are bound to see that nothing can be *kalos* *unless* it be the product of love. Deeds which are *kalos* are the outcome of a heart in which love reigns supreme. The outward beauty of the deed springs from the inward magnitude of the love within the heart.

There is no English word which fully translates *kalos*; there is no word which gathers up within itself the beauty, the winsomeness, the attractiveness, the generosity, the usefulness, which are all included in this word. Perhaps the word which comes nearest to it is the Scots word *bonnie*.

J. P. Struthers, that great Scottish preacher, used to say that it would do the Church more good than anything else in the world if Christians would only sometimes do a *bonnie* thing. He lived up to his own teaching. He lived in a manse in Greenock which was at the end of the road which led up to the hillside above the firth. The lads and lasses used to take that road at evening time. Struthers had a garden; and he used to pluck the flowers in it and make them up into little posies which he used to lay along his garden wall. And the lads knew that he meant them to take the posies and give them to the girls with whom they were walking along the road. That was an action which was the perfect illustration of this word *kalos*; and that is the kind of action which does the Church more good than most of the great works of theology that ever were written.

Scholarship can baffle; learning can bewilder; efficiency can chill; aggressiveness can antagonize. That which tugs at men's hearts and pulls them to Christ is the winsome attractiveness in Jesus Christ himself, the attractiveness which ought to reside in those who claim to be his.

If we would serve Christ in his Church, there must be on our lives that winsome beauty which will entitle us, too, to the title of *kalos*, loveliest of all the words which describe the Christian life.

KATAGGELLEIN

THE WORD OF AUTHORITY

THE word *kataggellein* means to *announce* or *to proclaim*; but the characteristic flavour of the word is that the announcement or the proclamation is made *with authority*. In classical Greek it is used of *proclaiming war* or *announcing a festival*.

In the papyri a widow makes an official *pronouncement* regarding the appointment of a representative to look after her interests in consequence of her husband's death. It is used of the *announcement* of an emperor's accession to the throne. Always the word carries with it weight and authority.

In the NT the word is used 15 times. It is used of the prophets *foretelling* the coming of Christ and the events of the early days (Acts 3.24). It is used of the work of Jesus in that he *showed* light to the people and to the Gentiles (Acts 26.23). It is Paul's word of praise that the faith of the Roman church is *spoken* of throughout the world (Rom. 1.8). The words and actions of the Sacrament are said to *show forth* the death of Christ (I Cor. 11.26).

But the main interest of the word lies in the fact that it is one of the great NT words for *preaching*. In Acts 15.36 we are told that Paul and Barnabas plan to revisit the churches to which they have *preached* (*kataggellein*).

Now the interest of the word lies in the examination of *the things which were preached*, for these are the things which are proclaimed *with authority*. What then were the things which the early preachers preached with authority, the things they preached as certainties, the things they preached as part of the unalterable and authoritative message of the Christian faith?

(i) They proclaimed *the word of God*. It is said that Paul and Barnabas *preached* (*kataggellein*) the word of God in the synagogues of Cyprus (Acts 13.5). It was the word of God that Paul *preached* at Berea (Acts 17.13). Preaching is not the proclamation of a preacher's private opinions; still less is it the public airing of his doubts; it is the proclamation of the word of God. 'Tell me of your certainties,' said Goethe, 'I have doubts enough of my own.'

(ii) They proclaimed *Christ*. Paul does not care how the preaching is done so long as Christ is *preached* (Phil. 1.16, 18). It is Christ whom he himself *preached* (Col. 1.28). In the early days the preachers did not deal with things on the circumference of the faith; they proclaimed the facts of the life, and the death, and the resurrection of Jesus Christ. Their primary aim was to confront men with Christ.

(iii) They proclaimed through Jesus *the resurrection from the dead* (Acts 4.2). The message of the preacher was the defeat of death. They preached a risen Christ, and they preached a life that was indestructible.

(iv) They proclaimed *the Messiahship of Jesus*. It was Paul's message that 'this Jesus whom I *preach* to you is Christ' (Acts 17.3). It was the message of the early preachers that in this man Jesus God's promises were fulfilled, that eternity had invaded time, that heaven's rule had begun.

(v) They proclaimed that *the way was open to the God whom men had ever sought but never found*. It was Paul's proclamation that he brought to the Athenians news of the God who to them had always been the unknown God (Acts 17.23). The time of guessing and groping had gone, and the time of knowing had come. The time of searching was ended, and the time of finding had come. George Borrow tells us that once when he was on one of his tours he was surrounded by some gipsies, who cried out: 'Give us God! Give us God!' Not knowing what to do, he put his hand in his pocket and scattered some money amongst them. But they disregarded the money. 'Not your money,' they said. 'Give us God!' It was God whom the early preachers claimed to give to men.

(vi) They proclaimed *a gospel*. It was the gospel which the preacher preached; it was good news (I Cor. 9.14). Any preaching which ultimately depresses a man is wrong, for preaching may begin by cutting a man to the heart with the sight and the realization of his sins; but it must end by leading him to the love, the forgiveness and the grace of God.

The very word which is so often used for preaching shows that in the early preaching there was nothing apologetic, nothing diffident, nothing clouded with doubts and misted with uncertainties. It was preaching with authority; and the things it preached with authority are still the basis of the message of the preacher today.

KATALLASSEIN

THE WORD OF RECONCILIATION

THERE is in the writings of Paul a group of words which are of extreme importance, because he uses them to express the central experience of the Christian faith.

All these words are compound forms made from the simple verb *allassein* which means *to change*. In classical Greek *allassein* itself can be used to express *changing* shape, or colour, or appearance. It can also be used in the sense of to *exchange* or to *barter*; and it can frequently be used of *taking one thing in exchange for another*. It is, for instance, used of one who in misfortune exchanges one sorrow for another.

This simple verb *allassein* is not uncommon in the NT. Stephen is charged with teaching that Jesus will *change* the accepted customs of the Jews (Acts 6.14). The heathen have *changed* the glory of God for lifeless, corrupted and polluted images (Rom. 1.23). Paul tells the people of Corinth that we shall all be *changed* (I Cor. 15.51). When Paul realizes the danger of perversion of the faith among the Galatians, he wishes to *change* his voice, and to adopt the accent of sternness and rebuke (Gal. 4.20). The word is used of *changing* a garment in Heb. 1.12. *Allassein* then can be used of almost any kind of *change*.

This word *allassein* acquires certain compound forms. In ordinary classical Greek the commonest of the compound forms is the form *katallassein*, and *katallassein* is one of the great Pauline words also. But we must go on with the examination of this group of words in ordinary secular Greek before we come to their use in the NT.

Katallassein in ordinary secular Greek acquires the almost technical sense of *changing money*, or *changing into money*. Plutarch tells how four Syrian brothers stole the king's gold vessels in Corinth and how bit by bit they *changed* them into money (Plutarch, *Aratus* 18). The corresponding noun *katallagē* has the same sense of *exchange*, especially the exchange of money.

Katallassein then begins to acquire a wider sense of exchanging any one thing for another. Aristotle, for instance, speaks of professional and mercenary soldiers who are willing to *barter* their lives for trifling gain (Aristotle, *Nicomachean Ethics* 1117b 20).

But then *katallassein* takes a still further step and it begins to mean, more than anything else, *the change of enmity into friendship*. Clytæmnestra reminds Agamemnon how he had been responsible for the death of her former husband and her children and then says: '*Reconciled* to thee and to thy house, a blameless wife was I' (Euripides, *Iphigeneia at Aulis* 1157). Sophocles speaks of a man *making his peace* with heaven (Sophocles, *Ajax* 744). Thucydides tells how in the Sicilian wars Hermocrates pled with the warring sections to set aside conflicting claims, and become *reconciled* with each other (Thucydides, 4.59). Xenophon tells of a man who had made war on Cyrus and who had then *become his friend again* (Xenophon, *Anabasis* 1.6.1). In all these cases the verb is *katallassein*.

So then in classical Greek *katallassein* becomes characteristically the word of the bringing together again of people who have been estranged. In a papyrus a man who is apparently a father who has had a difference with a member of his family, asks the question from an oracle: 'Am I to be *reconciled* to my offspring?'

Even before the NT used it *katallassein* is the word of reconciliation.

We now turn to *katallassein* and to its kindred words in the NT. With only two exceptions these words are used always of the restoration of the relationship between man and God.

The first exception is I Cor. 7.11 where Paul lays it down that a woman who has left her husband must not marry another, but must be *reconciled* to him. The other case is the single usage in the NT of the kindred word *sunallassein*. It is used in Acts 7.26 of Moses when he tried *to set at one* the two Israelites who were quarrelling in Egypt. Even when this word is used in connexion with human relationships, it always refers to the restoration of a broken friendship and an interrupted fellowship.

It is only Paul who uses this group of words in the NT: and he always uses these words of the restoration of the relationship between man and God.

In Rom. 5.11 he speaks of Jesus Christ through whom we have now received the *atonement* (*katallagē*). In Rom. 11.15 he explains the casting away of the Jews by saying that the casting away was necessary for the *reconciling of* the world (*katallagē*). In II Cor. 5.18, 19 he speaks of the ministry and the word of *reconciliation* (*katallagē*).

In Rom. 5.10 he says that while we were enemies we were *reconciled* to God by the death of his Son (*katallassein*). In II Cor. 5.18-20 there is a whole series of uses of this word. God has *reconciled* us to himself by Jesus. God was in Christ *reconciling* the world unto himself. We pray you to be *reconciled* to God.

Twice Paul uses a kind of intensified form of this word,

apokatallassein. In Eph. 2.16 he tells how Jesus Christ has *reconciled* Jews and Gentiles to each other, and both to God; and in Col. 1.21 he tells how Jesus Christ has *reconciled* all things and all men to God.

(i) First and foremost, Paul sees the work of Jesus Christ as above and beyond all else a work of reconciliation. Through that which he did, the lost relationship between man and God is restored. Man was made for friendship and fellowship with God. By his disobedience and rebellion he ended up at enmity with God. That which Jesus did took that enmity away, and restored the relationship of friendship which should always have existed, but which was broken by man's sin.

(ii) It is to be carefully noted that Paul never speaks of God being reconciled to men, but always of men being reconciled to God. The most significant of all the passages, II Cor. 5.18-20, three times speaks of God reconciling man to himself. It was man, not God, who needed to be reconciled. Nothing had lessened the love of God; nothing had turned that love to hate; nothing had ever banished that yearning from the heart of God. Man might sin, but God still loved. It was not God who needed to be pacified, but man who needed to be moved to surrender and to penitence and to love.

(iii) Here then we are face to face with an inescapable truth. The effect of the Cross—at least in this sphere of the thought of Paul—was on man, and not on God. The effect of the Cross changed, not the heart of God, but the heart of man. It was man who needed to be reconciled, not God. It is entirely against all Pauline thought to think of Jesus Christ pacifying an angry God, or to think that in some way God's wrath was turned to love, and God's judgment was turned to mercy, because of something which Jesus did.

When we look at it in Paul's way, it was man's sin which was turned to penitence, man's rebellion which was turned to surrender, man's enmity which was turned to love, by the sacrificial love of Jesus Christ upon the Cross. It cost that Cross to make that change in the hearts of men.

(iv) One thing remains to be said. If all this is so—and it is so—the ministry of the Church is a ministry of reconciliation, as indeed Paul said it was (II Cor. 5.19, 20). The function of the preacher is to convey to men, not the announcement of the threat of God's wrath, but the proclamation of the offer of God's love. The message of the preacher must ever be: Look at that Cross and see how much God loves you. Can you hold back in face of a love like that?

The very essence of Christianity is the restoration of a lost relationship. The summons of Christianity is to return to a God whose love men spurned, but whose love is ever waiting for men to come home. The task of the preacher is to break men's hearts at the sight of the broken heart of God.

KATARTIZEIN

THE WORD OF CHRISTIAN DISCIPLINE

THE great practical interest of *katartizein* lies in the fact that it is the word used in Gal. 6.1, for, as the AV puts it, 'restoring' a brother who is taken in fault. If, then, we can penetrate into its meaning it will greatly assist us in forming a correct view of the method and purpose of Christian discipline.

In classical Greek it has a wide variety of meanings, all of which can be gathered together under one or other of two heads. (i) It means 'to adjust, to put in order, to restore'. Hence it is used of pacifying a city which is torn by faction; of setting a limb that has been dislocated; of developing certain parts of the body by exercise; of restoring a person to his rightful mind; of reconciling friends who have become estranged. (ii) It is used of 'equipping or fully furnishing someone or something for some given purpose'. So it is used of fitting out a ship and it is used of an army, fully armed and equipped, and drawn up in battle-array. Its uses in the papyri do not add greatly to our insight into its meaning. There, too, it is used of something 'prepared for a given purpose or person'. It is, for instance, so used of clothes which have been made and prepared for some-one to wear.

In the NT it is used about thirteen times, twice in quota-tions from the OT (Matt. 21.16; Heb. 10.5). It has three main lines of usage.

(i) It is the word which is used of the disciples 'mending their nets' (Matt. 4.21; Mark 1.19). It may possibly there mean that they were 'folding up the nets'. But whether it means mending or folding up the idea is that the nets were being prepared for future use.

(ii) There is a set of passages in which the basic meaning is that of equipment. In Luke 6.40 it is said that a scholar cannot turn out better equipped than his teacher. Rom. 9.22 speaks of vessels of wrath equipped for destruction.

(iii) There is a set of passages in which the AV trans-lates it 'to perfect' (II Cor. 13.11; I Thess. 3.10; Heb. 13.21; I Pet. 5.10).

(iv) There is one passage in I Cor. 1.10 where the AV translates it 'perfectly joined together'. It is there used of the drawing together of the discordant elements in the Corinthian Church; and the idea could be either that of setting together dislocated and broken limbs, or that of calming and pacifying the warring elements in a disturbed city.

Now when we take this and apply it to Christian dis-cipline certain most significant things emerge. (i) It is clear that Christian discipline is never meant to be merely retributory punishment; it is not simply vengeance on the evil-doer. (ii) Discipline is meant to 'mend' a man and to 'repair' him. It regards him more as something which has been damaged or injured than it does as a deliberate sinner. (iii) Discipline is meant to 'equip' him better to meet his temptations and to meet the battle and the demands of life. It regards him as a man ill and inadequately equipped and it regards the duty of the Christian society as being that of sending him out better able to deal with the things which defeated him. (iv) It regards the evil-doer as one imperfectly constructed to deal with life and it calls on the Christian community to give him a more perfect knowledge and more perfect strength to overcome evil and to do the right.

So, then, when we study this word, we see that Christian discipline is never vengeful and retributory and sadistic. It is always constructive. It is applied always and only for the sake of helping the man who has erred to do better.

KATHAROS

THE LIFE THAT IS CLEAN

Katharos, which means 'pure' or 'clean', is one of the great Greek words. It occurs about 24 times in the NT; but before ever it became a Christian word it had a rich variety of meanings, all of which contribute something to its meaning for us.

(i) Let us look at *katharos* in classical Greek. (*a*) It began in Homer by meaning simply 'physically clean', as a man's body or clothes are clean. (*b*) It goes on to mean 'pure', in the sense of free from any admixture. Often it is used of clean water; sometimes it is used of the sunlight and of the clean wind; it is the word for 'white' bread; it is regularly used of grain that has been winnowed, of metals that are without alloy and of feelings that are unmixed. Every one of these meanings contributes something to the full Christian meaning of the word. (*c*) It is used in the sense of 'free from debt'. A man who has paid all his accounts and taxes and on whom no man has a claim is *katharos*. To make someone *katharos* is to give him a discharge from a debt or to acquit him of a charge. (*d*) It means 'free from all guilt and pollution'. It is used of innocent hands, of a body and a soul that are morally clean. (*e*) It means 'ceremonially clean', that is to say fit to approach God, or fit for the worship of God. So it is used of the altar, of the sacrifice, of the worshipper who has carried out the correct ritual, of the days on which sacrifice might be offered. It describes something which is fit for the service of God. (*f*) It means 'pure in blood' or 'genuine'. It is used of someone whose race is pure; it is used of a saying whose authenticity cannot be doubted.

(ii) Let us look at *katharos* in the papyri. (*a*) It is used of all kinds of things in the sense of 'clean', 'pure', 'without blemish'. A man writes, 'I have examined the goat and I certify it with my seal as *katharos*, unblemished, physically perfect.' A man promises, 'I will give you back the fields as *katharos*, clean, as I got them.' (*b*) It is used of a document that is corrected and 'free of errors'. It would be the word for a corrected proof. (*c*) It is used of 'the conditions of entry to a temple'. 'First, and greatest of all, the worshippers must have their hands and their minds pure and sound, and must have no terrible thing upon their consciences.'

(iii) Now let us look at it in the NT. (*a*) It is used of physical cleanness. The linen sheet in which they laid Jesus' body was *katharos* (Matt. 27.59; cp. Matt. 23.26; Rev. 19.8). (*b*) It is used in the sense of 'clean' with the meaning, when used of persons, that they are fit for God's service and worship, and when used for things, that they are fit for the Christians to use (John 13.10; Luke 11.41; Rom. 14.20; Tit. 1.15). (*c*) It is used in the sense of 'innocent of any crime' (Acts 18.6; 20.26). (*d*) It is used of 'the heart and the conscience' being pure and clean (I Tim. 1.5; 3.9; II Tim. 1.3; 2.22; I Pet. 1.22). (*e*) It is used of a worship which is fit to be offered to God (James 1.27).

But the instance in the NT which means most to us is its use in the Beatitude, 'Blessed are the *katharoi* (plural) in heart, for they shall see God' (Matt. 5.8). How are we to explain this, and what meaning are we to give *katharos* here? A word is always known by the company it keeps. There are four Greek words with which *katharos* is often closely associated. (*a*) There is *alēthinos*, which means 'real', 'genuine', as opposed to that which is unreal and, as we would say, a fake. (*b*) There is *amigēs*, which means 'pure', 'unmixed'. This word is used, for instance, of pure, unalloyed pleasure. And it is used of a roll which has in it the work of only one author. (*c*) It is used with *akratos*. This is the word that describes pure wine or pure milk which has not been adulterated by water. It is pure in the sense of 'neat', completely unadulterated. (*d*) It is used with *akēratos*, which is the word that describes unalloyed gold, hair which has never been shorn, an unmown meadow, a virgin whose chastity has never been doubted.

Now all these words basically describe something which is pure from every taint and admixture of evil. How then shall we translate, Blessed are the *katharoi* in heart? We must think of it this way—Blessed are those whose motives are absolutely unmixed, whose minds are utterly sincere, who are completely and totally single-minded. What a summons to self-examination is here! Here is the most demanding Beatitude of all. When we examine our motives with honesty, it will humiliate us, for an unmixed motive is the rarest thing in the world. But the blessedness is to the man with the motive that is as pure as clean water, and with the single-mindedness which does everything as to God. That is the standard by which this word and this Beatitude demand that we should measure ourselves.

KOINŌNIA, KOINŌNEIN AND KOINŌNOS

THE CHRISTIAN FELLOWSHIP

In the NT there is a great group of words all of which have to do with the basic idea of 'fellowship'. There is the word *koinōnia*. In classical Greek *koinōnia* means an association or a partnership. Plato uses the phrase the *koinōnia* of women with men for 'co-education'. Human *koinōnia* is the Greek for human society. The word is also used to express the idea of community. Plato says, 'There must be a certain *koinōnia* between pleasure and pain.' In later Greek *koinōnia* is used as the opposite and contrast to *pleonexia*, which is the grasping spirit which is out for itself. *Koinōnia* is the spirit of generous sharing as contrasted with the spirit of selfish getting. In the contemporary colloquial Greek *koinōnia* has three distinctive meanings. (i) It means very commonly a 'business partnership'. In a papyrus announcement a man speaks of his brother 'with whom I have no *koinōnia*', no business connexion. (ii) It is used specially of 'marriage'. Two people enter into marriage in order to have '*koinōnia* of life', that is to say, to live together a life in which everything is shared. (iii) It is used of a man's 'relationship with God'. Epictetus talks of religion as 'aiming to have *koinōnia* with Zeus'. So in secular Greek *koinōnia* is used to express a close and intimate relationship into which people enter. In the NT *koinōnia* occurs some eighteen times. When we examine the connexions in which it is used we come to see how wide and far-stretching is the fellowship which should characterize the Christian life.

(i) In the Christian life there is a *koinōnia* which means 'a sharing of friendship' and an abiding in the company of others (Acts 2.42; II Cor. 6.14). It is very interesting to note that that friendship is based on common Christian knowledge (I John 1.3). Only those who are friends with Christ can really be friends with each other.

(ii) In the Christian life there is a *koinōnia* which means 'practical sharing' with those less fortunate. Paul three times uses the word in connexion with the collection he took from his churches for the poor saints at Jerusalem (Rom. 15.26; II Cor. 8.4; II Cor. 9.13; cp. Heb. 13.16). The Christian fellowship is a *practical* thing.

(iii) In the Christian life there is a *koinōnia* which is a 'partnership in the work of Christ' (Phil. 1.5). Paul gives thanks for the partnership of the Philippians in the work of the gospel.

(iv) In the Christian life there is a *koinōnia* 'in the faith'. The Christian is never an isolated unit; he is one of a believing company (Eph. 3.9).

(v) In the Christian life there is a 'fellowship' (*koinōnia*) in the Spirit' (II Cor. 13.14; Phil. 2.1). The Christian lives in the presence, the company, the help and the guidance of the Spirit.

(vi) In the Christian life there is a *koinōnia* 'with Christ'. Christians are called to the *koinōnia* of Jesus Christ, the Son of God (I Cor. 1.9). That fellowship is found specially through the Sacrament (I Cor. 10.16). The cup and the bread are supremely the *koinōnia* of the body and the blood of Christ. In the sacrament above all Christians find Christ and find each other. Further, that fellowship with Christ is fellowship with his sufferings (Phil. 3.10). When the Christian suffers he has, amidst the pain, the joy of knowing that he is sharing things with Christ.

(vii) In the Christian life there is *koinōnia* 'with God' (I John 1.3). But it is to be noted that that fellowship is ethically conditioned, for it is not for those who have chosen to walk in darkness (I John 1.6).

The Christian *koinōnia* is that bond which binds Christians to each other, to Christ and to God.

There are two other great NT words in the *koinōnia* group at which we must look. The first is the verb *koinōnein.* In classical Greek *koinōnein* means 'to have a share in a thing'. It is used, for instance, of two people who have all things in common; it is used of 'going shares' with someone, and therefore of having 'business dealings' with him. It is used of 'sharing an opinion' with someone, and therefore agreeing with him. In the contemporary Greek of the papyri it has three main meanings. (i) It means to share 'in an action' with someone. For instance, when the authorities cannot track down some malefactors they come to the conclusion that those who 'share' in their misdeeds are sheltering them. (ii) It is used of sharing in 'a common possession'. For instance, all men are said to 'share' in human nature. (iii) It is used of the sharing of 'life'. A doctor puts up a tablet to a wife who had practised with him, for, he writes, 'I *shared* all life with you alone'.

When we turn to the NT, we once again see how wide this Christian sharing is. (i) All men share in 'human nature' (Heb. 2.14). There is a community between men simply in virtue of the fact that they are men. (ii) The Christians share in 'material things' (Rom. 12.13; 15.27; Gal. 6.6). It is interesting to note that of its eight appearances in the NT, four deal with this practical teaching. No Christian can bear to have too much while others have too little. (iii) It is used of sharing in 'an action' (I Tim. 5.22). We are partners with each other and with God. (iv) It is used of sharing 'an experience' (I Pet. 4.13). The man who suffers for his faith, in that very suffering shares the experience of Jesus Christ.

Koinōnos in classical Greek means a companion, a partner or a joint-owner. In the papyri it has come to be most commonly used of a business partner. For instance, a certain Hermes takes Cornelius as his *koinōnos* in a fishing lake to the extent of one-sixth of a share. A father complains to his son in regard to their allotment that their *koinōnos* is not doing his share of the work. It is to be remembered that in contemporary secular Greek the word is almost entirely a *business* word.

In the NT it occurs ten times. (i) It is used in the sense of a sharer 'in an action or course of action'. Jesus says that the Pharisees claim that if they had lived in the days when their fathers killed the prophets they would not have 'shared' in such an action (Matt. 23.30; cp. I Cor. 10.18; 10.20. (ii) It is used in the sense of 'a partner'. James and John are Peter's *koinōnoi* in the fishing business (Luke 5.10). Paul describes Titus as his *koinōnos* and *sunergos*, his *partner* and his fellow-worker (II Cor. 8.23). Paul's claim on Philemon, when he is pleading for Onesimus, is that Philemon in his *koinōnos* (Phil. 17). The Christian looks on all fellow-Christians as partners in a great work. For him to call a fellow man 'partner' is the most natural thing in the world. (iii) It is used in the sense of a sharer in 'an experience' (II Cor. 1.7; Heb. 10.33). Nothing happens to us alone. It happens to all men and it happened to Jesus Christ. Between Christ and man and man and man there is that sympathy of those who have passed through a common experience. (iv) Once it is used of man's sharing in the divine nature (II Pet. 1.4). Men share not only in the things of earth but in the glory of heaven.

Surely there is no more gracious group of words than this. The Christian shares in the manhood of all men; he shares in the common experience of joy and tears; he shares in the things divine and in the glory that shall be; and all his life he must be a sharer of all he has, for he knows that his true wealth lies in what he gives away.

LEITOURGIA

THE CHRISTIAN SERVICE

Leitourgia, from which comes our English word 'liturgy', and its kindred words form a group of words of unsurpassed interest. In classical and Hellenistic Greek these words go through four stages of meaning. (i) In the very early days *leitourgein*, the verb, meant to undertake some service of the state voluntarily and of one's own free will, voluntarily to shoulder some public task in order patriotically to serve the state. (ii) Later *leitourgein* came to mean to perform the services which the State laid upon citizens specially qualified to perform them. The services were the same, but now instead of being voluntary they have become compulsory. Certain duties were liable to be laid on any citizen who possessed more than three talents, that is about £700.

Four typical such duties were: (*a*) *Chorēgia*, which meant the supplying of all the expenses to maintain and train a chorus for the great dramatic performances. (*b*) *Gymnasarchia*, which meant the paying of the expenses involved in the training of outstanding athletes for the games. (*c*) *Architheōria*, which was the defraying of the expenses of embassies sent out by the state on solemn or sacred occasions. (*d*) *Triērarchia*, which meant the shouldering of all the expenses of a trireme or warship in time of national crisis. Still later, especially in Egypt, nearly all municipal duties were *leitourgiai*. The state picked out a suitable man and laid on him the duty of serving in some capacity his town or village or county. (iii) Still later *leitourgein* came to describe any kind of service. It is used, for instance, of dancing girls, flute-players, musicians who are hired for some entertainment; of a workman working for any master; and even, strangely enough, of a prostitute giving her services. (iv) In NT times *leitourgein* was the regular word for the service that a priest or servant rendered in a temple of the gods. So we read of 'Thaues and Taous, the twins, who *serve* in the great temple of Serapis at Memphis'.

In the NT the words have three main uses. (i) They are used of the service rendered by man to man. So Paul, when he is set on taking the collection for the poor saints of Jerusalem, uses *leitourgein* and *leitourgia* (Rom. 15.27; II

Cor. 9.12). He uses them of the service of the Philippians and of Epaphroditus to himself (Phil. 2.17, 30). To serve others is a 'liturgy' laid on the citizen of the Kingdom by God. (ii) They are used of specifically religious service (Luke 1.23; Acts 13.2). They are actually used of the high-priestly work of Jesus himself (Heb. 8.6; 8.2). Our Church work is a 'liturgy' again laid on us by God. (iii) There are two specially interesting uses in Paul. (*a*) The magistrate, the person in power, is called by Paul a *leitourgos* (Rom. 13.6). A man's public service must be done for God. (*b*) Paul uses it of himself when he calls himself Jesus Christ's *leitourgos* to the Gentiles (Rom. 15.16). Just as Athens in the old days sent out its *leitourgoi* to represent the state, so Paul is sent by God to the Gentiles. Perhaps the most interesting fact of all about the word *leitourgos* is that in later Greek it came simply to mean a 'workman', for that simple fact has in it the great truth that all work is a 'liturgy' laid on men by God, and that the commonest task is glorious because it is done for him.

The great fact about *leitourgia* is that it has a double background. (i) It describes voluntary service, spontaneously shouldered. (ii) It describes that service which the state lays compulsorily upon its citizens. The Christian is a man who works for God and men, first, because he desires to, with his whole heart, and second, because he is compelled to, because the love of Christ constrains him.

LOGOS

THE WORD OF THE CHRISTIAN MESSAGE

THE word *logos* means *word*. The Fourth Gospel uses *logos* in a technical sense when it calls Jesus *The Word*; but before we come to that special usage we wish to study its ordinary usage in the NT. Naturally it is one of the commonest of all Greek words, but, common as it is, the more we study it, the more we shall see a wealth of meaning.

Ho logos, the word, becomes almost a synonym for the Christian *message*. Mark tells us that Jesus preached the *word* to the crowds (Mark 2.2). In the parable the seed that the sower sowed was *the word* (Mark 4.14). It was the work of Paul and his friends to preach *the word* (Acts 14.25). Most often this word is said to be *the word of God* (Luke 5.1; 11.28; John 10.35; Acts 4.31; 6.7; 13.44; I Cor. 14.36; Heb. 13.7). Sometimes it is *the word of the Lord* (I Thess. 4.15; II Thess. 3.1). And once it is *the word of Christ* (Col. 3.16). Now genitives in Greek can be either *subjective* or *objective*. If these genitives are *subjective* the phrases mean the word which God gave, the word which the Lord gave, and the word which Christ gave. If they are *objective*, they mean the word which tells about God, or about the Lord, or about Christ. In all probability both the subjective and the objective meanings are involved in these phrases. This means to say that the Christian message, the *logos, the word*, is something which came from God; it is not the discovery of man, but the gift of God; and it is something which tells about God, something which man could not have discovered for himself.

The very fact that the word *logos* is used for the Christian message is very significant. It means *a spoken message*, and therefore it means that the Christian message is not something which is learned from books, but something which is transmitted from person to person. Papias, the second-century Christian writer, says that he learned more from the living and abiding voice than from any book. The Christian message comes far more often through the living personality than through the printed or the written page.

This *word*, this *logos*, has certain functions.

(i) The word *judges* (John 12.48). An old catechism asks what will happen if the truths recounted in it are disregarded. Its answer is that condemnation will follow, and a condemnation all the greater because the reader has read this book. To have heard the truth is not only to have received a privilege; it is also to have had a responsibility laid upon us.

(ii) The word *purifies* (John 15.3; I Tim. 4.5). It purifies by exposing evil and by pointing to good. It rebukes that which is wrong and exhorts to that which is right. It purifies in the negative sense by seeking to eradicate old faults; and it purifies in the positive sense by exhorting to new virtues.

(iii) Through the word *belief* comes (Acts 4.4). No man can believe in the Christian message until he has heard the Christian message. The word is that which gives a man the opportunity to believe; and, having heard the word himself, there is laid upon him the duty of giving others the same chance to hear it, that they also may believe.

(iv) The word is *the agent of rebirth* (I Peter 1.23). One thing is true, as G. K. Chesterton said, 'Whatever man is, he is not what he was meant to be.' He has to be changed so radically that the change can only be called a new birth, and the word is the first agent in that tremendous re-creating change.

The study of the word *logos* becomes of primary importance when we study what the NT says we must do with this *logos*.

(i) The *logos* must be *heard* (Matt. 13.20; Acts 13.7; 13.44). The duty of listening is laid upon the Christian. Among the many voices of the world he must tune his ears to hear the message which is the message of God. He will never give himself the opportunity to know unless he gives himself the opportunity to hear.

(ii) The *logos* must be *received* (Luke 8.13; James 1.21; Acts 8.14; 11.1; 17.11). There is a hearing which is a purely external thing. Either the tide of words flows over the hearer and his hearing leaves no effect upon him, or he listens and dismisses the whole matter as having nothing to do with him. The Christian message must not only be listened to, but must be taken into the heart and mind and inwardly digested.

(iii) The *logos* must be *held on to* (Luke 8.13). The Greeks described time by an adjective which means 'time which wipes all things out'. Any word can be heard, and for a time accepted, and then obliterated by the passage of time. The Christian message must be deliberately retained. It must be held in the forefront of the mind, thought about, meditated on, so that it is retained and not lost.

(iv) The *logos* is something *to abide in* (John 8.31). There is always a circle of thoughts and ideas in which a man lives and moves and has his being; in which he rests his life and by which he directs his activities. The Christian message must be the thing in which and by which a man lives.

(v) The *logos* must be *kept* (John 8.51; 14.23; I John 2.5; Rev. 3.8). It is a message which is not knowledge for the mind alone; it is direction for life. It issues not in speculation but in action. Its demand is obedience. It is not only a knowledge to think about; it is an ethic and a law to be obeyed.

(vi) The *logos* must be *witnessed to* (Acts 8.25; Rev. 1.2). It is something to which a man's whole life must bear witness. He can only prove that he has accepted it by living it. It is something which in any society he must be prepared to show that he accepts. It is something of which his whole life and action must say, 'I know and bear witness that this is true.'

(vii) The *logos* is something which must be *served* (Acts 6.4). It is something which brings its duties. It is not only something which a man accepts for himself, but something which he is bound to wish to bring to others. It is not only something which brings wealth to his own soul; it is also something for which he must be prepared to spend his whole life.

(viii) The *logos* is something which must be *announced*. Two words are specially used. II Tim. 4.2 uses the word *kērussein*, which is the word that is used for a herald making a proclamation. Acts 15.36 and 17.13 use the word *kataggellein* which is the word that is used for making an official and an authoritative pronouncement. The proclamation must be made with authority and with certainty. The proclamation is so made because, when we announce the Christian message to others, we are not saying, 'I am saying this,' we are saying, 'Thus saith the Lord.'

(ix) The *logos* must be spoken *with boldness* (Acts 4.29; Phil. 1.14). Some time ago a book was published with the suggestive title, *No More Apologies*. It may well be that we have been too anxious to meet the world halfway, that we have tried too much to attune the Christian message to the world's ears, that we have watered it down, and emasculated it in order to make it less demanding and therefore more attractive. There should be a certain uncompromising quality in our proclamation of the *logos*.

(x) The *logos* must be *taught* (Acts 18.11). The Christian message begins with proclamation, but it must go on to explanation. One of the gravest weaknesses of the Church is that so many people do not know what Christianity really means and believes and stands for; and one of the gravest faults in preaching is that it so often exhorts a man to be a Christian without teaching him what Christianity is. Teaching is an essential part of the Christian message.

(xi) The *logos* must be *acted upon* (James 1.22). The Christian message is not something exclusively for the calm of the study, for the dissection of the lecture room, for the mental acrobatics of the discussion group. It is something which has to be lived out in day-to-day living.

(xii) The *logos* may involve *persecution and suffering* (I Thess. 1.6; Rev. 1.9). It is not likely that in this country we shall have to die for our faith; but we shall have to live for it, and there may well be times when we have to choose between what is easy and what is right.

If our relationship to the *logos* involves obligations, it will inevitably be liable to failures.

(i) The *logos* may be *disbelieved* (I Peter 2.8). It may be disbelieved either because the hearer thinks it too good to be true, or because, in wishful thinking, he does not want it to be true, because it condemns his life and seeks to change him.

(ii) The *logos* can both be *snatched away* and *choked* (Matt. 13.22; cp. Mark 4.15). The temptations, the impulses and the passions of life can make a man forget the Christian message as soon as he has heard it. The activities, the cares and the pleasures of life can take up so much of a man's life and time that the Christian message is choked out of his life because there is no room left for it to breathe.

(iii) The *logos* can be *corrupted* and *adulterated* (II Cor. 2.17; 4.2). Whenever a man begins to listen to himself and stops listening to God, his version of the Christian message will be distorted and inadequate. Whenever he forgets to test his ideas and conceptions by the Word and the Spirit of God, he will produce a version of the Christian message which is his and not God's. If he goes on doing that he may well end by loving his own little system better than he loves God's truth.

(iv) The *logos* can be rendered *ineffective* (Mark 7.13). It is fatally easy to explain the Christian message away, to overlay it with human interpretations, to complicate its simplicities with conditions and reservations and explanations. Whenever we regard the Christian message as something with which to make terms rather than something to which to surrender we are in danger of making it ineffective. Without 'yieldedness' to the message the message cannot have its full effect.

When we begin to examine the NT content of the Christian message, we begin to appreciate, as never before, the riches of this faith which is offered to us. The word *logos* is used in the NT with at least seven different genitives which express that in which the message consists. Let us look at them.

(i) The Christian message is *a word of good news* (Acts 15.7). It brings to us tidings about God which set the heart singing for joy. The discovery of love is always the greatest day in a man's life; and the Christian message leads a man to discover nothing less than the love of God.

(ii) The Christian message is *a word of truth* (John 17.7; Eph. 1.13; James 1.8). The whole of life is the search for truth. 'What is truth?' said jesting Pilate, and would not stay for an answer. That may be so, but life is intolerable if there are no fixed stars in it. The Christian message is that which makes a man sure.

(iii) The Christian message is *a word of life* (Phil. 2.16). The Christian message is that which enables a man to stop existing and to begin living. It gives him life with a capital L.

(iv) The Christian message is *a word of righteousness* (Heb. 5.13). It tells a man where goodness lies; it shows him what goodness is; it gives him new standards for life; and it enables him to reach them and gives him the power which is not his own power to achieve them.

(v) The Christian message is *a word of reconciliation* (II Cor. 5.19). The very essence of it is that God is not our enemy but our friend. It is not that God needed to be reconciled to us; the NT never puts it that way; it is we who needed to be reconciled to God. The great gift of the Christian message is that it removes the estrangement between man and God and makes possible the greatest friendship of all.

(vi) The Christian message is *a word of salvation* (Acts 13.26). It is a word of rescue. It rescues a man from the evil bonds which bind him. It strengthens him to defeat the temptations of evil and to do the right. It rids him of the punishment which is his by right, if God were to treat him only with justice and not with love. It lifts a man out of the deadly situation in which he finds himself in this life, and in which he ought in justice to find himself in the life to come.

(vii) The Christian message is *a word of the Cross* (I Cor. 1.18). It is the story of one who died for men. It is the story of a love which did not stop until it reached the very limits of sacrifice, and which thereby proved that there is nothing that God will not dare and suffer and sacrifice for the sake of man. The heart of the Christian *logos* is the Cross.

In the NT there is one technical use of the word *logos*. It occurs in the Prologue to the Fourth Gospel, and it culminates in that great saying, 'The *Word* (*logos*) was made flesh and dwelt among us' (John 1.14). This is one of the greatest sayings in the NT and we shall have to dig deep if we wish to grasp something of its meaning.

(i) We must begin by remembering that in Greek *logos* has two meanings. (a) It means *word*, and (b) it means *reason*, and these two meanings are always intertwined.

(ii) We must begin with the *Jewish* background of this idea. In Jewish thought a word was more than a sound expressing a meaning; *a word actually did things*. The word of God is not simply a sound; *it is an effective cause*. In the creation story God's *word creates*. God said, Let there be light, *and there was light* (Gen. 1.3). By the *word* of the Lord the heavens were made . . . for he spake and it was done (Ps. 33.6, 9). He sent his *word* and healed them (Ps. 107.20). God's *word* will accomplish that which God pleases (Isa. 55.11). Always we must remember that in Jewish thought God's *word* not only *said* things; it *did* things.

(iii) There came a time when the Jews forgot their Hebrew; their language became Aramaic. It was necessary that the scriptures should be translated into Aramaic. These translations are called the Targums. Now in the simplicity of the OT human feelings, actions, reactions, thoughts are ascribed to God. The makers of the Targums felt that this was far too human; and in such cases they used a circumlocution for the name of God. They spoke not of God but of the *Word*, the *memra* of God. This is the kind of thing that happened. In Ex. 19.17 the Targums say that Moses brought the people out of the camp to meet with the *memra*, the *Word* of God, instead of, quite simply, with God. In Deut. 9.3 it is God's *Word*, the *memra*, which is a consuming fire. In Isa. 48.13 we read, Mine hand hath laid the foundations of the earth; and my right hand hath spanned the heavens. In the Targums this becomes, by my *Word*, my *memra*, I have founded the earth, and by my strength I have hung up the heavens. The result of all this was that the Jewish scriptures in their popular form became full of the phrase, The *Word*, the *memra*, of God; and the word was always *doing* things; not merely *saying* things.

(iv) Now let us remember that *Word* and *Reason* are locked together. In Jewish thought there is another great conception—the conception of *Wisdom* (*sophia*). This is specially so in the Old Testament in Proverbs. By *Wisdom* God founded the earth (Prov. 3.13-20). The great passage is in Prov. 8.1-9. There wisdom is from everlasting, before the earth came into being: she was with God in the day of creation. This idea was much developed in the books between the Testaments. In Ecclus. 1.1-10 there is the picture of *Wisdom* who was created before all things and who is intertwined with creation. In the Wisdom of Solomon, *Wisdom works* all things (8.5). God made all things by his *Word* and man by his *Wisdom* (9.1, 2). *Wisdom* was God's instrument in creation and is woven throughout all the world.

So in Jewish thought we have two great conceptions at the back of the idea of Jesus as the *Word*, the *logos* of God. First, God's *Word* is not only *speech*; it is *power*. Second, it is impossible to separate the ideas of *Word* and *Wisdom*; and it was God's *Wisdom* which created and permeated the world which God made.

By the end of the first century the Christian Church was faced with an acute problem in communication. The Church had been cradled in Judaism, but now she had to present her message to a Greek world, to which the categories of Judaism were quite alien. As Goodspeed puts it:

'A Greek who felt like becoming a Christian was called upon to accept Jesus as the Christ, the Messiah. He would naturally ask what this meant, and would have to be given a short course in Jewish apocalyptic thought. Was there no way in which he might be introduced directly to the values of Christian civilization without being for ever routed, we might even say detoured, through Judaism? Must Christianity always speak in a Jewish vocabulary?' Round about A.D 100 there was a man in Ephesus called John who saw this problem. He was perhaps the greatest mind in the Christian Church; and suddenly he saw the solution. *Both Jew and Greek possessed the conception of the logos of God.* Could the two ideas not be brought together? Let us see the Greek background with which John had to work.

(i) Away back in 560 B.C there was a Greek philosopher called Heracleitus, who also lived in Ephesus. He conceived of the world as what he called a *flux*. Everything is in a state of change; there is nothing static in the world. But if everything is changing all the time, why is the world not an absolute and complete chaos? His answer was that 'all things happen according to the *logos*'. In the world there is a reason and a mind at work; that mind is the mind of God, God's *logos*; and it is that *logos* which makes the world an ordered cosmos and not a disordered chaos.

(ii) This idea of a mind, a reason, a *logos* ruling the world fascinated the Greeks. Anaxagoras spoke of the mind (*nous*) which 'rules over all things'. Plato declared that it was God's *logos* which kept the planets in their courses, and brought back the seasons and the years in their appointed times. But it was the Stoics, who were at their strongest when the NT was being written, who passionately loved this conception. To them this *logos* of God, as Cleanthes said, 'roamed through all things'. The times, the seasons, the tides, the stars in their courses were ordered by the *logos*; it was the *logos* which put sense into the world. Further, the mind of man himself was a little portion of this *logos*. 'Reason is nothing else than a part of the divine spirit immersed in the human body,' said Seneca. It was the *logos* which put sense into the universe and sense into man; and this *logos* was nothing other than the mind of God.

(iii) This conception was brought to its highest peak by Philo, who was an Alexandrian Jew, and who had the aim of joining together in one synthesis the highest thought of Jew and Greek. To him the *logos* of God was 'inscribed and engraved upon the constitution of all things'. The *logos* is 'the tiller by which the pilot of the universe steers all things'. 'Every man is akin in understanding to the divine *logos*.' 'The *logos* is the high priest which sets the soul before God.' The *logos* is the bridge between man and God.

Now we can see what John was doing when he uttered his tremendous statement, 'The *Word* was made flesh.'

(i) He was clothing Christianity in a dress that a Greek could understand. Here is a challenge to us. He refused to go on expressing Christianity in outworn and Judaistic categories. He used categories that his age knew and understood. Again and again the Church has failed in that task through mental laziness, through fear to cut adrift from the past, through shrinking from possible heresy; but 'the man who would discover a new continent must accept the hazard of sailing upon an uncharted sea.' If we are ever to tell people about the Christian message we must tell it in language that they can understand. That is precisely what John did.

(ii) He was giving us a new Christology. By calling Jesus the *logos*, John said two things about Jesus. (a) Jesus *is* the creating power of God come to men. He does not only *speak* the word of *knowledge*; he *is* the word of *power*. He did not come so much to *say* things to us, as to *do* things for us. (b) Jesus is the incarnate mind of God. We might well translate John's words, 'The mind of God became a man.' A word is always 'the expression of a thought' and Jesus is the perfect expression of God's thought for men.

We should do well to rediscover and to preach again Jesus Christ as the *logos*, the *Word* of God.

LUTRON, LUTROUN AND
APOLUTRŌSIS

THE DEBT AND ITS PAYMENT

THERE is a group of NT words which all have to do with the idea of ransom and redemption, of deliverance and freedom won and purchased at a price. These words have been so influential in moulding the conception of the work of Jesus Christ, and of the idea of the atonement, that it is absolutely necessary to study them in detail. We begin with the word *lutron*.

(i) In classical Greek the word occurs mostly in the plural (*lutra*) and its basic meaning is 'the price of release'. The title of the 24th book of the *Iliad* is *Lutra Hektoros*, 'the ransoming of Hector', and it tells the story of the ransoming of the dead body of Hector, the Trojan champion, after it had been captured by the Greeks. So in classical Greek there are a whole series of phrases—*labein lutra tinos*, to receive a ransom for someone, *lutra didonai tinos*, to give a ransom for someone, *aneu lutrōn aphienai*, to let go without a ransom, and the phrase *huper lutrōn* describes a sum paid 'as a ransom'. Nearly always in classical Greek the word is quite literal; it means the price paid to effect someone's deliverance. The late Greek lexicon *Suidas* defines *lutron* quite simply as *misthos*, which means 'pay' or 'price', and goes on to amplify it by saying that it means 'Those things which are offered for freedom in order to ransom a man from barbarian slavery'. Very rarely in classical Greek it has a semi-metaphorical sense. Once it occurs in Aeschylus, the tragic poet, 'What *lutron* can there be for blood which has fallen upon the ground?' (*Choephoroi* 48). There it means, What release can there be for the guilty from the wrath and the defilement which follow upon shed blood?

(ii) Now to any NT writer this word would have two

backgrounds. It would have a background from OT thought and usage. In the Septuagint the word occurs about eighteen times. If a man was the owner of an ox which was known to be dangerous and the ox gored and killed someone, because it had not been properly confined, the man's own life was forfeit unless he paid a *lutron*, 'blood money', to ransom himself (Ex. 21.30). If a man deliberately murdered another there could be no *lutron* for him, he must be executed (Num. 35.31, 32). If an Israelite in his poverty sold himself to a wealthy sojourner a wealthier relative could buy him out, and the price was a *lutron* (Lev. 25.51). A jealous man set on vengeance will accept no *lutron* in place of revenge (Prov. 6.35). *Lutron* is the ransom of captives taken in war (Isa. 45.13). But in the OT the word has one specially interesting use. According to the Jewish law the first-born of man and every creature was sacred to God. Num. 3.13 traces this back to God's sparing of the first-born sons of the Jews on the night of the first Passover in Egypt. If all the first-born sons were dedicated to the special service of God it would disrupt life altogether and so there was a ceremony called 'The Redemption of the First-born', by which the parents could buy back their son by a payment of five shekels to the priests (Num. 18.16). Now that payment is regularly called a *lutron* (Num. 3.12, 46, 48, 49, 51; 18.15).

It may be laid down, as a general rule, that in the Greek OT the word *lutron* never has anything other than a literal meaning. It always means a payment which releases a man from an obligation which otherwise he was bound to fulfil. In the OT the *lutron* may be paid by the man himself, or it may be paid by someone for him; but always it is a price and a payment which releases him from a debt and a liability which otherwise he would have been bound to satisfy.

We now turn to the background which *lutron* had in Greek thought and practice. In the contemporary Greek of the NT times it has two main uses. (*a*) It is regularly used of 'the price which is paid to redeem something which is in pledge or in pawn' (b) It is regularly used of 'the purchase price paid or received for the liberation of a slave'. So a papyrus reads, 'I have given Helene her liberty and I have received *huper lutrōn autēs*, as the purchase price for her,' and then follows the actual sum of money received.

Now here we have to take account of another Greek custom in NT times which gives to NT language one of its most vivid pictures. There are two other NT words that we must bring in here—*agorazein* or *exagorazein*, which means 'to buy', and *timē*, which means 'price'. In I Cor. 6.19, 20, Paul says, 'Know ye not . . . that ye are not your own? For ye are bought (*agorazein*) with a price (*timē*)?' In I Cor. 7.23 he writes, 'Ye are bought (*agorazein*) with a price (*timē*); be not ye the servants of men?' In Gal. 3.13 he says that 'Christ has redeemed (*exagorazein*) us from the curse of the law'. In Gal. 4.4, 5 he says that God sent his Son 'to *redeem* them that were under the law'. In Gal. 5.1 he says, as it should be translated, 'For freedom (*ep'eleutheria*) did Christ set us free.' And in Gal. 5.13 he says, 'Ye were called for freedom (*ep'eleutheria*).' There are a great many Greek inscriptions which speak about a person being sold to a God, e.g., to Athene, to Asclepius, to Apollo. There was one special way in which a Greek slave could obtain his freedom. He could scrape and save, perhaps for years, such little sums as he was able to earn; and, as he saved the money, he deposited it little by little in the temple of some god. When he had laboriously amassed his complete purchase price, he took his master to the temple where the money was deposited. There the priest paid over to the master the purchase price of freedom, and the man who had been a slave became the property of the god and therefore 'free of all men'. There is an inscription on the wall of the temple of Apollo at Delphi like this: 'Apollo the Pythian, *bought* from Sosibus of Amphissa, for freedom (*ep'eleutheria*) a female slave, whose name is Nicaea, with a price (*timē*) of three minae of silver and a half-mina. Former seller according to the law: Eumnastus of Amphissa. The price (*timē*) he hath received. The purchase, however, Nicaea has committed to Apollo, for freedom (*ep'eleutheria*).' The purchase price was paid and Nicaea was the property of Apollo and free of all men. It is precisely this to which Paul indirectly refers when repeatedly he calls himself and others *doulos Christou*, 'the slave of Christ'. He has been bought by Christ and has become his property. It is very significant how Paul uses the very phrase *ep'eleutheria*, 'for freedom', which occurs again and again in these inscriptions. The purchase price is paid and the Christian belongs to Christ and is therefore free from all the powers which held him.

(iii) Now in the NT itself this word *lutron* occurs twice. In Mark 10.45 and Matt. 20.28 Jesus says that he came to give his life a *lutron*, 'a ransom', for many. There is one other kindred word which is used, the word *antilutron*. In I Tim. 2.6 we read of Christ Jesus who gave himself an *antilutron*, 'a ransom', for all. *Antilutron* is a very rare word. It is worth noting in the passing that in the Orphic literature it is used to mean an 'antidote', and 'remedy'. Christ's death, we could understand it, is the 'antidote' for the poison, and the 'remedy' for the disease of sin.

There are still other words which we must carefully examine. But, even at this stage, we can lay this down—that Jesus Christ by his life and by his death released man from an obligation, a liability and a debt which otherwise he would have been bound to pay, and delivered him from a bondage and a slavery, by paying the purchase price of freedom which he himself could never have paid.

We must now consider the verb *lutroun*.

(i) In Greek, verbs have three voices and not, as in English, only two. In Greek a verb can be active or passive, as in English, but it can also be middle. Generally speaking, the middle voice has a kind of semi-reflexive sense; it means to do something for oneself, for one's own interest, or pleasure or profit. So in classical Greek the word *lutroun* has really three meanings. (i) In the active *lutroun* means to 'hold to ransom'. (ii) In the passive it means 'to be ransomed'. (iii) In the middle it means 'to ransom for oneself', that is 'to redeem' or 'rescue' by paying the necessary price. It is to be noted that the whole background of the word is 'captivity'. It has always got to do with rescuing, redeeming, liberating, ransoming a man or a thing from some hostile power which has him or it in its possession.

(ii) In the papyri the characteristic use of *lutroun* is 'to redeem a pledge'. It can be used of redeeming a person's clothes or cloak or property which have been deposited in pawn or pledge with someone. Again the word has this idea of getting something back into the possession of its rightful owner, rescuing something from the power and possession of an alien possessor.

(iii) In the Septuagint the word is very common, occurring more than 65 times. It has certain characteristic usages. (*a*) It is constantly used of 'God's redeeming of Israel from slavery in Egypt'. In Ex. 6.6 it is God's promise, 'I will redeem you with a stretched-out arm.' Over and over again the people are reminded that God 'redeemed' them 'out of the house of bondmen' (Deut. 7.8; 13.5). It is God's command that they must never forget that they were bondmen in the land of Egypt and that he 'redeemed' them (Deut. 15.15; 24.18). (*b*) It is constantly used of 'redeeming', 'buying back the first-born from the special service of God' (Ex. 13.13; 34.20). (*c*) It is constantly used of 'redeeming something that has been pledged and pawned' (Lev. 25.25, 30, 33). (*d*) In Israel a man could 'devote' something to God. He could devote an animal, a house, his money, even himself to the exclusive possession of God. That is what Jephthah did when he sacrificed his daughter to God (Judg. 12.29-40). Now it might be that after a man had devoted something to God he might want that thing back for his own use. He could get it back by making certain payments to the priests; and *lutroun* is used for buying back the thing that has been devoted to God

(Lev. 27.15-33). (e) It is to be noted that once again *lutroun*, so far, always describes the process of getting back something which has passed into the power and possession of someone else. But in the Septuagint the word has one very special use which is not literal at all. Over and over again *lutroun* is the word which is used in the Psalms and in the Prophets for God's deliverance and preservation of his people in the time of their trouble and distress. It is the Psalmist's prayer, '*Redeem* Israel, O God, out of all his troubles' (Ps. 25.22; cp. 26.11; 69.18; 130.8). It is the Psalmist's great thanksgiving that God has so redeemed him. 'Thou hast redeemed me, O Lord God of truth' (Ps. 31.5). It is God who *redeems* his life from destruction (Ps. 103.4; 55.18). This usage goes on into the prophets (Isa. 43.1; 44.22; Jer. 15.21; 50.34). So much so is this the case that *ho lutroumenos* (the present participle of the verb), 'the redeeming one', becomes almost a technical name for God. We will see more clearly and vividly what this means if we translate it, not 'redeem' but 'rescue'. God is the redeemer who rescues man from the troubles which have him in their grip.

(iv) In the NT the word occurs three times. In Luke 24.21 the grief-stricken wayfarers tell the unrecognized Jesus that they had hoped that Jesus would have been the one who would 'redeem' Israel. In Tit. 2.14 Jesus died that he might rescue us from all lawlessness. In I Pet. 1.18 the Christians are said to have been 'rescued' from their vain way of life.

We have still one other great NT word to examine. But once again we have arrived at the same conclusion. The word *lutroun* expresses the 'redeeming', 'rescuing' of a man from a power or a situation which has him in its grip and from which he is powerless to free himself.

Apolutrōsis is one of the great NT words. It literally means a 'ransoming' or a 'redeeming', but this time we are dealing with a word which has practically no history. It is only used in very late Greek, and that very rarely. When it is used it is used of the ransoming of captives taken in battle. In the papyri no instances at all are quoted. In the Septuagint it occurs only once—in Dan. 4.30 where it is used of the recovery of Nebuchadnezzar from illness. But in the NT it is used ten times and all its usages are significant. We will look at the most significant of them.

(i) It is used of our 'redemption from sin', and always in connexion with the work of Jesus Christ. In Eph. 1.7 Paul says that the Christian has 'redemption' through the blood of Jesus Christ, 'the forgiveness of sins'. Exactly the same phrase is used in Col. 1.14. The same idea occurs in Heb. 9.15. The forgiveness of sins is indissolubly connected with the death of Christ.

(ii) It is used of 'the new relationship of friendship' into which man enters with God through the work of Jesus Christ. Paul speaks of the Christian entering into the right relationship with God, freely, by his grace, through the 'redemption' which is in Jesus Christ (Rom. 3.24).

(iii) It implies, not only forgiveness for past sins, but 'new, changed life for the future'. It implies adoption into the family of God (Rom. 8.23). For us Christ is made wisdom and justification and consecration and 'redemption' (I Cor. 1.30). *Apolutrōsis* looks, not only backwards to forgiveness, but forwards to a re-created life.

(iv) *Apolutrōsis* does not end with this life. It is eschatological. It is the foretaste of a process and a glory which will find their consummation in the coming of Christ and in the heavenly places (Luke 21.28; Eph. 4.30).

This redemption which was wrought by the death of Christ makes possible for us forgiveness of sins, a new relationship with God, a new life upon earth, and in the end the glory of heaven.

Now let us enquire what is implied in all these words which have to do with 'ransom', 'redemption', 'rescue', 'liberation'.

(i) They all imply that man was in captivity, in slavery, in subjection to an alien power. There was something which had man in its grip.

(ii) They all imply that by no conceivable means could man have effected his own liberation or rescue. He was helpless in the grip of a power and a situation which he could not mend and from which he could not break away.

(iii) His liberation was effected by the coming of Jesus Christ who paid the price which was necessary to achieve it.

(iv) Nowhere in the NT is there any word of to whom that price was paid. It could not have been paid to God because all the time God was so loving the world. It was in fact God's love that sent Christ into this world. It could not have been paid to the devil for that would put the devil on an equality with God. All that we can say is this—it cost the life and death of Christ to liberate man from the past, the present and the future power of sin. Beyond that we cannot go, but although thought may be baffled, experience shows that it cost the life of Jesus Christ to bring us home to God.

MAKROTHUMIA

THE DIVINE PATIENCE

THE noun *makrothumia* and the verb *makrothumein* are characteristically biblical words. They do not occur in classical Greek at all, and only very seldom in later Greek. They are indeed characteristically *Christian* words, for, as we shall see, they describe a Christian virtue which to the Greek was no virtue at all. In the NT *makrothumia* occurs fourteen times and *makrothumein* ten times. The AV varies between 'long-suffering' and 'patience'. These words have two uses.

(i) They describe the 'steadfast spirit which will never give in'. It is that spirit of 'patience' and faith which will ultimately inherit the promise. It was because Abraham 'patiently endured' that he in the end received the promise

(Heb. 6.15). 'Patience' is a virtue that the Christian must have as he waits for the Day of the Lord, and he may learn it from the 'patience' of the farmer as he waits for the crop, and from the 'patience' of the prophets who never gave up their hope in God (James 5.7-10). On this I Mac. (8.4) has a very illuminating use of the word. In that passage, as Trench points out, the Roman supremacy over all the world is ascribed to the Roman 'policy and patience'. And by that is meant, 'the Roman persistency which would never make peace under defeat'. The Christian must have this *makrothumia* which can endure delay and bear suffering and never give in.

(ii) They describe the 'attitude that a man should have towards his fellow-men'. This is the typically NT use of the words. Chrysostom defined *makrothumia* as the spirit which could take revenge if it liked, but utterly refuses to do so. Lightfoot explained it as the spirit which will never retaliate. Now this is the very opposite of Greek virtue. The great Greek virtue was *megalopsuchia*, which Aristotle defined as the refusal to tolerate any insult or injury. To the Greek the big man was the man who went all out for vengeance. To the Christian the big man is the man who, even when he can, refuses to do so.

(a) This patience with men is the characteristic of the 'Christian minister'. It is that very quality which Paul claims to be the proof of real apostleship (II Cor. 6.6; cp. I Tim. 1.16; II Tim. 3.10). No one can ever lead and guide and direct a Christian congregation without this patience, this *makrothumia*.

(b) It is the characteristic of the 'Christian preacher' (Tit. 2.2). Without it the preacher would be driven to pessimistic despair and to that irritability which wrecks preaching.

(c) It ought to be the characteristic of 'every Christian', 'every Church member'. It is included in the fruit of the Spirit (Gal. 5.22). Without it men cannot walk worthily of their Christian calling (Eph. 4.2; Col. 3.12). It must be exercised towards all men (I Thess. 5.14). It is one of the great characteristics of love (I Cor. 13.4). There can be no such thing as a Christian fellowship without *makrothumia*.

(iii) And the reason for that is just this—that *makrothumia* is the great characteristic of God (Rom. 2.4; 9.22). It was God's *makrothumia* which delayed in the days of Noah until the ark was built (I Pet. 3.20). It is that very *makrothumia* which is responsible for man's salvation (II Pet. 3.9, 15). If God had been a man he would long ago have taken his hand and, with a gesture, would have wiped out the world, but in his 'patience' he bears with the sins the follies and the disobedience of men.

The great obligation which rests on the Christian is just this—he must be as patient with his fellow-men as God has been with him.

MERIMNA AND MERIMNAN

THE RIGHT AND THE WRONG CARE

THE noun *merimna* means *care, thought* or *anxiety*, and the verb *merimnan* means *to take thought for*, or *to be anxious about*. It is very important that we should correctly understand the real meaning of these two words, because the whole Christian attitude to life and to living depends on a correct understanding of them.

Both words are quite frequent in the NT. The noun *merimna* is the word that is used for the *cares of this world* which choke the life out of the good seed of the word (Matt. 13.22; cp. Mark 4.19 and Luke 8.14). It is used by Luke in the warning that the coming of Christ must not find us overcharged with surfeiting and drunkenness and *cares of this life* (Luke 21.34). It is used by Peter when he bids his friends cast all their *care* upon God (I Peter 5.7). It is used by Paul when he says that the heaviest burden of all that is upon him is the *care* of all the churches (II Cor. 11.28). We must note right at the beginning that from these uses it can be seen at once that *merimna* is a word that has a double flavour, for obviously the *cares of life* which choke the seed are not the same thing as the *care of all the churches* which was laid upon the heart of Paul.

When we turn to the verb *merimnan* we find that its most important use is in the Sermon on the Mount.

In the Sermon on the Mount it is used in Matt. 6.25, 27, 28, 31, 34; cp. Luke 12.22, 25, 26. In every case the AV translates it *to take thought for*. '*Take no thought* for your life' (Matt. 6.25). '*Take no thought* for the morrow' (Matt. 6.34). Now it is to be noted that the AV was the first, and is the only, version to use this translation. Wiclif translated it: 'Be not *busy* to your life.' Tyndale, Cranmer and the Geneva Bible all translate it: 'Be not *careful* of your life,' in which translation *careful* has it literal meaning, *full of care*. The RV has: 'Be not *anxious* for your life.' Moffatt has: 'Do not *trouble* about what you are to eat and drink in life.' Weymouth has: 'I charge you not to be *over-anxious* about your lives.' The NT in Plain English has: '*Worry* no more about your life.' Rieu has: 'I bid you not to *fret* about your life.' The RSV has: 'Do not be *anxious* about your life.' Schonfield in The Authentic New Testament has: 'Do not *vex yourselves* about what you are to eat or drink.' It is obvious that this is a commandment of Jesus about the meaning of which we must be clear, for it is a commandment which affects our whole attitude to life.

Before we come to discuss the meaning of it we must go on to look at the other NT uses of the word. *Merimnan* is used in Luke when Martha is said by Jesus to be *careful* about many things (Luke 10.41); and when the disciples are bidden to *take no thought* how they will answer the charges that will be brought against them (Luke 12.11). *Merimnan* is used quite frequently by Paul. He uses it several times in I Cor. 7.32-34. In that passage he is insisting that the Christian must concentrate on the Second

Coming of Christ, which, at that time, he expected at any moment. The unmarried man and woman *care for* the things that belong to the Lord; but the married man and woman *care for* the things of the world, and *care* more how they may please each other than how they may please God. In I Cor. 12.25 *merimnan* is used of the *care* that members of the Church should have for one another. In Phil. 2.20 it is used for the *care* with which Timothy will concern himself for the highest interests of the Philippian church. In Phil. 4.6 Paul uses *merimnan* when he bids the Philippians: '*Be careful* for nothing.'

It is clear again that *merimnan*, like *merimna*, has a double flavour. The *care* for our fellow Christians is obviously a different thing from the *care* for the things of this world.

We must now go on to look at the meaning of these words in secular Greek that we may better interpret their meaning in the NT.

In classical Greek *merimnan* at its simplest can simply mean *to be occupied with*. In Sophocles' play, Oedipus asks the herdsman in what labour or in what way of life he is *employed* (*merimnan*) (Sophocles, *Oedipus Tyrannus* 1124). The noun *merimna* is sometimes joined with *lupē*, which means *grief*. In Euripides' *Ion*, Ion finds Creusa weeping at the shrine and asks her: 'How cam'st thou, lady, 'neath such *load of care*?' (Euripides, *Ion* 244). The word can and does denote real distress and trouble of mind.

In ordinary Greek the word *merimnan* can be used to describe a man thinking about his work, or a philosopher puzzling about his problems. Xenophon tells how Socrates criticized those who tried to understand the movement of the heavens and how God contrives them. He said that he who *would meddle with these matters* (*merimnan*) ran the risk of losing his sanity as completely as Anaxagoras, who took an insane pride in his explanation of divine machinery (Xenophon, *Memorabilia* 4.7.6). He tells how

Socrates had no time for the theorists who *worry about* the ultimate nature of things (Xenophon, *Memorabilia* 1.1.4). He tells how Socrates said to Pericles: 'I think that *you take much trouble* (*merimnan*) that you may not unconsciously lack any knowledge useful to a general' (Xenophon, *Memorabilia* 3.5.23). In his life of Cyrus, Xenophon tells how Cyrus at the end of his days left to Tanaoxares a position of less responsibility than the kingship. It would save him from *being cumbered about with the many cares* which come from responsibility and ambition (Xenophon, *Cyropædia* 8.7.12).

Once again we have this double meaning. Once again we can see that there is a care and an anxiety which is a right and an honourable thing; and there is a care and an anxiety which is a distracting, a distressing and an evil thing.

We now turn to our last source of information, to the contemporary Greek of the papyri. It so happens that the letters of the ordinary people in NT times quite often use the words *merimna* and *merimnan*.

A wife writes to her absent husband: 'I cannot even sleep because night and day my one *worry* (*merimna*) is your safety.' A mother, on learning that her son is well, writes: 'That is all my prayer and all my *anxiety*' (*merimna*). A soothsayer warns a client that he will be involved in many *anxieties* (*merimnai*) and distresses. Anacreon writes: 'When I drink wine my *worries* (*merimnai*) go to sleep.' In the Letter of Aristeas there is the question (271): 'What preserves a kingdom?' And the answer is: '*Care* (*merimna*) and watchfulness to see that no injury is inflicted by those who are set in positions of authority over the people.' An absent member of the family writes home: 'I am now writing in haste to prevent you being anxious (*merimnan*), for I will see to it that you are not worried.' The word *amerimnia* means *safety, security, the state of being unworried*. When two men have business dealings, the one writes to the other: 'For your *security* (*amerimnia*) I have issued to you this contract.' The contract has been drawn up and ratified so that the other partner to the deal will not worry.

So then this study of the meaning of the words *merimna* and *merimnan* in secular Greek has brought us once again to the same conclusion. There is a right and a wrong thought, a right and a wrong anxiety, a right and a wrong carefulness.

It remains now to go back to the NT and see just what that right and that wrong anxiety are. First, let us look at the wrong anxiety.

(i) The anxiety and the worry which come from too much involvement in the affairs of the world is always wrong (Matt. 13.22; cp. Mark 4.19 and Luke 8.14; Luke 21.34). When a man gets so involved in the things of time that he has no time for the things of eternity he is in a dangerous position. When he gives so much thought and care and concentration to the things of the earth that the things of heaven are crowded out he is in a perilous situation. A man may be so much with men that he has no time to be with God. He may have so many words to say to men that he has no time to pray to God. Be it noted, his engagement in the world may be with things which in themselves are not bad things, but 'the second best can often be the worst enemy of the best.'

(ii) Worry about the future is always wrong. It is wrong because it is *blind*; it fails to see God's bounty in the world; if God cares for the birds and the flowers, surely he will care for men (Matt. 6.25, 26, 28-30). It is wrong because it is *useless*. Worry never achieved anything (Matt. 6.27). It is wrong because it is essentially *irreligious* (Matt. 6.32). A Gentile may worry, but not a Christian. It is wrong because it merely *incapacitates a man from meeting problems when they do come* (Matt. 6.34). Worry does not make a man more able to face a situation; it makes him less able to face it.

(iii) Worry is wrong when it means the expenditure of energy on non-essentials. That was why Martha was wrong

(Luke 10.41). It was not a big meal Jesus wanted; it was peace before the Cross.

(iv) Worry about how to face the oppositions and the trials which come to a Christian is wrong (Luke 12.11). With the need there will come the power. God does not let down the man who is true to him.

(v) Worry about how to please the wrong people is wrong (I Cor. 7.32-34). It is not men whom we seek to please; it is God. And if a man fears God enough, he will never fear the face of any man.

(vi) The cure for worry is to cast oneself and all things upon God (I Peter 5.7; Phil. 4.6). In other words, the cure for worry is the realization that we are not left to handle life alone; we face it with God.

Second, let us look at the right kind of anxiety.

(i) It is right that we should take thought for *each other* (I Cor. 12.25). It may in fact often happen that the best way to forget our own worries is to shoulder someone else's. Life becomes an easier and a bigger thing when we feel the troubles of others more than we feel our own.

(ii) It is specially right to take thought for our fellow-Christians (Phil. 2.20). Timothy was the man who would take all thought for the needs of the Philippians. No Christian can be a happy when other Christians, of any colour or of any country, are in distress and persecution and need.

(iii) It is right to take thought for the Church of Christ (II Cor. 11.28). Paul's care for all the churches was at once his burden and his privilege. The Christian will ever think and plan how best he may serve his church.

It is true that we are told to take no thought for life and the morrow. But what is forbidden is disabling worry and not enabling foresight. It is the duty of a Christian man to do all that he can and to dare all that he can and to leave the rest to God. And at the same time it is the duty of a Christian man to have the same care and the same thought and the same anxiety for his fellow men, his fellow-Christians, and his church, as God himself has.

MESITĒS

THE ONE BETWEEN

Mesitēs is one of the great NT titles of Jesus. It is usually translated 'mediator'. It comes from the Greek word *mesos*, which, in this instance, means 'in the middle', and *mesitēs* therefore means 'a man who stands in the middle and who brings two parties together'. In the NT it is used in Gal. 3.19 of Moses, and in I Tim. 2.5; Heb. 8.6; 9.15; 12.24 of Jesus. It was just such a person for whom Job's whole soul cried out in his misfortune, when he said of himself and God, 'Neither is there any daysman, *mesitēs*, between us' (Job 9.33).

In classical Greek the word itself is not common, but the idea is very common. When it and its equivalents appear, they have two main meanings.

(i) They mean an 'arbiter'. Both Greek and Roman law believed strongly in arbitration. In Athens there was a body of men called The Forty, who were made up of four from each of the ten tribes. People who had disputes brought them to The Forty, and The Forty appointed an arbiter or mediator to settle them. The arbiters were composed of every Athenian citizen in his sixtieth year. An arbiter could not refuse the task if selected, and it was his duty, at all costs, to effect a settlement and a reconciliation between two parties who were at variance. In Rome there was a body of men called the *arbitri*. When a case was a matter of pure law it was tried by a judge, *judex*, but when it was a matter of equity, for instance, a matter of damages incurred or the like, it was settled by an 'arbiter', whose duty it was to bring the dispute to an end. An arbiter, a mediator, a *mesitēs*, is therefore fundamentally a person whose duty it is to bring together two people who are estranged and to wipe out the differences between them. That is what Jesus did between us and God.

(ii) They mean 'a sponsor', 'a guarantor', 'a surety'. A man who went bail for another person's appearance in court was so called. But the words are specially used of guaranteeing or standing surety for a debt. If a man wished to borrow from a bank he had to find someone to stand guarantor, a *mesitēs*. The *mesitēs* was a man who was ready to pay his friend's debt. Jesus is the *mesitēs* who stands good for our debt to God.

Always the *mesitēs* is the person in the middle who brings two people together. The Jews regularly used the term of Moses. In the Assumption of Moses (1.14) Moses is made to say of God, 'He designed and devised me, and he prepared me before the foundation of the world, that I should be the mediator of his covenant.' It was Moses who was the connecting link between Israel and God. In later times the Jews believed that the prayers of men were borne to God by angels. The Testament of Dan (6.2) says, 'Draw near unto God and unto the angel who intercedeth for you, for he is a mediator between God and man.' The Christian needs no human and no angelic mediator. Christ is for him the connecting link with God.

So when we call Jesus *mesitēs*, 'mediator', we remember three great things.

(i) Jesus is God's intermediary. He is the connecting link between God and man. He is the King's messenger, the one who stands between God and man, not to separate them, but to bring them together.

(ii) The great function of the mediator is to bring together people who are at variance. Again and again the papyri speak of the appointment of a *mesitēs* to effect an agreement between people who are estranged. It is Jesus' work to break down the barrier between God and man.

(iii) If a mediator is to be effective, he must perfectly represent both parties. Irenaeus described Jesus thus, *hominibus ostendens deum, deo autem exhibens hominem*, that is, he showed God to men and exhibited men to God. The very word shows us the great mystery of Christ, that at one and the same time he is perfectly God and perfectly man. That is why he, and he alone, is the only mediator between God and man.

PAIDAGŌGOS

THE GUARDIAN OF CHILDHOOD'S DAYS

THE word *paidagōgos* occurs in the NT in only two passages; but it is a word the correct understanding of which is essential, if Paul's thought is to be understood. In I Cor. 4.15 Paul says to the Corinthians that they may have ten thousand *paidagōgoi*, but they have not many fathers; that it is he who is their true father in the Christian faith. There, the AV translates the word 'instructors'; Moffatt translates 'thousands to superintend'; the RSV translates 'guides'. In Gal. 3.24, 25 the AV says that the law was our 'schoolmaster' (*paidagōgos*) to lead us to Christ . . . but after faith comes we are no longer under a *paidagōgos*. There Moffatt translates, the law 'held us as wards in discipline'. And the RSV has it that the law was our 'custodian'. None of these translations is fully satisfactory, for the very good reason that the *paidagōgos* carried out a function to which there is nothing precisely corresponding in our educational system.

Up to the age of seven the Greek boy was almost exclusively in his mother's charge. But even then, if there was a *paidagōgos* in the household, he had his say. Socrates in Plato's *Protagoras* (325 c) says of the child: 'Mother and nurse and father and *paidagōgos* are quarrelling about the improvement of the child as soon as ever he is able to understand them.' It was when he went to school that the *paidagōgos* really took over the management of the boy and retained it till the boy was eighteen. The *paidagōgos* was not in our sense of the word a teacher at all. His duty was to accompany the boy to school each day and to see that he got there safely; to carry the boy's books and his lyre; to watch his conduct in school; to see to his conduct in the street; to train the boy in morals, in manners and in deportment. He must see that the boy walked modestly with downcast head in the streets; he must see that he gave place to older people and was becomingly silent in their presence; he must teach him to be well-mannered at table and to wear his clothes with grace. He had to teach him all the Greek meant by *eukosmia,* good manners, good deportment, pleasantness of life. K. J. Freeman says of the *paidagōgos* that he was 'a mixture of nurse, footman, chaperon and tutor'. When in the *Lysis* (208 c) Socrates is trying to teach the lad that life does not consist in doing what you like, there is a conversation like this. 'Are you your own master, or do they not even allow that?' 'Nay; of course they do not allow that.' 'Then you have a master?' 'Yes, my *paidagōgos*; there he is.' . . . 'And what does he do with you?' 'He takes me to my teachers.' It was an anxious and a most practical job, especially if the lad was a high-spirited and independent boy. Plato compares the relationship of the *paidagōgos* to his charge to that of an invalid to his health: 'He has to follow the disease wherever it leads, being unable to cure it, and he spends his life in perpetual anxiety with no time for anything else' (Plato: *Republic,* 406 a). Clement of Alexandria has a work called *The Paedagogus* in which he likens the Word to our *paidagōgos.* He says: 'The *paidagōgos* being practical, not theoretical, his aim is thus to improve the soul, and to train it up to a virtuous, not to an intellectual life'. Plutarch in his life of Quintus Fabius Cunctator tells how Fabius defeated Hannibal. He refused to join in battle but he dogged Hannibal's armies everywhere. 'Still he kept pace with them; when they marched he followed them; when they encamped he did the same.' There were those who wished for violent action and they taunted Fabius with being Hannibal's *paidagōgos*, 'since he did nothing else but follow him up and down and wait upon him' (Plutarch, *Life of Fabius* 5). Clearly the *paidagōgos* had a most constant and a most responsible task.

But here we have the very point of the matter. Sometimes the slave chosen to be *paidagōgos* was old and trusted. Sometimes he had the highest ideal of his task. It is told of a good *paidagōgos* that, when he was asked, 'What is your duty?' he replied, 'My duty is to make the good pleasant to the boy.' When Themistocles wished to send to Xerxes the secret message which lured him to his doom it was to Sikinnos, the *paidagōgos* of his sons, that he entrusted it, and afterwards rewarded him with wealth and the citizenship (*Herodotus* 8.75). Sometimes indeed the *paidagōgos* was the trusted family friend. But far oftener the *paidagōgos* was a most unsatisfactory figure. For too often he was chosen for his task, as Plutarch complains, because he was too old and feeble for any other.

Pericles is reported to have said when he saw a slave fall from a tree and break his leg: 'Lo, he is now a *paidagōgos*!' In Plato's *Alcibiades* (122 b) Socrates says to Alcibiades: 'Pericles gave you, Alcibiades, for a *paidagōgos* Zopyrus, the Thracian, a slave of his who was past all other work.' At the very end of Plato's *Lysis* the *paidagōgoi* arrive to take Lysis and Menexenus home. The conversation is not ended and the lads are unwilling to go. Plato goes on: 'Suddenly we were interrupted by the *paidagōgoi* of Lysis and Menexenus, who came upon us like an evil apparition with the lads' brothers, and bade them go home as it was getting late. At first we and the bystanders drove them off; but afterwards, as they paid no attention, but only went on shouting in their barbarous dialect, and got angry and kept calling the boys—they seemed to us to have been drinking rather too much at the Hermaea, which made them difficult to manage—we fairly gave way and broke up the company.' It is not a pretty picture, the picture of uncouth, drunken slaves with no pretensions either to morals or to culture. It is true that the other side sometimes appears. In a third century papyrus a mother writes to her son: 'Let you and your *paidagōgos* see to it that you go to a fitting teacher,' and she ends the letter, 'Salute your much honoured *paidagōgos*, Eros.' But the balance is very much the other way.

In any event the *paidagōgos* existed for no other reason than to make his charge independent of his care. Xenophon in his work on Sparta (3.1) writes: 'Whenever they emerge from childhood to youth, they cease from *paidagōgoi*, they cease from teachers. No one governs them any more, but they let them go as masters of themselves.' When Paul spoke of the law as our *paidagōgos* to bring us to Christ, in the very phrase he affirmed that the law was an inadequate, unsatisfactory thing, doomed to come to an end. It was another way of saying that Christ is the end of the law.

PARAGGELIA AND PARAGGELLEIN

THE WORDS OF COMMAND

Paraggelia and *paraggellein* are characteristically words of command. *Paraggelia* is a noun which means *an order, an instruction, a charge, a command*; and *paraggellein* is a verb which means *to charge, to instruct, to give* or *to pass on an order*. The great interest of these words lies in the background against which they are used. They have five different areas and spheres within which they are used.

(i) First and foremost, they are *military* words. *Paraggelia* is distinctively *a command issued to soldiers*. *Paraggellein* is distinctively the word used of *a general issuing a word of command*, and of that word of command being passed from commander to commander, from rank to rank and from man to man.

Xenophon tells how in battle Cyrus armed himself, and *passed the word to others* to do the same (Xenophon, *Anabasis* 1.8.3). He tells how on the occasion of a ceremonial parade Cyrus gave an *order* to his first captain to take up his position at the head of the line, and *to transmit the same order* to the second captain, and so on (Xenophon, *Cyropædia* 2.4.2). He tells how the officers were to bid the corporals each one *to announce* it to his squad (Xenophon, *Cyropædia* 4.2.7). *Paraggelia* and *paraggellein* are characteristically words of military command.

(ii) They are *legal* words. They are the words which are used of summoning a man to court, or of citing him to appear in a certain place that he may give account for the things that he has done, or of laying certain legal injunctions upon him, which he must satisfy and obey.

In the papyri one man writes to another to tell him that, now that he has received the written *paraggelia, instruction,* he must take thought for the cultivation of his fields. The warning is issued that if certain people disobey this *paraggelia, injunction,* they will pay the penalty of their disobedience. An official is directed to serve warning upon a man, so that he may have a written *summons* to appear wherever the prefect shall hold his court. An official is instructed to give *written notice* to a man who is arraigned for murder and other crimes to appear before the court in three days' time.

The words develop a general sense of giving instructions or injunctions to a person. For instance, *paraggellein* is used in the papyri of ordering someone out of the house, of telling a person to go to a certain street, of giving notice of a certain obligation. The legal and the military sense meet in the kindred word *paraggelma,* which can be used for a *mobilization order.*

(iii) They are *ethical words.* They are used of the instructions that the ethical teacher gives to his disciples. Clement of Rome writes of God: 'He who has *ordered* us not to lie, how much more will he not lie himself' (I *Clement* 27.2).

When Aristotle is talking about individual judgments on individual people, he says that they cannot be dealt with by rule, because there is no science and no set of *rules* which can be used (Aristotle, *Nicomachean Ethics* 1104a 7). The ethical rules of life are *paraggeliai*.

(iv) They are words of *technique*. The rules of grammar, the rules of literary composition or of oratory are *paraggeliai* or *paraggelmata*. Longinus insists that there are rules for great art, and he writes: 'First of all, we must raise the question whether there is such a thing as an art of the sublime or the lofty. Some hold that those are entirely in error who would bring such matters under *the precepts of art, paraggelmata*' (Longinus, *On the Sublime* 2.1). These words describe the laws and the rules of any technique or of any art.

(v) They are *medical* words. *Paraggellein* is the word that is used of a doctor *prescribing* for a case. They describe the instructions which a man must obey if he is to enjoy or to recover his health.

Now we must turn to the use of these words in the NT itself.

Within the NT itself the word *paraggelia* is used five times. In Acts 5.28 it is used of the command of the Sanhedrin to Peter and John not to preach or to teach in the name of Jesus. In Acts 16.24 it is used of the magistrates' command to the Philippian gaoler to keep Paul and Silas secure in prison. In I Thess. 4.2 it is used of the instructions which Paul gave to the church at Thessalonica. And in I Tim. 1.5 and 1.18 it is used of Paul's instructions to Timothy.

The verb *paraggellein* is much more frequently used. In the Synoptic Gospels, in Matt. 10.5 and Mark 6.8, it is used of the commands of Jesus to his disciples before he sent them out on their mission of preaching and teaching and healing. These commandments are, as it were, Jesus' marching orders to his men. In modern language, they are being briefed for the expedition on which they are being sent.

Similarly, in Acts 1.4 it is used of Jesus' command to his disciples to wait in Jerusalem until the Holy Spirit should come upon them. In Matt. 15.35 and Mark 8.6 it is used of Jesus' command to the crowd to sit upon the grass before the feeding of the five thousand.

In Luke 5.14 it is used of Jesus' instructions to the leper after he had healed him. In Luke 8.29 it is used of Jesus' command to the evil spirit to come out of the Gerasene demoniac. In Luke 8.56 it is used of Jesus' instruction to Jairus and his wife not to talk of the miracle of the raising of their daughter.

In Luke 9.21 it is used of Jesus' command to his disciples not yet to spread abroad their discovery that he was the Christ. The notable thing is that in the Synoptic Gospels the verb *paraggellein* is never used of anyone except Jesus. It is the characteristic word for his instructions to his people.

We now look at the word in the rest of the NT. It occurs sometimes in its normal secular use of the command issued by a higher authority to a subordinate. In Acts 4.18; 5.28, 40 it is used of the command of the Sanhedrin to Peter and John to stop preaching. In Acts 15.5 it is used of the command of the Pharisees to observe the ceremonial law. In Acts 16.23 it is used of the command of the Philippian magistrates that Paul and Silas should be thrown into prison. In Acts 23.22, 30 it is used of the instructions of the Roman captain to the young man who had given him information regarding the plot to assassinate Paul. All these usages are the normal secular usages. They are all commands of the military or the civil authority.

But the word becomes of great interest when we examine its remaining uses. We discover that it is the regular word for Christian instruction, and that it is the word which is uniquely characteristic of the commands and the instructions and the training which Paul gave to his friends and converts.

It is used of Paul's command to the evil spirit to come out of the Philippian slave girl in Acts 16.18. In I Cor. 7.10

it is used of Paul's insistence that the marriage bond is not to be broken, a command which he says comes from the Lord. In I Cor. 11.17 it is used of Paul's instructions to the Corinthian church regarding the Lord's Supper. In I Thess. 4.11 it is used of Paul's command to the Thessalonians to be quiet and to mind their own business. In II Thess. 3.4, 6. 10, 12 it is used of a whole series of commandments of Paul to the Thessalonian church.

Paraggellein is a word which is almost characteristic of the Pastoral Epistles. It is used of the instructions given to Timothy in I Tim. 1.3; of the work which Timothy must do, that he must *command* and teach these things (I Tim. 4.11); of the charge which is to be made to the widows concerning how they must live (I Tim. 5.7); of the solemn charge to Timothy to keep the commandments (I Tim. 6.13); and of the charge to the rich not to be proud because of their riches (I Tim. 6.17).

We have now reached the most interesting and significant fact that *paraggellein* is the characteristic word for the commandments of Jesus to his people, and for the instruction of Paul to his converts in the early Church. We must now go on to see what the significance of that fact is for the Christian life.

The very fact that these words are so often and so consistently used tells us certain things about the Christian and about the Christian life. We have seen that these words have five backgrounds, five areas and spheres which define their use.

(i) They are the words of *military command*. The Christian must regard himself as a soldier; he must regard himself as a man under orders; he must regard himself as a man having a definite commission; he must regard himself as a man on a campaign.

The Christian must therefore see himself, not as a man who is in the world to do as he likes, but as a man who is in the world to do as his commander orders. Further, the Christian must not see himself as an individual, but as a member of an army, a unit in the task-force of Jesus Christ. Too much independence and too much individualism are alike forbidden by these words.

(ii) They are the words of *legal summons*. The Christian must regard himself as a man under responsibility; he must regard himself as a man who is answerable for all that he does. The Christian is a man under judgment. His life must be aimed not to satisfy himself, not to please his fellow-men, but to stand the scrutiny of God.

(iii) They are the words of *the ethical teacher*. The Christian must regard himself as a man under instruction and discipline; as a man learning the laws and the rules of life. The foolish man is the man who thinks that he knows it all already; the wisest man is the man who knows that he does not know.

The Christian will be invited to direct his life by many standards, the standards of business practices, the standards of worldly wisdom, the standards of human cleverness; his one standard must be the teaching of Jesus Christ.

(iv) They are the words of *instruction in technique*. The Christian has not only to learn a series of ethical laws; he has to learn the art of living the Christian life. His study is not confined to the class-room or the library or the dis-cussion circle or the prayer group. He is under the obliga-tion, not only to learn, but also to live Christianity. He is learning, not only a theology for thought, but also a tech-nique for living.

In *Prayers for the Lambeth Conference of 1948* there is this prayer: 'Almighty God, give us grace to be not only hearers but doers of thy holy word, not only to admire but to obey thy doctrine, not only to profess but to practise thy religion, not only to love but to live thy gospel. So grant that what we learn of thy glory we may receive into our hearts and show forth in our lives, through Jesus Christ our Lord.'

Therein is summed up the Christian duty. Technique may nowadays be a word which is belittled, but there is not only a theology but also a technique of the Christian life.

(v) They are the words of *medical treatment*. Epictetus called his lecture-room 'the hospital of the sick soul'. He called his teaching 'the medicines of salvation'. Men are sick in soul and must come to Jesus Christ for healing. No doctor can heal any man unless that man submits to the doctor's treatment, accepts the doctor's prescription, and obeys the doctor's instructions. The Christian is the man who has realized the sickness of his soul, who has come to Christ for a cure, and who is determined to submit his life to the treatment which Christ prescribes.

So these words *paraggelia* and *paraggellein* tell us that the Christian is the soldier of Christ, the man on trial before Christ, the disciple of Christ, the trainee of Christ and the patient of Christ.

PARAKLĒTOS

THE WORD OF THE HOLY SPIRIT

Paraklētos is one of the great characteristic words of the Johannine writings. In the Fourth Gospel it is used as a title of the Holy Spirit in 14.16; 14.26; 15.26; 16.7; and in the First Epistle it is used of Jesus as the advocate who pleads our cause with the Father (I John 2.1). Clearly it is a word of quite special importance; but when we look at the efforts of translators to render it into English, equally clearly it is a word of quite special difficulty. In the passage in the First Epistle the translators are almost unanimous in rendering *paraklētos* by the word *advocate*. The only exception is the Twentieth Century New Testament, which renders it *one who pleads our cause*, which is simply a description of the work which an advocate does. But in the Fourth Gospel itself the translations are many and varied.

The AV translates it *comforter*; the RV retains the word *comforter*, but the margin gives *advocate* and *helper* and notes that the Greek is *paraclete*. The RSV translates it *counsellor*. J. B. Phillips translates it *someone to stand by you*. Ronald Knox translates it *he who is to befriend you*. Moffatt, Torrey and the Twentieth Century New Testament all translate it *helper*. Clearly this is a difficult word to translate. We shall come to see that the difficulty lies in the fact that the word means so much that there is no single English word by which it can be adequately translated.

The English translation *comforter* goes all the way back to Wiclif; but it must be noted that Wiclif was using the word *comforter* with a width of meaning which in modern English it does not possess. The proof of this is that Wiclif translates Eph. 6.10, 'Be ye *comforted* in the Lord.' The word there is *endunamoun*, which has in it the same root as the root of the word *dunamis*, which means *power*, and which is the word from which the English word *dynamite* is derived. In point of fact Tyndale translated Eph. 6.10, 'Be strong in the Lord,' a translation which has survived down to the present day. This same word, *endunamoun*, is used in I Tim. 1.12 where once again Wiclif translates, 'I do thankings to him that *comforted* me.' Tyndale has, 'I thank him who has *made me strong*,' and the AV has, 'I thank him who hath *enabled* me.' In modern English the word *comforter* has to do exclusively with comfort and consolation and sympathy in sorrow and in distress; but in Wiclif's time it was much more closely connected with its root, the Latin word *fortis*, which means, *brave*, *strong*, *courageous*. So we may note to begin with that when Wiclif translates *paraklētos* by the word *comforter* he was certainly not saying that the sole, or even the main, function of the Holy Spirit was to comfort and console in our sense of the words; he was meaning that the function of the Holy Spirit was to fill a man with that Spirit of power and courage which would make him able triumphantly to cope with life. It is in fact a great misfortune that the narrowing of the word *comforter* has resulted in an undue narrowing of our conception of the work of the Holy Spirit.

It is again to be noted that even the early Fathers have difficulty with the word *paraklētos*. Origen would translate it *consoler* in the Gospel and *advocate* in the Epistle. Cyril of Jerusalem would translate it *consoler*, because the Spirit helps our infirmities and makes intercession for us. Hilary and Jerome both translate it *consolator*, again stressing the idea of *consolation*. Tertullian varies. Sometimes he merely transliterates into *paracletus*; sometimes he has *advocatus*, an advocate to plead our cause; and once he has the very unusual word *exorator* which means a *successful suppliant*, one who obtains by entreaty.

Let us then see if we can come at something of the riches of the meaning of this word.

Paraklētos itself is a word which is passive in form. It means literally *one who is called in*. But although it is passive in form it is almost always *active in meaning*, because the thing that gives it its meaning is the purpose and the function for which the person is called in. He is always called in in order that he may do something, that he may render some service. Therefore the word is a word with a *passive form* but an *active meaning*.

If that be so we shall come best at its meaning by examining first of all the verb *parakalein* from which *paraklētos* is derived.

(i) At its most general *parakalein* means *to call in, to summon*. So a man is said to call in an *ally* (*summachos*) (Herodotus, 7.158); to call in a *counsellor* to give advice (*sumboulos*) (Xenophon, *Anabasis* 1.6.5); to call in an *advocate* to plead a case in the law courts (*sunēgoros*) (Aeschines, 2.184). It is also used of calling upon a man *to undertake a public duty* such as the duty of gymnasiarch, whose duty it was to maintain and train a team at his own expense to run in the torch race. Finally, it is used of calling in the gods as *helpers* (*boēthoi*) (Epictetus, 3.21.12). It is clear that in every case the summons is to help, to service, to assistance. Therefore at its widest a *paraklētos* is a person who is called in to help in a situation with which a man by himself cannot cope. It is true that the basic meaning of *paraklētos* is *helper*, but we must now try to put some more definite content into the meaning of the help which is sought and given.

(ii) Let us look next at one of the rare meanings of the word *parakalein*. In ordinary secular Greek the word *parakalein* very rarely means to *comfort*, in the sense of to *console*. But it does have that meaning in the Septuagint. It is so used in Ps. 71.21, 'Thou shalt increase my greatness and *comfort* me on every side.' It is the word which is used in the great passage in Isa. 40.1, 2, '*Comfort ye, comfort* ye, my people, saith your God.' In the two later versions of the Septuagint, those of Aquila and Theodotion, *paraklētos* is the word used in Job 16.2, 'Miserable *comforters* are ye all.' It is then possible to take *paraklētos* to mean *one called in to comfort and to console*; but two things have to be noted. First, it is by far the rarest meaning of the word. Second, even if it be taken in that sense, it still has the background of a comfort which makes a man able to stand on his two feet and face life. In Job 4.4 the Moffatt translation is, 'Your words have kept men on their feet,' and that is a description of the effect of the comfort which *parakalein* describes.

(iii) In ordinary secular Greek by far the most characteristic usage both of *parakalein* and *paraklētos* is in connexion with help given in some kind of legal trial. In Greece the *paraklētos* was the friend of the accused person, called in to speak in support of his character, in order to enlist the sympathy of the judges in his favour. In Demosthenes it can be used for the counsel for the defence. It means someone who will present someone else's case to some other person or to some other authority in the most favourable light. Diogenes Laertius (4.50) tells about the answer of the philosopher Bion to a man who was a talkative nuisance. Bion said: 'I will do my best for you if you send *paraklētoi, representatives,* to plead your case, and if you don't come yourself.' The *paraklētoi* would put a much more effective case than the man himself. Philo (*In Flaccum* 4) tells how the Alexandrian Jews wished to find someone to plead their case with the Roman Emperor; they in fact wished the city of Alexandria to plead it for them. He says: 'We must find a more powerful *paraklētos, advocate,* by whom Gaius will be brought to a favourable disposition towards us.' The *Epistle of Barnabas* (20) speaks of those who are *paraklētoi, advocates,* of the wealthy and the unjust, and accusers of the poor. Philo (*De Josepho* 40) tells of the answer of Joseph to his brethren when they were in obvious terror that he would revenge himself upon them, 'I grant you free forgiveness for all that you have done to me; you need no one else to intercede for you, no other *paraklētos.*' Philo speaks of God himself creating and blessing the world (*De Mund. Opif.* 6), 'employing no *paraklētos, adviser, helper*—for who else was there—but only himself, did God resolve that he ought to bless the world with his benefits.' The *Second Letter of Clement* (6) says: 'Who will be our *paraklētos* if we are found doing that which is not right?' That is to say: 'Who will speak for us, plead for us, take up our cause against the justice of God?' In the Letter of the Churches of Lyons and Vienne (quoted in Eusebius, *Ecclesiastical History,* 5.1) when certain of the Christians were on trial for their faith, Vettius Epagathus, one of the Roman officials, himself confessed to being Christian, and was thereupon called the *paraklētos* of the Christians, the advocate of the Christian cause.

This usage of the word became transliterated into later Jewish language. The Targum, that is the authorized translation, of Job 33.23 says that in order to redeem man from going down into the pit, a special angelic agency, a mediator, an interpreter, a *paraklētos* is necessary.

The later Rabbis wrote the word *paraklētos* in Hebrew letters and used it quite freely. 'He who fulfils one precept of the Law gains for himself one *paraklētos, advocate*; he who commits one transgression gains to himself one *katēgoros, accuser*.' 'In the heavenly judgment a man's *paraklētoi, advocates*, are repentance and good works.' 'All the righteousness and mercy which an Israelite doeth in the world, are great peace and great *paraklētoi, advocates*, between him and his Father in heaven.'

There is no doubt that this is the meaning of *paraklētos* in I John 2.1. Jesus is the prisoner's friend. He is the one who will plead our cause. He is the one who will plead and intercede for us. He is the counsel for the defence. The Jew had the hopeless task of putting forward as his defence before God his own good works and his own obedience to the Law. The Christian has the supreme defence—the advocacy of Jesus Christ himself. It is he who ever liveth to make intercession for us.

(iv) The meaning of advocate for the defence is both fitting and adequate for *paraklētos* in I John 2.1; but it is not so fitting in the Gospel. There the *paraklētos* is the Spirit of truth (14.16); there the Spirit is the interpreter and the teacher and the remembrancer (14.26); there the Spirit is the one who will testify of Christ (15.26); there the Spirit comes when Jesus goes away (16.7). In the Gospel, as Dr. G. H. C. Macgregor finely puts it, the Spirit is Christ's *alter ego*. The *paraklētos*, the Spirit, is the constant, illuminating, strengthening, enabling presence of Jesus. Now it so happens that there is still another meaning of *parakalein* which will give us the key. *Parakalein* not infrequently means to *exhort* or *to urge*. It is used by Xenophon for exhorting men to the fairest deeds (*Anabasis* 3.1.24). It is used by Plato for exhorting men to apply their minds to think about things (*Republic* 535b); it is used by Isocrates of urging men to remember (3.12). It is fairly frequently used of inciting a person to a certain action or emotion.

But above all *parakalein* is used of *exhorting troops who are about to go into battle*. Aeschylus (*Persae* 380) says of the ships sailing into battle; 'The long galleys cheered (*parakalein*) each other, line by line.' Euripides (*Phoenissae* 1254) describing the plans for battle says: 'So did they hail them, *cheering* them to fight.' Xenophon uses it of urging the soldiers to embark upon the ships and to set out on an adventurous voyage (*Anabasis* 5.6. 19). Polybius uses it of Lutatius addressing his troops before a naval battle with the Carthaginians (1.60.5). He uses it of Demetrius rallying his men and addressing the ranks before they embarked upon battle (3.19.4). And the word he uses of embarking upon battle is *diakinduneuein*, which means *to accept the risk of battle*.

Again and again we find that *parakalein* is *the word of the rallying-call*; it is the word used of the speeches of leaders and of soldiers who urge each other on. It is the word used of words which send fearful and timorous and hesitant soldiers and sailors courageously into battle. A *paraklētos* is therefore an *encourager*, one who puts courage into the faint-hearted, one who nerves the feeble arm for fight, one who makes a very ordinary man cope gallantly with a perilous and a dangerous situation.

Here then we have the great work of the Holy Spirit. To put it in modern language, the Holy Spirit makes men able to cope with life. The Holy Spirit is in fact the fulfilment of the promise, 'Lo, I am with you always even unto the end of the world' (Matt. 28.20).

It is quite clear that the translation *comforted* which in the days of Wiclif was perfectly adequate and correct for *paraklētos* has now become much too narrow and much too limited. To limit, even by suggestion, the work of the Holy Spirit to consolation and to comfort is sadly to belittle the work of the Spirit. By the study of the word *paraklētos* we have come to see the wide scope in time and eternity of the *paraklētos*.

(i) The word *paraklētos* always means someone called in to help and to render some service; therefore the Holy Spirit is essentially the helper of men.

(ii) The word *paraklētos* has a great Septuagint back-

ground to that kind of comfort and consolation in distress
which keeps a man on his feet, when, left to himself, he
would collapse. It is the comfort which enables a man to
pass the breaking-point and not to break.

(iii) The word *paraklētos* has a great background in
Greek law. The *paraklētos* was the prisoner's friend, the
advocate and counsel for the defence, the man who bore
witness to his friend's character when he most needed it,
and when others wished to condemn him; therefore when
we describe the glorified Christ as our *paraklētos* we mean
that he is there to speak for us before God.

(iv) The word *parakalein* is the word for exhorting men
to noble deeds and high thoughts; it is especially the word
of courage before battle. Life is always calling us into battle
and the one who makes us able to stand up to the opposing
forces, to cope with life and to conquer life is the *paraklētos*, the Holy Spirit, who is none other than the presence
and the power of the risen Christ.

PAROUSIA

THE ARRIVAL OF THE KING

THE Greek word *parousia* has become naturalized in
English as a technical term for the Second Coming of
Christ. The use of the word in the secular Greek contem-
porary with the NT is extremely interesting.

(i) In classical Greek it means quite simply the 'presence'
or the 'arrival' of persons or things. It can be used in such
phrases as the 'presence' of friends or the 'presence' of
misfortunes. A man takes an oath that he will fulfil a certain duty in the presence of the brothers and the bishops.
Quite often Paul uses *parousia* in that simple non-technical
sense. He rejoices at the *parousia*, the 'arrival' of Stephanas

(I Cor. 16.17). He is comforted by the *parousia* of Titus (II Cor. 7.6). He urges the Philippians to be as obedient in his absence as they were during his *parousia* with them (Phil. 2.12). The Corinthians fling the taunt at him that, however impressive his letters may be, his bodily *parousia*, presence, is weak (II Cor. 10.10).

(ii) But, characteristically, in the NT *parousia* is the word for the Second Coming of Christ (Matt. 24.3, 27, 37, 39; I Thess. 2.19; 3.13; 4.15; 5.23; II Thess. 2.1, 8, 9; James 5.7, 8; II Pet. 1.16; 3.4, 12; I John 2.28). Let us study the contemporary secular use of the term to see what kind of picture it would convey to the minds of the early Christians.

In the papyri and in Hellenistic Greek *parousia* is the technical word for the arrival of an emperor, a king, a governor or famous person into a town or province. For such a visit preparations have to be made. Taxes are imposed, for instance, to present the king with a golden crown. For the visit of Ptolemy Soter to the village of Cerceosiris 80 artabae of corn have to be collected. Always the coming of the king demands that all things must be ready.

Further, one of the commonest things is that provinces dated a new era from the *parousia* of the emperor. Cos dated a new era from the *parousia* of Gaius Caesar in A.D. 4, as did Greece from the *parousia* of Hadrian in A.D. 124. A new section of time emerged with the coming of the king.

Another common practice was to strike new coins to commemorate the visitation of the king. Hadrian's travels can be followed by the coins which were struck to commemorate his visits. When Nero visited Corinth coins were struck to commemorate his *adventus*, advent, which is the Latin equivalent of the Greek *parousia*. It was as if with the coming of the king a new set of values had emerged.

Parousia is sometimes used of the 'invasion' of a province by a general. It is so used of the invasion of Asia by Mithradates. It describes the entrance on the scene of a new and conquering power.

Lastly, *parousia* is used of the visitation of a god. It is used, for instance, of the visit of the god to a sufferer, who was healed, in the temple of Aesculapius, the god of healing. On the political side, the *parousia* of the king or governor or emperor was often an occasion when petitions were presented and wrongs were righted. The word describes a healing and a correcting visitation.

With all this in our minds let us return to the NT and see how the idea of the *parousia* is used.

(i) It is used as the basis of a demand to preserve life blameless against the coming of the king. The preparations must be made (I Thess. 3.13; 5.23; I John 2.28).

(ii) It is used as a reason for patience (James 5.7, 8). The day is coming when the coming of the King will right all wrongs.

(iii) It is spoken of as something to desire and to pray for (II Pet. 3.4, 12). R. L. Stevenson tells of a byreman, who said that he never wearied of his unattractive work because 'he that has something ayont (beyond) need never weary'. He who awaits Christ has the something beyond.

Deissmann says that the word precisely expresses the text, 'Behold, thy King cometh unto thee' (Zech. 9.9; Matt. 21.5). The Christian is one who awaits a king.

PENTHEIN

THE WORD OF GODLY SORROW

Penthein, the verb which means *to sorrow*, is by no means an unusual Greek word. In the NT it occurs nine times.

Jesus said that it was not possible that the friends of the bridegroom should *mourn* while the bridegroom was still with them (Matt. 9.15). Paul rebukes the Corinthian church because its members did not *mourn* for the man whose sin had shamed the church (I Cor. 5.2.). Paul's fear is that he will have cause *to bewail* the sinners, if he comes again to Corinth (II Cor. 12.21). In James the sinners are invited to return to God, and to be afflicted, *to mourn*, and to weep (James 4.9). Three times in the Revelation the word is used of the *mourning* which shall follow the destruction of the great Babylon (Rev. 18.11, 15, 19).

But the most important use of this word is in the Beatitudes. Luke has it: Woe to you that laugh now! For ye shall *mourn* and weep (Luke 6.25). And Matthew has it: Blessed are they that *mourn* for they shall be comforted (Matt. 5.4).

There are two most significant things about this word.

(i) *Penthein* is the strongest word for mourning in the Greek language. It is the word which in all ages of Greek is used for mourning for the dead, or for one who is as if he were dead. So it is used in Homer (*Iliad* 19.225) and in Herodotus (4.95). So Sophocles speaks of Oedipus shaken with the spasms of *agonizing* memory (Sophocles, *Oedipus Tyrannus* 1320).

In the Septuagint it is the word which is used for Jacob's *mourning* when he thinks that Joseph is dead and gone for ever (Gen. 37.34); and it is the word which is used for David's *mourning* when his son Absalom met his tragic death (II Sam. 19.1).

In the papyri again it is connected with the *mourning* of death and of unbridgeable separation. In one papyrus it is laid down: The *mourning* women shall wear dark raiment. In another a husband who is separated from his wife writes: I wish you to know that ever since you left me I have been in *mourning*, weeping by night, and *mourning* by day.

There is no stronger word of mourning in the Greek language than *penthein*.

(ii) It must have been noticed in the examples quoted

how often *mourning* and *weeping* (*penthein* and *klaiein*) are associated. The second significant fact about *penthein* is that it described *the mourning which cannot be hidden*.

It describes, not only a grief which brings an ache to the heart, but also a grief which brings tears to the eyes. *Penthein* describes the sorrow which cannot be concealed.

This then is the word which the NT uses for a Christian's *mourning for his sin* (Matt. 5.4; I Cor. 5.2; II Cor. 12.21; James 4.9). The Christian sorrow for sin must be not only a gentle, vague, sentimental regret that something has gone wrong; it must be a sorrow as acute as sorrow for the dead.

It must be a sorrow which is not hidden, but which emerges in the tears and the confession of the truly penitent heart. It is a sorrow which realizes what Carlyle called 'the infinite damnability of sin', and which is broken in heart when in the Cross it sees what sin can do.

One of the great conversion stories of modern times is the story of how the Japanese murderer Tokichi Ishii was converted by reading the NT when he was in prison. He was a man of the most savage cruelty, bestial and sub-human in the terrible crimes that he had committed.

He was converted by reading a Bible which two Canadian women left with him, when they could not get even a flicker of human response to anything they said to him. He read it, and when he came to the prayer of Jesus: 'Father, forgive them, they know not what they do,' he says: 'I stopped. I was stabbed to the heart, as if pierced with a five-inch nail.' His sorrow for his sin was the sorrow of a broken heart.

The word *penthein* tells us that we have not even begun on the Christian way until we take sin with such serious-ness that our sorrow for it is like the mourning of one who mourns for the dead. Christianity begins with the godly sorrow of the broken heart.

PHOBOS

THE RIGHT AND THE WRONG FEAR

Phobos means 'fear', and in all ages of Greek *phobos* is
what is sometimes known as 'a middle word'. That is to
say, the word itself is quite neutral, and, according to the
way in which it is used and the context in which it occurs,
it can have either a good or a bad meaning, and can describe something which is useful and praiseworthy, or evil
and contemptible. In Greek *phobos*, 'fear', can be the
characteristic either of the coward or of the truly religious
man.

In classical Greek *phobos* has three main meanings. (i) In
Homer it nearly always means 'panic' or 'flight'. Panic-
stricken flight,' says Homer, 'which is the companion of
chilliing *phobos*, fear' (*Iliad*, 9.2). *Phobos* in early Greek
has always in it the idea of running away, of fleeing panic-
stricken from the battle. The passive of the corresponding
verb, *phobeisthai*, means 'to be put to flight', and it is the
opposite of the verb *hupomenein*, from which comes *hupomonē*, and which means 'to stand fast' and 'to endure'.
The word has in it that failure of nerve which makes a man
take to his heels and flee. (ii) More generally in classical
Greek *phobos* means 'fear' in the widest sense of the term.
It is the opposite of *tharros*, which means 'courage'.
(iii) Lastly, in classical Greek, *phobos* means 'awe' or
'reverence' for some exalted ruler and especially for some
divinity or some god. It is the feeling which a man experiences in the presence of someone who is infinitely his
superior.

In the NT the word is common and occurs about 47
times. First of all, let us look at it in the Synoptic Gospels
and in Acts.

It is used of the reaction of the disciples when they saw
Jesus walking on the water (Matt. 14.26) and when he

stilled the storm (Mark 4.41). It is used of the reaction of the people after the healing of the paralysed man (Luke 5.26), after the raising of the widow's son at Nain (Luke 7.16), after the healing of the Gerasene demoniac (Luke 8.37). It is used of the feeling of Zacharias when he saw the angel of the Lord beside the altar (Luke 1.12), and of the spectators when Zacharias recovered his speech (Luke 1.65). It is used of the shepherds when they heard the song of the angels (Luke 2.9). It is used of the guards at the tomb when the angel rolled the stone away (Matt. 28.4), and of the women as they went home after seeing the empty tomb (Matt. 28.8). It is used of the feelings of men in the midst of the shattering events of the last days (Luke 21.26).

In Acts it is used of the feeling in men's minds when they saw the signs and wonders and felt the power in the early Church (Acts 3.43). It is used of the reaction of the people after the death of Ananias and Sapphira (Acts 5.5, 11). It is used of the discomfited heathen exorcists at Ephesus (Acts 19.17). The Church is said to walk in the *phobos*, the 'fear', of the Lord (Acts 9.31).

In not one case in the Synoptic Gospels or Acts is *phobos* used in a bad sense. In every case it describes the feeling in a man's heart when he is confronted with the divine power in action. It always describes the feelings of a man when he finds himself in the presence of what Otto called 'the wholly other', when he finds himself face to face with something outside and beyond and different from himself, something which he cannot understand.

There is here the truth that there can be no religion without reverence. Between man and God there is 'intimacy' but not 'familiarity'. It describes the feeling of the man who is 'lost in wonder, love and praise'. It describes that awe which comes upon the creature in the presence of the Creator. In a famous sentence Swinburne wrote: 'Glory to man in the highest, for man is the master of things.' *Phobos* is the very opposite of that, for, in its highest sense, *phobos* is the essential reverence of man in the presence of God.

In the rest of the NT the word *phobos* is a much more complicated word. It can have both a good and a bad sense. Let us start with the good sense.

(i) In many cases the word 'fear' translates *phobos* in the AV where the meaning is rather 'reverence' than 'fear'. We have already seen that in Acts 9.31 it is said the Churches were 'walking in the fear of the Lord', that is, the Christians were living reverent lives. It is Paul's condemnation of the heathen world that there is no 'fear of God' before their eyes (Rom. 3.18). Reverence, respect for God, was entirely lacking. Peter talks about passing the time of your sojourning here 'in fear' (I Pet. 1.17). A man must be ready to give a reason for his hope in meekness and 'fear' (I Pet. 3.15). In this sense *phobos* describes the feeling of the man who is living in the shadow of eternity, who is always conscious of God, who never forgets that he will give account for the things he does.

(ii) This *phobos*, this 'reverence', this 'awareness' of God, is the source of certain great things. It is the source of 'the chaste life' (I Pet. 3.2). This awareness of God necessarily exercises an antiseptic influence on life.

(iii) This *phobos* is the source of 'holiness' (II Cor. 7.1). Because God is holy, God's man must be holy too. There must be a difference in the Christian life and that difference finds its motive power and mainspring in the sense of God.

(iv) This *phobos* is connected with the 'godly sorrow' that brings repentance (II Cor. 7.11). Repentance must have as one of its roots the feeling of inadequacy, of failure, of unworthiness in the presence of the holy perfection of God. That feeling produces in the first instance *phobos*, the sense of abasement of the creature in the presence of the Creator.

(v) This *phobos* is the source of Christian effort (Phil. 2.12). The Christian must work out his own salvation with *phobos*, 'fear', and trembling. The sense of the judgment which he faces, the sense of the goal which he may miss, the sense of the crucial importance of life and living, the sense of the necessity of in some way seeking to deserve the love of Christ, all combine to fill the Christian with an awed wonder and a trembling eagerness, and a passionate effort.

(vi) This *phobos* is the basis of the 'mutual respect' and 'mutual service' which Christians are bound to render to each other (Eph. 5.21). All Christians live in the presence of God. All must be conscious, not only of their own salvation, but also of the brother for whom Christ died. Christians, because of their common reverence for God, also reverence each other.

(vii) This *phobos* can be 'the motive power of persuasion' (II Cor. 5.11). It is because he knows the *phobos* of God that Paul seeks to persuade the Corinthians. It is altogether wrong completely to excise the threat from the Christian message. Christianity always comes to men with a promise and an offer, but any promise can be disbelieved and any offer can be refused, and there is a necessary consequence of refusal and disbelief.

(viii) The Pastoral Epistles have one rather special instance of *phobos*. Christian discipline is to be publicly exercised that others may see it and 'fear' (I Tim. 5.20). It is an interesting thought that Christian discipline is to be exercised not only for the sake of the man who has sinned, but also as a means of warning the man who has not sinned to abide in the right way.

It can easily be seen that NT thought traces many of the greatest things to this *phobos*, this 'reverence', this constant 'awareness' of the presence of God.

We may now turn to the other side of *phobos*, the side in which *phobos* is an evil thing.

(i) Before we turn to the really bad side of *phobos* we must look at two things which are not bad in themselves, but which could become bad. *Phobos* describes the 'natural shrinking' from some difficult task. So Paul uses *phobos* of his own feelings regarding the unhappy situation in the church at Corinth (I Cor. 2.3; II Cor. 7.5). Such a *phobos* is natural and inevitable. The more sensitive a man is the more acutely it will come to him. In itself it is nothing to be ashamed of, but it becomes a bad thing if it stops a man doing what he knows he ought to do and facing what he knows he ought to face.

(ii) *Phobos* is used of the feeling of 'respect' a man should have in the presence of human authority. The Corinthians received Titus with *phobos* (II Cor. 7.15). The NT repeatedly enjoins that those who are in positions of authority in the State and the Church must receive the *phobos* which is their due (Rom. 13.7; Eph. 6.5; I Pet. 2.18). But it is to be noted that this respect must never become subservience. Caesar must always receive his things, and God must always receive his.

(iii) And now we come to the definitely bad side of *phobos*. There is a *phobos* which is characteristically the bad man's emotion (Rom. 13.3). In the face of authority the upright man has nothing to fear. *Phobos* is the child of evil-doing.

(iv) There is the *phobos*, the 'fear', of dying (Heb. 2.15). An American journalist set high in the list of his personal rules for life, 'Never to allow myself to think of death.' It was Dr Johnson who declared that the fear of death was so naturally ingrained into man that life was one long effort to keep it at bay. That is a *phobos* from which the Christian hope must deliver a man. The Christian cannot be haunted by the fear of death.

(v) *Phobos* and legalism go hand in hand. Legalism reduces a man to being a slave instead of a son, and the characteristic feeling of the slave is *phobos*, 'fear' (Rom. 8.15). It was Paul's belief that a religion dominated by law cannot issue in anything else but fear. But the Christian holds a faith dominated by grace, in which he is a son of love and not a slave of law.

(vi) The cure for *phobos*, 'fear', is love (I John 4.16, 18). Perfect love ejects fear from life. Fear, said John, has torment (I John 4.18). Fear has to do with punishment, but Christianity teaches us to think not so much of the vengeance as of the love of God, not so much of the punishment as of the forgiveness of God.

When we put that saying of Paul and that saying of John together we get a very interesting and suggestive thought. Together they go to prove that fear is the sign of an inadequate religion. When fear becomes the motive power of religion it means that a man is thinking of religion in terms of law and of God in terms of vengeance. In Christianity there is both law and judgment, but when they become so dominant that they oust grace and love from a man's thoughts they issue in an inadequate religion.

(vii) *Phobos*, 'fear', is the cowardice which prevents a man from bearing the Christian witness he ought to bear. This is a characteristic usage of the Fourth Gospel. Fear of the Jews kept men from confessing their faith in Jesus (John 7.13). It made Joseph of Arimathaea remain a secret disciple (John 19.38). It kept the disciples terrified and behind locked doors after the crucifixion (John 20.19). It is that which may prevent a man in time of trouble from showing whose he is and whom he serves (I Pet. 3.14). *Phobos* destroys the essential heroism of the Christian faith.

In the NT *phobos* is one of the great words. There can be no religion at all without the awe of the creature in the presence of the Creator. The feeling of reverence, the awareness of God, is at once the prophylactic against sin, the dynamic of the Christian life, and the mainspring of Christian effort. But when reverence turns to fear in the lower sense of the term then religion becomes a stunted and inadequate thing, which, because it has lost its grace, has lost its glory.

PLEONEXIA

THE SIN OF GREED

Pleonexia is a sin which the NT again and again most un-
sparingly condemns. The word occurs in Mark 7.22; Luke
12.15; Rom. 1.29; II Cor. 9.5; Eph. 4.19; 5.3; Col. 3.5; I
Thess. 2.5; II Pet. 2.3, 14. The regular AV translation is
'covetousness'. Once, in Eph. 4.19, the AV translates it
'greediness'. The RSV retains 'covetousness' in most passages but translates 'greedy practice' in Eph. 4.5 and
'greed' in the II Peter passages. Moffatt varies more. He
retains 'covetousness' in Luke 12.15, but his regular translation is 'lust', which he uses in seven of the passages.
Once, in I Thess. 2.5, he uses 'self-seeking'.

Pleonexia in all ages of Greek is an ugly word, and
always it has a certain basic idea behind it which none of
the translations wholly bring out, because it cannot be
brought out in any one word. In classical Greek it means
'an arrogant greediness', the spirit which tries to take
advantage of its fellow-men. The corresponding verb,
pleonektein, means 'to defraud' or 'overreach'. Polybius,
the Greek historian, has one suggestive use of the word.
The Stoics had a phrase by which they described 'that
which is fitting'—*ta kathēkonta*—by which they meant
that kind of conduct which a good man ought to produce.
Polybius says that the man who is guilty of this covetous
conduct uses methods which are not fitting for a man to
use. *Pleonexia* was a word which was much in the vocabulary of the ordinary people and it is common in the
papyri. There it is connected with conduct which is 'quite
shameless', with 'overreaching ambition', with 'violence',
with 'injustice', with the 'cupidity' for which a man in
his better moments will be sorry, with the 'rapacity' of a
dishonest official who is out to fleece the district of which
he is in charge. By the Latin moralists it is defined as *amor*

sceleratus habendi, 'the accursed love of possessing'. Theodoret, the early commentator, describes it as 'the aiming always at getting more, the snatching at things which it does not befit a man to have'. Cicero defined *avaritia*, which is the Latin equivalent, as *injuriosa appetitio alienorum*, 'the unlawful desire for things which belong to others'.

Now let us see if we can classify the NT usages so that we may arrive at the basic quality of this sin.

(i) In Rom. 1.29 *pleonexia* is the sin of the godless world. It is the sin of the world, of the society, of the man who has turned his back upon the laws of God. It is the very opposite of the generosity of the love of God and of the charity of the Christian life.

(ii) In Luke 12.15 it is the sin of the man who evaluates life in material terms, who thinks that the value of life lies in the number of things that a man possesses, the man whose one desire is to get and who never even thinks of giving.

(iii) In I Thess. 2.5 and in II Pet. 2.3 it describes the sin of the man who uses his position to take advantage of, 'to make merchandise of' the people he ought to serve, the man who sees his fellow-men as creatures to be exploited and not as sons of God to be served.

(iv) In Col. 3.5 it is identified with idolatry. *Pleonexia* is the worship of things instead of God. A threepenny-piece is a little thing, yet if it is held before the eye it will blot out the vastness of the sun. When a man has *pleonexia* in his heart he loses sight of God in a mad desire to get.

(v) In passage after passage it is connected with sexual sin (Mark 7.22; Rom. 1.29; Eph. 4.19; 5.3; II Pet. 2.14). Here is the very essence of the word. The essence is not the sexual sin. The essence is the desire to have what is forbidden, the desire to take what should not be taken, the giving of rein to appetites and desires which are against the laws of God and man.

Lightfoot (on Rom. 1.29) defines *pleonexia* as 'the disposition which is ever ready to sacrifice one's neighbour to oneself in all things, not in money dealings merely'. *Pleonexia* is the sin of the man who has allowed full play to the desire to have what he should not have, who thinks that his desires and appetites and lusts are the most important thing in the world, who sees others as things to be exploited, who has no god except himself and his desires.

POIKILOS

THE MANY-COLOURED WORD

THE word *poikilos* is not in itself one of the great NT words. For the most part its usage in the NT requires no comment; but *poikilos* is worth studying for one single NT occurrence of it.

In secular Greek *poikilos* basically means *many-coloured*. It is frequently so used of natural objects. A leopard skin is said to be *poikilos*, many-coloured. A snake is said to be *poikilos*; the word describes the iridescent quality of the snake's skin. The plumage of birds is said to be *poikilos*; the word describes the many-coloured sheen of the feathers. Red granite stone is said to be *poikilos*; the word describes the many-coloured glint of the granite as the light strikes upon it.

Poikilos goes on to describe, not only natural objects, but things made and manufactured by the hands of men. It means *wrought in various colours, cunningly made*. So, in describing cloth, it is the opposite of self-coloured. It describes a many-coloured carpet; it describes a richly embroidered robe of many colours. It describes the cunningly-wrought metal work of an elaborately embossed shield.

Poikilos goes a step further. It describes anything which is *intricate* or *complex*. So it can describe an elaborately compounded medicine, or a complex and complicated law.

From this it goes on to describe a person who is subtle, artful, wily, resourceful to meet any occasion or any emergency.

In this sense it can even descend to a rather bad meaning, and it can describe a person who is too clever and too subtle, a person full of tricks and stratagems to further his own ends and to get his own way.

It can be seen that in secular Greek *poikilos* is a vivid and a many-coloured word.

As we have said, in the NT the great majority of the cases where it occurs have no particular interest. It is the word which the AV commonly translates *divers*. Jesus healed those who were sick of *divers*, *poikilos*, diseases (Matt. 4.24; Mark 1.34; Luke 4.40). The Pastoral Epistles speak of silly women, led away with *divers*, *poikilos*, lusts (II Tim. 3.6); and of the *divers* lusts and pleasures characteristic of the heathen life (Titus 3.3).

The writer to the Hebrews speaks of *divers* miracles of God (Heb. 2.4); and of *divers* and strange doctrines (Heb. 13.9). James speaks of *divers* temptations (James 1.2); and Peter uses the same phrase, but the AV in his case translates it *manifold* temptations (I Peter 1.6).

But there is one occasion on which Peter, with a touch of sheer genius, uses this word *poikilos* to describe *the grace of God*. The AV translates it the *manifold* grace of God (I Peter 4.10). When we remember what *poikilos* means, this is a tremendous thought.

(i) *Poikilos* means *many-coloured*; therefore to speak of the grace of God as *poikilos* means that there is no colour in the human situation which the grace of God cannot match. It matters not whether a man is living in the gold of the sunshine of joy or success, or in the sombre black of sorrow and pain, there is that in the grace of God which can match his situation. No possible situation can arise in life which the grace of God cannot match and answer. The grace of God is a many-coloured thing with that in it which can match and meet every possible situation in life.

(ii) *Poikilos* means *artful, clever, resourceful*; therefore to speak of the grace of God as *poikilos* means that no possible problem can arise to which the grace of God cannot supply the solution; no possible task can be laid upon us which the grace of God cannot find a way to do. There is no possible set of circumstances, no possible crisis, emergency or demand through which the grace of God cannot find a way, and which the grace of God cannot triumphantly deal with and overcome. There is nothing in life with which the grace of God cannot cope.

This vivid word *poikilos* leads our thoughts straight to that many-coloured grace of God which is indeed sufficient for all things.

PŌROUN AND PŌRŌSIS

THE HARDENING OF THE HEART

Pōroun is the verb and *pōrōsis* is the noun which are used in the NT to express the idea of what the AV calls 'the hardening of the hearts of men'. These words are interesting, not only for their history, but also for a most suggestive shift of meaning which they undergo.

At the back of both of them there is the word *pōros*. *Pōros* is used in a variety of senses. Basically it means a kind of stone, which Theophrastus in his work on stones describes as a stone like Parian marble in colour and in texture but lighter. Aristotle used the word for a stalactite, one of these solidified drippings of water in a cavern. In the papyri the word is used of the kind of stone that is used to pack the foundation course of a building. Medically the words have certain technical uses. *Pōros* means the chalk stone that forms in the joints and paralyses action. It also means a stone in the bladder; and *pōrōsis* means the process by which a callus forms at the joining of the break when fractured bones unite. *Pōrōsis* does not mean a callus on the skin, as, for instance, a callus formed on the hand by digging; the Greek for that is *tulē*, which is not a NT word. *Pōrōsis* is the much harder and much more irremovable bone callus that forms when a fracture unites. In all these cases it is easy to see that the basic meaning of the word is an impenetrable hardness, a hardness like bone or even marble.

The words then acquire two different sets of meanings. (i) They are used in connexion with something which has 'lost all power of sensation'. Athenaeus has a queer story of Dionysius of Heracles. He became overfat from over-eating. He became subject to fits of coma. His surgeons could only arouse him by pricking him with long needles. And even then certain parts of his body had lost all power of feeling because the fat had lost its sense of feeling. It had become *pepōrōmenē*, which is the perfect participle passive of the verb *pōroun*. The words have now become definitely connected with 'loss of feeling'. (ii) The words become connected with the idea of 'blindness' and 'inability to see'. The word *pōroun* is the only one of the group which occurs in the Septuagint, and it only occurs once, in Job 17.7 where the AV has it: 'Mine eyes *have grown dim* by reason of sorrow.'

So then we may say that at the back of them this group of words has three ideas—the idea of 'hardness', the idea of 'lack of the power to feel', and the idea of 'blindness', lack of the power to see. With this background in our minds we turn to the NT.

Pōroun and *pōrōsis* together occur eight times in the NT.

(i) They describe the mental condition of a man 'who cannot see the lesson that events are designed to teach him'. In Mark 6.52 the disciples were bewildered when Jesus came to them walking on the water because they did not see the meaning of the miracle of the loaves and fishes, because their hearts were 'hardened' (*pepōrōmenē*). When they were crossing the lake, they were worried about the fact that they had forgotten to bring bread with them. This episode in Mark follows the feeding of the four thousand; and Jesus asked them why they were so worried about having no bread. 'Have you your hearts yet hardened?' He asks (*pepōrōmenē*) (Mark 8.17). The word here describes the blind insensitiveness which will not learn a lesson. We sometimes say that things make no 'impression' on a person. Now there were certain Greek thinkers who believed that things did literally make an 'impression' on the mind. It was as if words and sights and ideas impinged on the soft, wax-like substance of the mind, and literally left an 'impression'. But clearly if the mind becomes hardened there can be no such thing as an 'impression' on it. Here the word describes unteachability. It describes the man who is so wrapped up in his own little world that nothing from any other world can touch him, the man whose mind is shut to all ideas but his own, the man who is impervious to the lessons that events are designed to teach him.

(ii) They describe the mental condition of the man 'who has made himself incapable of seeing the meaning of God's word for him'. Paul says of the Jews that their minds are 'blinded' when they hear the word of God read to them (II Cor. 3.14). A man can lose any faculty if he will not use it. Darwin lamented the fact that he had lost the power to appreciate music and poetry, because he had given all his time to biology. He said that if he had life to live over again he would keep that faculty of appreciation alive. If a man erects his ideas into supreme authority for long enough he will in the end be incapable of receiving the ideas of God.

(iii) They describe 'the attitude of the Jews' to God. In spite of the miracles they did not believe in Jesus because God had blinded their eyes and 'hardened' their hearts (John 12.40). These are the words that Paul twice uses to describe what had been happening to Israel throughout all her history (Rom. 11.7, 25). They describe the man who stubbornly takes his own way, who is deaf to the appeal of

God, because he has been busy making God in his own image. They describe the man who thinks he knows better than God.

(iv) The immoralities of the Gentile world are due to the fact that their understandings were darkened because of the *pōrōsis* of their hearts (Eph. 4.18). The idea is that they have so long stifled conscience that conscience has ceased to function. Conscience has petrified. It is so calloused that it has no sensitiveness left.

(v) When Jesus was about to heal the man with the withered hand in the Synagogue and when he saw the bleak looks of the orthodox because the deed was going to be done on a Sabbath he was grieved at the 'hardness' (*pōrōsis*) of their hearts (Mark 3.5). There are two things there. (*a*) They had so long identified religion with rules and regulations that they could not recognize real religion when they saw it. (*b*) They had so legalized religion that they had forgotten human sympathy. Because they had so long taken their way and not God's way they were completely insensitive alike to the appeal of God and the appeal of human need.

Whenever a man sets his own ideas in the place that God should take, whenever he stubbornly goes his own way, he is on the way to a condition in which his heart is petrified, in which his heart and his conscience have become insensitive and when his eyes are blind.

PRAUS AND PRAOTĒS

CHRISTIAN GENTLENESS

THE word *praus* is the word which is used in the Beatitude which says, Blessed are the *meek* (Matt. 5.5). This adjective occurs three other times in the NT. Twice it is used of Jesus himself (Matt. 11.29; 21.5). The other occasion is in I Pet.

3.4. The noun *praotēs* is the word which is used for 'meekness' in Paul's account of the fruit of the Spirit (Gal. 5.23). Its other occurrences are I Cor. 4.21; II Cor. 10.1; Gal. 6.1; Eph. 4.2; Col. 3.12; II Tim. 2.25; Tit. 3.2; James 1.21; 3.13; I Pet. 3.15. The AV without exception translates the adjective by 'meek' and the noun by 'meekness'. Moffatt has 'humble' in the Beatitude; 'modesty' in the James passages; and 'gentle' or 'gentleness' in all the others. He never retains the translation 'meek'. The American RSV has 'humble' once, in Matt. 21.5; 'meek' or 'meekness' five times, included among which is the Beatitude; and 'gentle' or 'gentleness' in the remaining passages.

In classical Greek this is a lovely word. Of things it means 'gentle'. It is used, for instance, of a gentle breeze or a gentle voice. Of persons it means 'mild' or 'gracious'. Menander has a fragment in which he says, 'How sweet is a father who is *mild* and young in heart.' It would be true to say that in classical Greek it is a word with a caress in it. Indeed Xenophon uses the neuter plural of the adjective in the sense of caresses. It is characteristically a kindly and a gracious word.

Aristotle discussed it. For Aristotle every virtue consisted in the mean which lies between the two extremes. He defined *praotēs* as the mean between *orgilotēs* and *aorgēsia*, that is to say, the mean between excessive anger and excessive angerlessness. He said that it was the secret of equanimity and composure. We might put it this way—the man who is *praus* is the man who is always angry at the right time and never angry at the wrong time.

That brings us to the use of *praus* which really illumines the whole matter. In Greek *praus* is used in one special sense. It is used—as is *mitis* in Latin—for a beast which has been tamed. A horse which was once wild but which has become obedient to the bit and to the bridle is *praus*.

Now herein lies the secret of the meaning of *praus*. There is gentleness in *praus* but behind the gentleness there is the strength of steel, for the supreme characteristic of the man who is *praus* is that he is the man who is under perfect control. It is not a spineless gentleness, a sentimental fondness, a passive quietism. It is a strength under control. Num. 12.3 tells us that Moses was the 'meekest' man upon the earth, but that same Moses was a man who could act with decision and blaze with anger when the occasion arose.

To such a character no man can attain by himself and his own efforts. *Praotēs* is strength under control, but it would be wrong to say that the man who is *praus* is perfectly *self*-controlled. He is perfectly *God*-controlled, for only God can give him that perfect mastery. It should be our prayer that God will make us *praus*, masters of ourselves, for only then can we be the servants of others.

PROSAGEIN AND PROSAGŌGĒ

THE WORD OF INTRODUCTION

THE verb *prosagein* means 'to bring to', and the noun *prosagōgē* means 'a way of entrance, access' or 'introduction'. Together they are used eight times in the NT, and of these eight times four have reference to the work of Jesus for men. On four occasions the word *prosagein* is used in a quite ordinary way. In Matt. 18.24 it is used of 'bringing' the debtor into the presence of the master. In Luke 9.41 it is the word that Jesus uses when he commands the epileptic boy to be 'brought' to him. In Acts 16.20 it is used of 'bringing' Paul and Silas into the presence of the magistrates at Philippi. In Acts 27.27 it is used of land 'drawing near' during the storm. *Prosagein* is used once of the special work of Jesus. In I Pet. 3.18 it is said that Christ died that he might 'bring' us to God. *Prosagōgē* is always used in the NT of the work of Jesus. In Eph. 2.18 it is said that through him we both, Jew and Gentile, have 'access' to the Father. In Eph. 3.12 it is said that in Jesus we have boldness and 'access' to God with confidence. And in Rom. 5.2 it is said that through Jesus we have 'access' by faith into this grace in which we stand.

The great interest of these words, when they are used of the work of Jesus, comes from the many pictures which lie behind them.

(i) *Prosagein* is used in the Septuagint of bringing sacrificial victims to God (Lev. 3.12; 4.4; 8.14). It is the word which is used of bringing to God something which is especially dedicated to his use and his service.

(ii) *Prosagein* is used in the Septuagint for bringing chosen men into the presence of God that they may be ordained as priests for his worship and his service (Ex. 29.4).

(iii) In the heathen world in the time of the NT many people found their way closer to God in the Mystery Religions than through any other of the pagan faiths. The Mystery Religions were like passion plays which the worshipper was only allowed to see after a long period of preparation. After this period he became an initiate. When he did become an initiate, he was brought into the presence of the sacred mysteries by a person called the *mustagōgos*, and the technical word for 'bringing him in' is *prosagein*. The word describes the bringing of someone into the presence of something specially sacred and holy.

(iv) In secular Greek *prosagein* is regularly used of 'introducing' a speaker into the presence of the *dēmos*, the assembly of the people, or into the *boulē*, the senate or council. It is regularly used of 'introducing' ambassadors to the assembly of the people when they came to seek terms; and it is regularly used of 'bringing a person into' a court of justice and before a judge. *Prosagein* is then the word which is used of introducing a person into the presence of some higher authority.

(v) But *prosagein* has a very special usage. It is specially used of 'introducing a person into the presence of a king'.

Xenophon tells how prisoners in chains were 'brought into the presence' of Cyrus the king (Xenophon, *Cyropædia* 3.2.12). He tells how Cyrus expected anyone who wanted anything from him to get into favour with his friends and, through them, to ask for a *prosagōgē*, 'an introduction to the royal presence' (*Cyropædia* 7.5.45). He tells how Sacas, the cup-bearer, had the office of 'introducing' (*prosagein*) to Astyages those who had business with him, and of keeping out those whom he thought it not expedient to admit (*Cyropædia* 1.3.8). There was, in fact, an official at the Persian court called the *prosagōgeus*, the introducer, whose function it was to introduce people into the royal presence.

Every single use of the words lights up the work that Jesus does for men. Jesus is the person who introduces us into the royal presence of God. With him alone we can enter into that presence without fear, he is God's introducer. When he introduces us to that presence he introduces us to the supreme authority for our lives; he introduces us into the presence of the holiest and the most sacred of all; he introduces us that, through him, we may dedicate our lives as a sacrifice to the service of God. Can we think of Jesus better than as the one who 'introduces' us into the presence of God that we may receive God's grace and give to God our willing service?

There remains one special use of *prosagōgē* at which we must look. In Rom. 5.2 we read that through Jesus we have 'access', *prosagōgē*, into the grace in which we stand. Now *prosagōgē*, when it means 'access' or 'introduction', is always used of introduction to 'persons', therefore this use is slightly different. In Hellenistic Greek *prosagōgē* is used of 'a place for ships to put in'. Plutarch speaks of a general who drew up his troops on terrain in front of the sea where there was no *prosagōgē*, no place for ships to put in (*Aemilius* 13). In Sophocles (*Philoctetes* 236) we find the phrase, 'What need made you put in (*prosagein*) to Lemnos?' The likelihood is that in this Romans passage *prosagōgē* is used in this sense, and that the phrase means, 'Jesus opened to us a way into the haven of God's grace.' The idea is that we are storm-tossed by sin and sorrow and trouble and temptation, and Jesus offers us the way into the harbour, the haven, the shelter of God's grace. We are like storm-tossed mariners who would make shipwreck of life unless Jesus took over the piloting of the ship of life and steered it out of the storm into the safe haven of the grace of God.

PROSLAMBANESTHAI

THE WORD OF WELCOME

Proslambanesthai is a verb which means 'to lay hold on, or to take to oneself'. In the NT it occurs eleven times. In Matt. 16.22 and Mark 8.32 it is used of Peter 'laying hold' of Jesus when Jesus first foretold his coming death. In Acts 27.33 it is used of 'taking food'. In Acts 17.5 it is used of the Thessalonian Jews 'laying hold of', or 'enlisting the help of' the corner-boys of Thessalonica to cause a riot against Paul and his company. In Acts 28.2 it is used of the people of Malta 'receiving' Paul and the ship's company when they were shipwrecked. These usages are perfectly straightforward. It is the remaining instances which are of special interest.

In Acts 18.26 *proslambanesthai* is used of Aquila and Priscilla 'taking Apollos to themselves' in order to explain the Christian way more fully to him. In Rom. 14.1 Paul uses it of 'receiving' into the fellowship of the Church the brother who is weak in the faith; and in Rom. 14.3 Paul says that God has 'received' us. In Rom. 15.7 Paul uses it when he says that all Christians ought 'to receive' one another. And in Philem. 17 he uses it when he urges Philemon 'to receive' the runaway slave Onesimus as he would have received Paul himself. From these usages we see that *proslambanesthai* is an almost technical word for 'receiving someone into the Christian Church and fellowship and faith'.

Let us see the flavour of the word so that we can perhaps understand a little more fully what that Christian reception ought to mean.

(i) In the Septuagint *proslambanesthai* is often used of the way in which God receives his people. In Ps. 27.10 the Psalmist says that when his father and mother abandon him the Lord 'will take him up'. In Ps. 65.4 the Psalmist sings of the happiness of the man whom God chooses and 'takes to himself'. In I Sam. 12.22 it is used when Samuel says that the Lord has graciously 'taken Israel to himself' for a people. Here, then, is the first thing this word tells us. When we receive others we should receive them as God receives them. The same word is used for God's reception of his people and the Christian's reception of his fellow-man. In our welcome to others there must be all the generosity, the forgiveness, the sheer kindness of God.

(ii) In classical Greek it is used widely and regularly of 'taking someone to oneself as a helper'. It is used by Xenophon of a leader who receives as his helpers a new force of cavalry and infantry. He uses it of a leader who brings cities into alliance with himself either with or against their will. It is particularly used with three Greek words. It is used with *summachos*, which means 'an ally', with *sunergos*, which means a 'fellow-labourer', and with *koinōnos*, which means 'a partner in a business'. When we receive someone into the Church and the Christian fellowship we receive him as 'an ally' and a 'helper'. That means two things. (*a*) For us, it means that we must never receive anyone into the Christian fellowship without an honest attempt to see how his gifts may best be used for the good of the fellowship. The Church is full of people with gifts which have never been used. (*b*) For the person received, it means that he must enter the Christian fellowship, not with a view to resting back and doing nothing, but with a view to bringing all his strength and talents to bear on the Christian campaign. The Church is equally full of people who have gifts and will not place them at the disposal of the Church.

(iii) In papyrus Greek *proslambanesthai* has two specially significant usages. (*a*) It is used of 'welcoming a person into one's house and home'. When a person is received into the fellowship of the Church, he does not enter as a stranger into the midst of strangers; he enters as a member of a family into a family. Introductions are needless; there ought to be no strangeness to be bridged. The Church is a family, not a band of strangers who do not know each other. (*b*) In late Greek *proslambanesthai* is the technical term for 'enrolling a soldier into the army'. It is the word for receiving the enlisted man into the unit in which he is to serve. When a man enters the fellowship of the Church, he enlists in the army of Christ; he becomes a soldier of Christ.

The word *proslambanesthai*, the word of welcome and reception into the Christian Church, tells those who are inside the Church that they must welcome others as God welcomes them, that they must welcome them into the family of the Christian fellowship; and it tells those who enter that they must enter as allies and helpers, and as enlisted soldiers for the campaign of Christ.

PTŌCHOS

THE TRUE POVERTY

THIS word *ptōchos* is translated 'poor' in the AV of the Bible. That is a perfectly correct translation; but there is a wealth of meaning behind it. When Jesus read the lesson in the Synagogue at Nazareth, he chose the passage which said that the Spirit of the Lord was on the Servant of the Lord to preach the gospel to the 'poor' (Luke 4.18). When Jesus, as it were, stated his credentials to John's disciples, who had come asking if he really was the Anointed One, his answering statement culminates in the words, The 'poor' have the gospel preached to them (Matt. 11.5). The Beatitudes begin with the saying: 'Blessed are the poor in spirit' (Matt. 5.3). In all these cases it is the word *ptōchos* which is used.

In Greek there are two words for 'poor'. There is the word *penēs*, which simply describes the man for whom life and living is a struggle, the man who is the reverse of the man who lives in affluence. There is this word *ptōchos*. This word comes from the verb *ptōssein*, which means to cower or crouch; and it describes not simply honest poverty, and the struggle of the labouring man to make ends meet; it describes abject poverty, which has literally nothing and which is in imminent danger of real starvation. First, then, let us note that *ptōchos* does not describe genteel poverty but real, acute destitution.

But behind this Greek word *ptōchos*, there lie two Hebrew words, the words *ebion* and *ani*. Both these words have a most interesting and significant development of meaning. Their meaning has three stages. (i) They mean simply 'poor', in the sense of lacking in this world's goods (Deut. 15.4; 15.11). (ii) They go on to mean, because poor, therefore 'downtrodden and oppressed' (Amos 2.6; 8.4). (iii) It is then that they take their great leap in meaning. If a man is poor and downtrodden and oppressed, he has no influence on earth, no power, no prestige. He cannot look to men for help and when all the help and resources of earth are closed to him, he can only look to God. And, therefore, these words come to describe people who, because they have nothing on earth, have come to put their complete and total trust in God (Amos 5.12; Ps. 10.2, 12, 17; 12.5; 14.6; 68.10).

We are now in a position to come at the real meaning of the Beatitude, 'Blessed are the poor in spirit'. (i) It means: blessed is the man who has an utter sense of his own abject destitution in the sight of God, the man who feels not simply unsatisfactory, but who can only say, God be merciful to me, a sinner. (ii) But equally it means: blessed is the man who feels this sense of destitution and who has then put his utter and complete trust in God. So then the Beatitude means: blessed is the man who is conscious of a desperate need and who is utterly certain that in God, and in God alone, that need can be supplied. In the NT the 'poor' are those who realize their own abject helplessness and the wealth of the riches of the grace of God.

SEMNOS AND SEMNOTĒS

THE MAJESTY OF THE CHRISTIAN LIFE

THE adjective *semnos* and the noun *semnotēs* are characteristic words of the Pastoral Epistles. Only once does *semnos* occur outside the Pastoral Epistles. It is used in Phil. 4.8 in the phrase 'whatsoever things are *honest*'.

In the Pastoral Epistles *semnos* occurs three times. The deacons must be *grave* (I Tim. 3.8); the women, or perhaps it should be translated their wives, should have the same quality (I Tim. 3.11). The aged women must live *as becometh holiness* (Titus 2.3).

The noun *semnotēs* also occurs three times in the Pastoral Epistles. Prayer is to be made for kings and those in authority that we may live a quiet and peaceable life in all godliness and in all *honesty* (I Tim. 2.2). *Semnotēs*, *gravity*, is the quality which should be the outstanding quality of a good father (I Tim. 3.4), and of a good teacher (Titus 2.7).

Clearly this quality of *gravity* and *dignity* was meant to be the characteristic of the Christian life.

These words have a most notable background and atmosphere in secular Greek. It may truly be said that there are no more majestic words in the whole Greek language. Let us study their usage in ordinary Greek that we may see just what they demand of the Christian, and that we may understand the quality in which the Christian life is to be clothed.

(i) The word *semnos* is particularly connected with the gods. It means *revered, august, holy*. Apollo is called by Aeschylus *the august commander* (*The Seven against Thebes* 800). Poseidon is called *awful Poseidon* by Sophocles (*Oedipus Coloneus* 55).

The sacrifices of the gods are *holy* sacrifices (Pindar, *Olymp.* 7.42); the temple of Apollo is a *holy* house (Pindar, *Nem.* 1.72). In every case the word used is *semnos*, for *semnos* is a word with the majesty of divinity in it.

(ii) But there were certain gods of whom this word was specially used. It was specially used of the Erinyes, the Furies whose duty and task it was to avenge sin. So much so was this the case that these Furies were actually called the *semnai* (the feminine plural of the adjective). There were three of these grim goddesses, Allecto, 'she who never rests', Tisiphone, 'the avenger of murder', and Megaera, 'the jealous one', and once a man had sinned they were on his heels, and neither in this world or the next did they let him go. 'They are the avengers of every transgression of natural order, and especially of offences which touch the foundation of human society. They punish, without mercy, all violations of filial duty, or the claims of kinship, or the rites of hospitality; murder, perjury and like offences. . . . The punishment begins on earth and is continued after death.' The Erinyes, the Furies, the *semnai* were nothing less than the custodians of divine justice. There is much about them in Greek tragedy. Sophocles calls them '*majestic* swift-footed hounds of vengeance' (*Ajax* 837).

Euripides says of them: 'They are the *dread ones*; wise art thou to name them not.' The most terrible description of the *semnai* is in Aeschylus' play, *The Eumenides*. *Eumenides* means *The Gracious Ones*, and the Greeks called the Erinyes, the Furies, by that name in order to please them and to avert their wrath. There the chorus of the avengers says: 'No wrath from us creeps up on him who has clean hands, but unharmed he passes the age of his life; but whosoever sins, as this man has done, and seeks to hide the hands in murder dipped, to him we appear, true witnesses to the dead, come as the avengers of blood, avengers who cannot fail in their task' (Aeschylus, *The Eumenides* 313-320).

There is all the majesty of the divine in this word *semnos*, and it is the word which describes the characteristic quality of the Christian.

But these words have still other and illuminating uses.

(i) They are words which have to do with *royalty* and with *kingliness*. Herodotus tells how the Egyptians disapproved of the lax and drunken conduct of their king, and how they said: 'We would have you sit aloft upon a throne *of pride*' (Herodotus, 2.173). Euripides speaks of a '*proud* despot' (*The Suppliant Women* 384). Plato uses *semnos* to describe the 'most *important* and influential men in our cities' (Plato, *Phædrus* 257d).

Aristophanes in his skit *The Ecclesiazusæ*, in which the women take over the government and wipe out social distinctions, says, as Rogers translates it into English verse:

'By the side of the beauty so *stately and grand*
The dwarf, the deformed and the ugly shall stand.'

Xenophon uses the word *semnotēs* to describe the *magnificence* of the appearance of Cyrus, the Persian king, as he drove forth in state. *Semnos* and *semnotēs* have in them all the majesty of kingship and of royalty.

(ii) They are words which are very commonly used to

express that which is *stately* and *dignified* in language and in expression. Aristotle says that the metre of poetry which was called the heroic metre is *semnos, dignified* (Aristotle, *Rhetoric* 1408b 35).

Plato speaks of *stately* and wonderful tragic poetry (Plato, *Gorgias* 502b). Pindar speaks of untruths which are dressed in great language, and says, 'His falsehoods through winged artifice wear a flower of *dignity*' (Pindar, *Nem.* 7.22).

Herodotus speaks of using *high* language in the presence of a king (Herodotus, 7.6).

When Aristotle is discussing literary style, he writes: 'The merit of diction is to be clear without being commonplace. The clearest diction is that made up of ordinary words, but it is commonplace. . . . That which employs unfamiliar words is *dignified, semnos* and outside the common usage' (Aristotle, *Poetics* 1458a 21). Once again we come to this idea of solemnity and of dignity and of gravity and of weight.

(iii) Still another use of *semnos* and *semnotēs* is that they occur very frequently on sepulchral inscriptions. They are favourite words used in describing and paying tribute to those who have lived well and nobly and who are gone to their rest. Here then is still another great series of meanings which these words possess. Here is another atmosphere in which they moved.

They are used to express all the majesty of royalty and of kingship.

They are used to express all the weight and the dignity and the solemnity of speech at its highest and its best and its most moving. They are used to express all that is lovely and all that demands respect in life. No greater tribute can be paid to one who has passed on than to say he was *semnos* and lived with *semnotēs*, that on his life there was the royal dignity and the kingly majesty of goodness.

Aristotle, the greatest of the Greek ethical writers, and one of the great ethical teachers of all time, has much to say about the man who is *semnos* and the quality of *semnotēs*.

In the *Nicomachean Ethics* he talks of 'the great-souled man'. He says that it is characteristic of such a man 'never to ask help from others, or only with reluctance, but to render aid willingly; and to be haughty towards men of position and fortune, but courteous towards those of moderate station, because it is difficult and *distinguished* (*semnos*) to be superior to the great, but easy to outdo the lowly, and *to adopt a high manner* (*semnunesthai*, the verb from *semnos*) with the former is not ill-bred, but it is vulgar to lord it over humble people' (*Nicomachean Ethics* 1124b 21). The man who is *semnos* knows the time for dignity.

Aristotle says that if a man's desires are weak and not evil in any event, there is nothing *to be proud of* (*semnos*) in resisting them (*ibid.* 1146a 15).

Aristotle had a habit of defining every virtue as the mean, the happy medium, between two extremes. On the one hand there is an extreme of excess of a quality, on the other hand there is the extreme of defect of a quality, and in the middle there is the happy medium. So Aristotle defines that which is *semnos* as the mean between *areskeia* and *authadia*. *Areskeia* is the characteristic of the man who is so eager to please that he is like a fawning dog; *authadia* is the characteristic of the man who thinks so little of pleasing that he is like an ill-mannered boor. *Semnos* is the word which describes the man who carries himself towards other men with a combination of dignified independence and kindly consideration. He is the man who, as Aristotle said, is 'kindly and lovely in his gravity' (Aristotle, *Rhetoric* 1391a 28). He said that the man who was *semnos* was the man who was dignified without being heavily pompous.

When Plutarch was describing the great commander Nicias, he said of him that the '*dignity* (*semnotēs*) of Nicias was not of the harsh and offensive sort, but was blended

with much circumspection' (Plutarch, *Nicias* 2). In this
dignified gravity there was no arrogance; it was dignity and
courtesy combined.

It is easy to see what a great quality this word *semnos*
describes. It describes the divinity of the gods; it describes
the Furies, the Erinyes who are the agents of divine justice;
it describes the royalty of all true kingliness; it describes
that which is stately and dignified in words and speech and
conduct; it describes the characteristic of the man who
carries himself with the perfect blend of dignity and
courtesy, independence and humility to his fellow men.

R. C. Trench says that the man who is *semnos* 'has a
grace and dignity not lent to him from earth, but which he
owes to that higher citizenship which is also his'. The Latin
word for this *dignity* is *gravitas*, and Tertullian writes: '*Ubi
metus in Deum, ibi gravitas honesta,*' 'Where there is fear
towards God, there is honourable dignity' (Tertullian, *De
Praescriptione* 43).

Clement of Alexandria summed it up when he said that a
Christian man is *semnos* because his life is turned to the
divine (Clement of Alexandria, *Stromateis* 7.35.6). This
Christian kingliness and majesty and dignity come to a
man when his face is turned to God, for then the reflection of God shines in him.

It is of the greatest significance that the Pastoral Epistles
make so much of the majesty of the Christian life. They
were written in the missionary days of the early Church.
They were written when the Church was a little island of
Christianity surrounded by a pagan world. At such a time
it was not sermons but lives which won men for Christ.
And men were won for Christ by the sight of the sheer
majesty of the Christian life. So often the Christian life is
beset by pettiness. So often the professing Christian allows
little and petty things to disturb his own serenity and the
peace of the brethren. We should do well to think of this
essential majesty of the Christian life, and seek for more
of it in our own lives.

There is a famous incident from the greatest days of Roman history. Pyrrhus had sent Kineas as his ambassador to Rome, and Kineas had been received by the Roman senate; he returned to Pyrrhus and told him that he had seen and talked with 'an assembly of kings'.

To him the Roman senate seemed nothing less than an assembly of kings. That is what the Christian Church should be like. The Christian should be *semnos*; he should ever display in his life the majesty of Christian living.

SKANDALON AND SKANDALIZEIN

THE STUMBLING-BLOCK IN THE WAY

Skandalon is the word which the AV regularly translates 'stumbling-block' or 'offence', and *skandalizein* is the corresponding verb. The interest of this word lies in the fact that it has, not one, but two pictures behind it, and to differentiate between the two will often give us a much more vivid picture.

The word *skandalon* is not a classical Greek word at all. It is late Greek and is, in fact, much commoner in the Septuagint and in the NT than anywhere else. The classical equivalent is *skandalēthron*, which means 'the bait-stick in a trap'. The *skandalēthron* was the arm or stick on which the bait was fixed. The animal for which the trap was set was lured by the bait to touch or step on the stick; the stick touched off a spring; and so the animal was enticed to its capture or destruction. In classical Greek the word is used by Aristophanes for 'verbal traps' set to lure a person in an argument into defeat. It is therefore clear that the original flavour of the word was not so much 'a stumbling-block' to trip someone up as an 'enticement' to lure someone to destruction.

When we turn to the Septuagint we find that this distinction is still quite clear. The Greek word *skandalon* is used to translate two Hebrew words. (*a*) It is used to translate the word *michsol*, which quite definitely does mean a 'stumbling-block'. It is so in Lev. 19.14, 'Thou shalt not put a stumbling-block before the blind.' It is so used in Ps. 119.165, 'Great peace have they which love thy law; and nothing shall offend them.' That is to say, 'Nothing shall trip them up.' (*b*) It is used to translate the word *mokesh*, which definitely means 'a trap' or 'a snare'. So in Josh. 23.13 alliances with foreign nations are said to be 'snares' and 'traps'. In Ps. 140.5 the Psalmist says that the proud have hid a 'snare' for him, and cords; they have spread a 'net' by the wayside; they have set 'gins' for him. In Ps. 141.9 the Psalmist prays: 'Keep me from the snares which they have laid for me, and the gins of the workers of iniquity.' In Ps. 69.22 the Psalmist says: 'Let their table become a snare before them; and that which should have been for their welfare, let it become a trap.' The idea is that success and prosperity can become a snare instead of a blessing. In the Septuagint, then, the word *skandalon* has two ideas behind it. It means either a 'stumbling-block', something set in a man's path to trip him up, or 'a snare', 'a bait', 'a lure' to entice him astray and so to ruin him.

When we turn to the NT we find that the translators of the AV always took *skandalon* in the sense of 'stumbling-block', but when we go to the NT passages with the idea of the double meaning of *skandalon* in our minds, we find that in certain passages the other meaning gives a more vivid picture.

(i) There are some passages where either meaning is perfectly suitable. In Matt. 13.41 it is said that the Son of Man will remove all *skandala* from his Kingdom. When the Kingdom comes all the things which are calculated to make a man sin, all the things which could trip him up, all the things which would entice him and seduce him into the wrong way will be taken away. The Kingdom will be a state of things in which temptation will lose its power.

(ii) There are some passages where the meaning of 'stumbling-block' is more fitting, or where it is even essential. In Rom. 14.13 we are forbidden to put a 'stumbling-block' or 'occasion to fall' in our brother's way. The word that is used for 'occasion to fall' is *proskomma*, which means 'a barrier', 'a hindrance', 'a road-block'. It is the word that would be used for a tree that has been felled and laid across a road to block it. We must never do or allow anything which would be a road-block on the way to goodness. In Matt. 13.21 the shallow hearer of the word is said to be 'offended' (*skandalizein*) by persecution. Persecution is a stumbling-block that stops him on the Christian way. The Pharisees are 'offended' by Jesus and his words (Matt. 15.12). Jesus forecasts that all his disciples will be 'offended' because of him (Matt. 26.31). The false teachers put a 'stumbling-block' in the way of others (Rev. 2.14). The Jews find the cross of Christ 'a stumbling-block' and 'an offence' (I Cor. 1.23; Gal. 5.11). In all these cases, the words mean something which stops a man's progress, something which trips him up, something which bars the way to him. That something may come from the malicious action of others, or it may come from the prejudice and the pride of a man's own heart.

(iii) But there are certain cases where it gives a far better picture to take *skandalon* and *skandalizein* in the sense of a 'trap', a 'snare', a 'bait', an 'allurement', an 'enticement to sin'. Rom. 16.17 warns against those who cause divisions and 'offences' contrary to the doctrine which Christ's people have received. That is a warning against those who would 'lure' us from the way of true belief. I John 2.10 says: 'He that loveth his brother abideth in the light, and there is no *skandalon* in him.' That is to say, 'He would never entice and seduce anyone into sin.' Matt. 18.6 talks about the sin of 'offending' one of these little ones, and the next verse talks about the terribleness of 'offences'. It gives a much better picture to take *skandalon* and *skandalizein* there in the sense of luring and enticing the younger and the more impressionable people to sin. Matt. 5.29, 30 speak of the necessity of cutting off and plucking out the hand and the eye which 'offend' us. Clearly it is better there to take *skandalon* in the sense of 'that which lays a trap or snare to entice us into the ruin of sin'. If the desires of the hand and the eye are a bait to sin they must be eradicated.

When Burns went to learn flax-dressing in Irvine he met an older man who led him far astray. He said of him afterwards: 'His friendship did me a mischief.' That is precisely the meaning of *skandalon*. A *skandalon* is that which trips us up or that which lures us into sin. From our own lives such things must be rooted out; and God will not hold us guiltless if we bring such things into the lives of others.

SOPHIA, PHRONĒSIS, SUNESIS

THE MIND EQUIPPED

THE Greeks had three great words describing three great qualities of the mind; and if a man possessed these three qualities he had a mind equipped. The NT writers took over these three great words, for they were sure that the qualities which they describe were to be found in Jesus and in Jesus alone.

The first of these words is *sophia*. *Sophia* is generally translated *wisdom*; but the wisdom it describes is *the wisdom of ultimate things*. The Greek writings have many a great definition of *sophia*. The commonest definition is that *sophia* is 'the knowledge of things both human and divine and of their causes' (Clement of Alexandria, *Stromateis* 1.30.1).

Aristotle defined *sophia* as 'the most perfect of the modes of knowledge, not only of conclusions but also of first principles'. He said that *sophia* was 'consummated knowledge of the most exalted subjects' (Aristotle, *Nicomachean Ethics* 1141a 20).

Augustine said that *sophia* 'pertains to the knowledge of eternal things' (Augustine, *De Div. Quaest.* 2.2). Cicero said that *sophia*—which he translates *sapientia*—'is knowledge of things both human and divine' (Cicero, *Tusculan Disputations* 4.26) and he said that it was 'the chief of all the virtues' (Cicero, *De Officiis* 1.43). *Sophia* is that ultimate knowledge which is nothing else than the knowledge of God. *Sophia* is the furthest reach of the human mind.

It is to be noted that, although *sophia* can be perverted into a bad thing, *sophia* itself is always noble and always implies goodness. Plato said: 'All *wisdom* (*sophia*) which is divorced from justice and the rest of virtue is craftiness and not wisdom' (Plato, *Menex.* 19). Xenophon quotes Socrates as saying: 'Justice and every other form of virtue is *wisdom, sophia*' (Xenophon, *Memorabilia* 3.9.5). To the Greek *sophia, wisdom,* and goodness and nobility go hand in hand. The one cannot exist without the other.

The second of the three great words is *phronēsis*, which is usually translated *prudence*. The basic difference between *sophia* and *phronēsis* is that *sophia* is *theoretical,* and *phronēsis* is *practical; sophia* has to do with a man's mind and thought; *phronēsis* has to do with his life and conduct and action.

Aristotle defined *phronēsis* as 'truth . . . concerned with action in relation to the things that are good for human beings' (Aristotle, *Nicomachean Ethics* 1140b 20). He defined it as 'a virtue of mind by which men can come to wise decisions about the things which are called good and bad in relation to happiness' (Aristotle, *Rhetoric* 1366b 20).

Plutarch says that 'that virtue which considers what ought to be done and what ought not to be done is called *phronēsis*' (Plutarch, *De Virt. Mor.* 440 f.; he is really quoting a philosopher called Aristo). Plato defined it as 'that disposition of mind whereby we judge what is to be done and what is not to be done' (Plato, *Definitions* 4.11).

Cicero defined *phronēsis*—he translates it by the word *prudentia*—as 'knowledge of what things are to be sought and what things are to be avoided'. Philo defined *phronēsis* as 'the correct mean between craftiness and folly' (Philo, *De Proem. et Poen.* 14).

Phronēsis is an extremely practical virtue. A writer in one of the papyri speaks of '*phronēsis, prudence*, which increases a man's belongings'. There is a pessimistic papyrus poem which says: 'Whosoever thinks to prosper through *phronēsis, prudence*, his hopes are vain. For all things in this life happen not through, *phronēsis, prudence*, but through *tuchē, chance.*'

Very often the classical writers contrast and compare *sophia* and *phronēsis*. Philo says that *sophia* has got to do with the service of God; *phronēsis* has got to do with the arrangement of human life (*De Proem. et Poen.* 14).

Aristotle says that *sophia* has to do with the unchangeable things, whereas *phronēsis* has to do with changeable things, with what is expedient in any given set of circumstances (Aristotle, *Magn. Mor.* 1197a 34). Panaetius, the Stoic, said that *sophia* is the knowledge of things human and divine, but *phronēsis* is the knowledge of things good and evil and of things which are neither good nor evil (Diogenes Laertius, 7.92).

The third of the great Greek words of the mind is *sunesis*. *Sunesis* literally means a *uniting*, a *union*, a *bringing together*; and it would be true to say that *sunesis* is the *faculty of putting two and two together*. Aristotle said that *sunesis* was concerned only with judgment (Aristotle, *Nicomachean Ethics* 1143a 10). Demosthenes said that *sunesis* was a kind of conclusion, 'that by which fair and base things are distinguished'. When Thucydides is describing how the chances of war can be assessed he says that '*knowledge, sunesis*, fortifies courage' (Thucydides, 2.62). That is, an intelligent assessment of the situation gives ground and strength to courage. When he is talking of a barbarian nation, he admits their courage and their strength, but, he says, 'they are not on a level with other races in *general intelligence, sunesis,* and the arts of civilized life' (Thucydides. 2.97). They do not possess the developed faculty of judgment which civilized peoples possess. Aristotle says that children develop *sunesis.* 'Parents love their children as soon as they are born,' he says, 'but children only love their parents when time has elapsed and when they have acquired *understanding, sunesis,* or at least perception' (Aristotle, *Nicomachean Ethics* 1161b 26).

From all this we see that in its essence *sunesis* is critical. It is the power of distinguishing between different courses of action, different values of things, different relationships between people. *Sunesis* is the ability to test and to distinguish and to criticize and to evaluate and to form judgments.

So then we see that the mind equipped has three kinds of wisdom; it has the wisdom which can see and understand the ultimate and the infinite things; it has the wisdom which can deal with the practical problems of daily life and living; it has the wisdom which can judge and test things and choose the right aim and the right course of action in any actual situation.

It is interesting and important to note that over and over again the Bible joins together the theoretical wisdom which is in *sophia* and the practical wisdom which is in *phronēsis* and *sunesis.* On the Bible view of life a man needs both. Solomon prays that he may receive *wisdom, sophia,* and *understanding, phronēsis,* a wise and understanding heart (I Kings 3.12; 4.29). In the version of the same story in Chronicles, David prays that God may give Solomon *wisdom, sophia,* and *intelligence, sunesis,* and that is Solomon's prayer for himself (I Chron. 22.12; II Chron. 1.10). The four wise children in the Daniel story have knowledge and skill and learning and wisdom (Dan. 1.17). *Wisdow, sophia,* and *understanding, phronēsis,* both summon men to listen to them (Prov. 8.1). To keep

God's commandments is the sign of *wisdom* and *understanding* (Deut. 4.6). Isaiah talks of the *wisdom* of the wise man, and the *understanding, sunesis,* of the prudent man (Isa. 29.14).

The great interest of this is that the really wise man has both theoretical and practical wisdom. Anatole France said of certain scholars that they have ink in their veins instead of blood and that they have never looked out of the window. It is quite true that the picture of the wise man is often the picture of a man locked in his study and buried in his books and lost in his research, a man quite out of touch with life, and indeed quite inefficient in the day-to-day conduct of life, the man who is epitomized in the absent-minded professor. Both the Greek and the biblical view of life would say that such a man is an incomplete man because though he may have *sophia* he certainly has neither *phronēsis* nor *sunesis.* On the other hand, the common picture of the practical man is that he is so busy with the practical concerns of life that he has neither the time nor the inclination to trouble himself with theology or philosophy or just plain thinking. Again that man is incomplete because he may have *phronēsis* and *sunesis,* but he has not got *sophia.*

The great vision of biblical thought is the vision of a complete man who is wise in the things of eternity and efficient in the things of time.

We must now turn to consider these words in the NT itself, and with them we will consider their corresponding adjectives. The adjective of *sophia, wisdom,* is *sophos, wise.* The adjective of *phronēsis, prudence,* is *phronimos, prudent.* The adjective of *sunesis, understanding,* is *sunetos, understanding.*

(i) Wisdom is the property of God (Rev. 5.12). Jesus speaks of the wisdom of God (Luke 11.49); Paul also speaks of the wisdom of God (Rom. 11.33), and the manifold wisdom of God (Eph. 3.10). To know God is the only true wisdom.

(ii) Wisdom is the characteristic of Jesus (Rev. 7.12). Jesus grew in wisdom when he was a lad in Nazareth (Luke 2.40, 52). When he preached in Nazareth, the people asked where he had acquired the wisdom which was so evident in his words (Matt. 13.54; cp. Mark 6.2). He himself is wisdom, the wisdom of God (I Cor. 1.24, 30). In him are all the treasures of wisdom (Col. 2.3). Jesus is wisdom because he came to bring us the knowledge of God, which is the only wisdom which matters.

(iii) Wisdom is the distinguishing feature of the men who were great. Solomon had wisdom (Matt. 12.42; cp. Luke 11.31). Joseph had wisdom which kept him in the right way and raised him to greatness in Egypt (Acts 7.10). Moses was trained in wisdom (Acts 7.22). The qualifications of the first office-bearers in the Church, the Seven, were that they must be men full of the Holy Ghost and of wisdom (Acts 6.3). Stephen had a wisdom with which he confounded the Jews in his debates with them (Acts 6.10). The prophets and the wise men are classed together (Matt. 23.34). It is when a man knows God that he is really wise.

(iv) Wisdom is the mark of the Christian. It was the promise of Jesus that he would give his followers wisdom with which they could confront their enemies and their persecutors (Luke 21.15). It is Paul's prayer that God would give his people wisdom and prudence (Eph. 1.8), that God would give them the spirit of wisdom (Eph. 1.17). Wisdom is the object of Paul's prayers and of his teaching (Col. 1.9; 1.28). The Christian walks in wisdom (Col. 4.5). The man who produces works to fit his faith is the man of wisdom (James 3.13). The Christian has that wisdom which gives him an answer to his opponents and a solution to his problems. The Christian is wise unto that which is good (Rom. 16.19).

(v) Wisdom is connected with prayer and with the Holy Spirit and with God. The Seven were to be men filled with the Holy Spirit and with wisdom (Acts 6.3). God gives it to the man who lacks it (James 1.5). The real wisdom is heavenly (James 3.15). And we have already seen that Paul prays that wisdom should be given to God's people (Eph. 1.17; Col. 1.9). The word of wisdom in preaching is the gift of the Spirit (I Cor. 12.8). The only wisdom which matters is not man's discovery; it is God's gift.

(vi) And yet, though that be so, wisdom can be taught, for it is Paul's endeavour to teach it (Col. 1.28). There is a development in wisdom, for Paul speaks wisdom among the mature Christians (I Cor. 2.6, 7). There is clearly growth in wisdom. Although wisdom is not the discovery of the mind, it cannot be obtained without the strenuous activity of the mind. Real wisdom comes when the Spirit of God reaches down to meet the searching mind of man, but the mind of man must search before God will come to meet it. Wisdom is not for the mentally lazy even although it is the gift of God.

(vii) Wisdom reads the true meaning of things (Rev. 13.18; 17.9). God's messages are there for the man who has eyes to see and mind to understand. In this it is blessedly true that the man who seeks will find.

But great as wisdom is, it can degenerate. Especially in I Corinthians Paul has a great deal to say about the wrong kind of wisdom.

(i) The degenerate wisdom is worldly wisdom, wisdom of this world (I Cor. 1.20; 2.6; 1.26; 3.18). It is the kind of wisdom which knows well how to get on in this world and how to amass the treasures of this world, but has no knowledge of the things that matter.

(ii) It is a wisdom of words. It is a wisdom of words which in the end do nothing but obscure the Cross (I Cor. 1.17). Paul refuses to preach with the enticing words of man's wisdom (I Cor. 2.1, 4, 5, 13). When Paul so strongly condemned the worldly wisdom of words, he was speaking out of the situation of the world of his day. The Greeks had always loved words; and one of the well-known figures of the Greek world was the Sophist. The Sophist was the

orator who was as famous as a film star. The Sophist had
two faults. He was much more concerned with how he said
a thing than with what he was saying. It was cleverness
of speech with which he was primarily concerned; and his
first aim was to provoke applause. His one desire was to
display himself. Dio Chrysostom said of the Sophists:
'They are all agape for the murmur of the crowd. . . . Like
men walking in the dark, they move always in the direction
of the clapping and the shouting.' (Dio Chrysostom,
Oration 33). One of them said to Epictetus: 'I want your
praise.' 'What do you mean by my praise?' asked Epictetus.
'I want you to say Bravo! and Wonderful!' said the
Sophist (Epictetus, *Discourses* 3.23.24). Epictetus describes
the scene as the professor went round after the lecture
was done. 'What did you think of me today?' 'Upon
my life I thought you were admirable.' 'What did you
think of my best passage?' 'What was that?' 'Where I
described Pan and the Nymphs.' 'Oh, it was excessively
well done' (Epictetus, *Discourses* 3.23.11). He describes
another scene. 'A much larger audience today, I think,'
says the professor. 'Yes, much larger.' 'Five hundred, I
should guess.' 'Oh, nonsense, it could not have been less
than a thousand.' 'Why, that is more than Dio ever had;
I wonder why it was: they appreciated what I said, too.'
'Beauty, sir, can move even a stone.'

Paul knew the preachers and the teachers who were more
concerned with epigrams than truth, whose one desire was
to display their own cleverness and to awaken the applause
of the crowd. He knew the preacher and the teacher who
was thinking more of what men were thinking of him than
what God was thinking of him.

He knew the preacher and the teacher who was more
concerned that men should look at him than that men
should look at Christ. That is what Paul meant by the
wisdom of this world. It is not yet completely dead.

(iii) Such wisdom did not really know God (I Cor. 1.21).
It was seductive far more than it was instructive (I Cor.

2.4, 5). It was man's wisdom, not God's wisdom (I Cor. 2.13). It was the wisdom of the clever debater who was more concerned with a display of mental acrobatics than with the search for the truth (I Cor. 1.20). It was vain in the sense that it helped nobody and achieved nothing (I Cor. 3.20). In the end it was doomed to destruction and to the condemnation of God and to the demonstration of the folly which it in reality was (I Cor. 1.19; 1.27; 3.19).

The only true wisdom is the outcome, not of pride, but of humility. The only wise teaching points not at itself, but beyond itself. Wisdom ceases when a man's sole desire is to be clever. Preaching degenerates whenever it seeks for applause. Whenever the personality and methods of the teacher and the preacher obscure Christ then there is no wisdom in it, and it degenerates into the foolishness which in the end will receive the conviction and the condemnation it deserves.

Now let us look at the companion words, *phronēsis* and *phronimos*, *sunesis* and *sunetos*.

Phronēsis, the noun, only occurs twice in the NT, in Luke 1.17 and Eph. 1.8. But *phronimos*, its corresponding adjective, occurs more frequently. *Phronēsis*, as we saw, is the practical wisdom which sees what must be done and what must not be done in any given situation. The builder who built his house on a rock was *phronimos* (Matt. 7.24). The disciple in face of the world must be *phronimos* as a serpent (Matt. 10.16). The wise steward who orders the household well is *phronimos* (Matt. 24.45; cp. Luke 12.42). The virgins who remembered the oil for their lamps are *phronimos* (Matt. 25.2, 4, 8, 9). When Paul is addressing the Corinthians, he says in appeal to their common sense: 'I speak as to wise men' (*phronimoi*) (I Cor. 10.15).

This practical wisdom can on occasion degenerate into conceit (Rom. 11.25; 12.16; I Cor. 4.10; II Cor. 11.19). A man can become too impressed with his own cleverness. In Barrie's novel, *Sentimental Tommy*, when Tommy had done something clever at school, he used to come home and say to Elspeth, his admiring sister: 'Am I no' a wonder?' This practical wisdom can be like that.

There are two passages which specially show the meaning of *phronimos*. The serpent who seduced Adam and Eve in the garden is called *phronimos* (Gen. 3.1); and the unjust steward who first swindled his master and then took steps to safeguard his own ease and comfort is called *phronimos* (Luke 16.8). *Phronēsis* is above all the ability to deal with a given situation; it is the ability to see what needs to be done and to do it; it is the practical wisdom of the man who is never at a loss.

Sunesis and *sunetos* are not very frequent in the NT. The scribe answered Jesus that men are to love God with all their hearts, and *understanding*, *sunesis*, and soul and strength. The Jewish Rabbis were amazed at Jesus' *sunesis* when he was with them in the Temple Court (Luke 2.47). Sergius Paulus, the Roman governor, is described as *sunetos* (Acts 13.7). In Eph. 3.4 *sunesis* describes Paul's understanding of God's secret. In Col. 1.9 Paul prays that his people may have *sophia* and *sunesis*; and in Col. 2.2 *sunesis* can bring assurance. It is Paul's prayer for the young Timothy that God will give him understanding, *sunesis*, in all things (II Tim. 2.7). It too can be a worldly and conceited thing and when it does become so it will be destroyed (I Cor. 1.19). Jesus says that the great things are hidden from the wise and the prudent (*sophoi* and *sunetoi*) and revealed to babes (Matt. 11.25; cp. Luke 10.21).

The essence of *sunesis* is the critical faculty which, as Lightfoot puts it 'sees the bearing of things'. Its essence is discrimination and wise judgment. It can see the implications of a thing and the ultimate end of a course of action. It sees a thing, not only as it is at the moment, but as it will be.

The Christian equipment of the mind is a many-sided thing. There is the wisdom, *sophia*, which sees the ultimate truths of God; there is the practical wisdom, *phronēsis*, which sees what ought to be done in any given situation;

there is the discriminating, critical wisdom, *sunesis*, which can assess and evaluate every course of action which presents itself. The Christian is not only the dreamer whose thoughts are long, long thoughts and who is detached from this world; the Christian is not only the man of affairs who never thinks of ultimate things; the Christian is not only the shrewd evaluator of any policy or any situation. The Christian is all three. He has not only the vision to know God; he has the practical knowledge to turn that vision into action, and the sound judgment to see what course of action will best achieve his aim. The Christian is the only man who is dreamer and man of action at one and the same time.

SŌTĒRIA AND SŌZEIN

THE WORD OF SALVATION

In the Old Testament

THE noun *sōtēria* means 'salvation' and the verb *sōzein* means 'to save', and surely it is of paramount importance that we should find out what salvation and being saved mean. In classical Greek *sōtēria* means 'deliverance' or 'preservation'. It can be used for a man's safe return to his own home or his own country after an absence and a journey. It can mean a 'guarantee of safety' or a 'security against danger'. In the papyri by far the commonest meaning of *sōtēria* is 'bodily health'. For instance, a member of the family writes home, 'Write me a letter about your *sōtēria*,' or, as we would say, 'Let me know how you are.'

But it is only natural that we should look for the beginning of the meaning of *sōtēria* in the Septuagint, the

Greek version of the OT scriptures, for it was on it that so many of the early Christians were nurtured. It was the Bible of the Church before ever the NT was written and it coloured the thoughts and the language of the early Church all the time.

(i) In the Septuagint *sōtēria* means at its simplest 'general safety and security'. In the multitude of counsellors there is *sōtēria*, says the proverb (Prov. 11. 14). It is Jacob's bargain that if he comes again to his home in *sōtēria* Yahweh would be his God (Gen. 28.21). It is Joseph's promise that every man in whose sack the cup is not found shall return home in *sōtēria* (Gen. 44.17; cp. Gen. 26.31; Job. 11.20; 13.16; 30.15).

(ii) In the Septuagint *sōtēria* means 'deliverance from trouble in general'. The mockers say to the Psalmist, 'There is no *sōtēria* for him in God' (Ps. 3.2). God is the *sōtēria* of the Psalmist's countenance (Ps. 42.11). He prays to God to command *sōtēria* (Ps. 44.4). The man who waits on God will rejoice in his *sōtēria* (Isa. 25.9; cp. Ps. 20.6; Isa. 38.20; Jer. 25.35).

(iii) In the Septuagint *sōtēria* specially means 'deliverance from an enemy'. In the AV it is represented by such words as 'salvation', 'help', 'escape', 'victory'. It describes deliverance from the Philistines (Judg. 15.18), from the Ammonites (I Sam. 11.9, 13), from Syria (II Kings 13.5), from Egypt (II Chron. 12.7), from Moab (II Chron. 20.17). It describes Israel's divine deliverance from her enemies through all her history.

(iv) In the Septuagint *sōtēria* specially describes 'Israel's deliverance at the Red Sea'. 'Stand still,' says Moses, 'and see the *sōtēria* of the Lord which he will show to you today' (Ex. 14.13). Every deliverance was a *sōtēria* of the Lord, but the deliverance at the Red Sea was the *sōtēria par excellence*. There above all God's hand was seen in all its splendour and its strength.

(v) Sometimes in the Septuagint this *sōtēria* is 'eschatological', that is to say, it will find its full flowering and glory only in the new age which is to come. It is not something which exhausts itself in this world. It will be mighty to save in any world that will ever be (Isa. 45.17; 52.10; Jer. 3.23).

(vi) Consistently this *sōtēria* is connected with and attributed to God. Contrasted with it 'vain is the help of man' (Ps. 60.11; 108.12; 146.3). It is God who is characteristically the God of *sōtēria*, the God of 'salvation' (Ps. 18.46; 38.22; 51.14; 88.1). When the power of man is helpless, the *sōtēria* of God steps in. Man's extremity is always God's opportunity.

(vii) Lastly, we may note that this word *sōtēria* has a way of appearing in the midst of triumphant lyrical passages of singing thanksgiving. It appears in the Song of Moses after the crossing of the Red Sea (Ex. 15.2), in the Song of David after his deliverance from Saul (II Sam. 22.3, 36, 47, 51), in the Song of Hannah when she knew she was to have a son (I Sam. 2.1). It makes the man who experiences it sing for very joy.

So, then, the NT writers when they used *sōtēria* entered into a rich heritage, for already it described the saving, preserving, providential power of God in the crises of history and the crises of the individual life, a care which does not stop with this world, and a care which makes the man who is wrapped round by it sing with joy.

In the New Testament

Two of the older uses are repeated in the NT.

(i) *Sōtēria* is used of 'deliverance from enemies' (Luke 1.69, 71; Acts 7.25; Jude 25). It is to be noted that all these passages have a characteristically OT background.

(ii) Both noun and verb are used of 'bodily health and safety' in the NT. They are used of Paul's preservation in shipwreck (Acts 27.20, 34) and of Noah's construction of the ark for the saving of himself and of his family (Heb. 11.7).

But, having noted these older usages, we must now come

to the distinctive and characteristic NT usages of these words.

(i) *Sōtēria* is 'the aim of God' and 'the purpose of Jesus Christ'. The NT knows nothing of an angry God who has to be pacified into forgiving men. It knows nothing of a God whose attitude to men has somehow to be changed from wrath to mercy. In the NT the whole initiative of *sōtēria* is with God. God has not appointed us to wrath but to obtain *sōtēria* (I Thess. 5.9). God has from the beginning chosen men to 'salvation' (II Thess. 2.13). God will have all men to be 'saved' (I Tim. 2.4). It is the long-suffering of God which makes *sōtēria* possible (II Pet. 3.15). So much so is *sōtēria* a prerogative of God that it is ascribed to him in the doxologies of the Revelation (Rev. 7.10; 19.1). It is God himself who has 'saved' us (II Tim. 1.9). Christ Jesus came into the world to 'save' sinners (I Tim. 1.15). He came not to condemn the world, but that through him the world might be 'saved' (John 3.17). The prime mover in *sōtēria* is God.

(ii) For this very reason *sōtēria* may be refused. It is something which has to be worked out with fear and trembling (Phil. 2.12). Great as it is, it can still be neglected (Heb. 2.3). The NT never forgets that the perilous free-will of man can frustrate the saving purpose of God.

(iii) The place of Jesus in God's *sōtēria* is central. In no one else is *sōtēria*, and there is no other name in heaven or earth by which men may be saved (Acts 4.12). He is the *archēgos*, the pioneer, the trail-blazer of *sōtēria* (Heb. 2.10). He is the *aitios*, the moving and essential cause of *sōtēria* (Heb. 5.9). Without himself and his work *sōtēria* is not possible.

(iv) None the less he needs his human agents. It is Paul's aim to do something to 'save' some of the Jews (Rom. 11.14). He is all things to all men that he may 'save' some (I Cor. 9.22). He exhorts the believing partner in marriage not to leave the unbelieving one for perhaps the believer may 'save' the unbeliever (I Cor. 7.16). Paul's whole desire in God's sight is to 'save' men (I Cor. 10.33). He blames the Jews for hindering him in this work (I Thess. 2.16). Timothy is to take heed to himself and his teaching that he may 'save' himself and others (I Tim. 4.16). The man who converts a sinner 'saves' a soul from death (James 5.20). Jesus Christ needs lips to speak for him, hands to work for him, men to be his heralds.

(v) For this very reason the Christian message is certain things.

(a) The Christian message is 'the word of salvation' (Acts 13.26; Eph. 1.13). It is the good news of God's good will to men.

(b) The Christian message is 'the way of salvation' (Acts 16.17). It shows a man the path that leads to life and not to death.

(c) The Christian message is 'the power of salvation' (Rom. 1.16). It brings a man not only a task but also the strength to do it, not only a way but also the power to walk it, not only an offer but also the power to grasp it.

(d) The 'aim' of the Christian message is salvation (Rom. 10.1; II Cor. 6.1). The aim of the Christian message is not to hold a man over the flames of hell but to lift him up to the life of heaven.

We must now look at what we might call the NT elements of *sōtēria*, the things which bring 'salvation'.

(i) *Sōtēria* involves 'repentance'. A godly sorrow produces a repentance that works towards salvation (II Cor. 7.10). *Sōtēria* is something which has to be worked out with 'fear and trembling' (Phil. 2.12).

(ii) *Sōtēria* involves 'faith' (Eph. 2.8; II Tim. 3.15; I Pet. 1.9). It involves taking God at his word and casting oneself in utter trust on the offered mercy of God. It involves 'belief' (Rom. 1.16), the conviction that the promises of God in Christ are true, the willingness to stake one's life on the veracity of Jesus Christ. It involves 'hope' (Rom. 8.24). The repentance, the fear and trembling are not meant to move a man to despair but to move him to seek in radiant hope the remedy in Jesus Christ. Faith, hope and belief are all closely interlinked. They are all different expressions of the trust on which *sōtēria* is founded.

(iii) *Sōtēria* involves 'endurance'. It is he who endures to the end who will find *sōtēria* (Matt. 10.22; 24.13). The man who is daunted neither by opposition from without nor discouragement from within will in the end find salvation. He must be defeated neither by his own doubts nor by the arguments and seductions of others. His trust is something to which he must cling as to a life-belt in an overwhelming sea.

(iv) *Sōtēria* involves 'the love of truth' (II Thess. 2.10). It is something that the man who does not love the truth can never find. If a man shuts his eyes to the truth about himself he cannot be moved to the essential repentance. If he shuts his eyes to the truth about Jesus Christ he can never realize the finality of God's offer. And it is always true that there are none so blind as those who will not see.

(v) *Sōtēria* sometimes involves 'fear' (Jude 23). There is such a thing as a cleansing fear (Ps. 19.9). The fear of the Lord is the beginning of knowledge (Prov. 1.7). There is what someone has called 'the celestial shudder', the sudden spasm of fear at what we are, which drives us to find the hope of what in Christ we may be.

(vi) *Sōtēria* always involves 'grace'. It is founded on grace. By grace we are saved (Eph. 2.5). It was the conviction of the early Church that it was by the grace of the Lord Jesus Christ that they were saved (Acts 15.11). The sorrow of repentance, the shudder of fear, is met by the grace of the Lord Jesus Christ, and the very word is the final proof that *sōtēria* is a gift which we have not earned and could not earn but which comes to us from the sheer goodness and generosity of God.

(vii) *Sōtēria* involves 'the message of the cross' even if that message seems at first hearing foolishness (I Cor. 1.18), and it involves the fact that we must never forget that message, that it must remain printed for ever on our memories (I Cor. 15.2). It involves the sight of the cross and the constant memory of the cross, the realization of the love of God and a life lived in that realization.

(viii) The writer to the Hebrews alone has one further thing to say. He would say that *sōtēria* involves 'the continued work of Christ'. It is his vision that Christ ever liveth to make intercession for us (Heb. 7.25). With one of the greatest reaches of thought in the NT he still sees Christ pleading for men, carrying on his high priestly work, and still opening the way to God for men, the vision of a Christ who loved us from the first of time and who will love us to the last, and whose continued love is our eternal hope of *sōtēria*.

In many cases in the NT *sōtēria* occurs as it were without explanation and without qualification. It is used as a word of whose meaning everyone would understand at least something. Such passages are Luke 19.9; Acts 11.14; 16.30; I Cor. 3.15; II Cor. 2.15).

But if we are to get the full value and the full meaning out of this word, we must ask the question: What is a man saved from? What is the deliverance which *sōtēria* promises? Before we begin to examine the NT for this purpose we must note one thing. The verb *sōzein* means both to save a man in the eternal sense, and to heal a man in the physical sense. Salvation in the NT is 'total salvation'. It saves a man, body and soul.

(i) *Sōtēria* is salvation from 'physical illness' (Matt. 9.21; Luke 8.36, in both of which cases the verb is *sōzein*). Jesus was concerned with men's bodies as well as with men's souls. It is significant that the Church is rediscovering that today. Such salvation may not cure, but it always enables the sufferer to transmute the suffering into glory.

(ii) *Sōtēria* is salvation from danger. When the disciples were in peril they cried out to be 'saved' (Matt. 8.25; 14.30). This does not mean protection from all peril and from all harm, but it does mean that the man who knows that he is within the *sōtēria* of God knows, as Rupert Brooke had it, that he is 'safe when all safety's lost'. It is the conviction that nothing in life or in death can separate him from the love of God.

(iii) *Sōtēria* is salvation from 'life's infection'. A man is saved from a crooked and perverse generation (Acts 2.40). The man who knows the *sōtēria* of God has within him and upon him a prophylactic quality, a divine antiseptic which enables him to walk in the world and yet to keep his garments unspotted from the world.

(iv) *Sōtēria* is salvation from 'lostness'. It was to seek and to save the lost that Jesus came (Matt. 18.11; Luke 19.10). It was to rescue a man when he was on the way to a situation in which he would lose his life and lose his soul. It was to turn him from the way that led to the most deadly kind of death to the way that led to the most vital kind of life.

(v) *Sōtēria* is salvation from 'sin'. Jesus was called Jesus because he was to save his people from their sins (Matt. 1.21). By himself man is the slave of sin. He cannot liberate himself from it. He can diagnose his situation easily enough, but he cannot cure his disease. The saving power of Christ alone can do that. 'He breaks the power of cancelled sin. He sets sin's prisoner free.'

(vi) *Sōtēria* is salvation from 'wrath' (Rom. 5.9). The NT cannot be emptied of the conception of judgment. That conception is fundamental to it. Jesus Christ did something, God did something, which freed men from the wrath of injured holiness and transgressed justice. In Jesus Christ something happened which put a man into a new relationship with God.

(vii) One last thing we may note. *Sōtēria* is eschatological. That is to say, we can begin to enjoy it here and now, but its full impact and its full wonder will only come to us in the day when Jesus Christ is enthroned King of all the world (Rom. 13.11; I Cor. 5.5; II Tim. 4.18; Heb. 9.28; I Pet. 1.5; Rev. 12.10). It is quite true that the Second Coming of Christ is not a popular doctrine. But it does conserve the tremendous truth that this world is going some-where, and when the world reaches its final consummation so will *sōtēria* be finally perfected.

Sōtēria is that which saves a man from all that would ruin his soul in this life and in the life to come.

SPLAGCHNIZESTHAI

THE DIVINE COMPASSION

THERE are some words which bear within themselves the evidence of a kind of revolution in the realm of thought: and *splagchnizesthai* is such a word. It means *to be moved with compassion*. It is not a classical word, but it does contain a classical way of thought. *Splagchnizesthai* is the verb which comes from the noun *splagchna*, which means what are known as the nobler viscera, that is, the heart, the lungs, the liver and the intestines. The Greeks held these to be the seat of the emotions, especially of anger, of anxiety, of fear, and even of love. When Hercules is expressing his complaint to Admetus, he says: 'Unto a friend behoveth speech outspoken, Admetus, not to hide within the *splag-chna* (the breast, as we would say in English) murmurs unvoiced' (Euripides, *Alcestis* 1008-1010). When the Chorus are listening to Electra's lamentation, they say: 'My *splagchna* are overcast with gloom at thy speech' (Aeschylus, *Choephori* 413). So then in classical Greek the *splag-chna* mean the inner parts of man, which are the seat of the deepest emotions. It is from that idea that the verb *splag-chnizesthai* was formed in later Greek. It means *to be moved with compassion*, and, from its very derivation, it can be seen that it describes no ordinary pity or compas-sion, but an emotion which moves a man to the very depths of his being. It is the strongest word in Greek for the feel-ing of compassion.

In the NT the word never occurs outside the Synoptic Gospels; and except for three occurrences in the parables it is always used of Jesus. In the parables it is used of the master who had *compassion* on the servant who was unable to pay his debt (Matt. 18.33); of the *compassion* which made the father welcome home the prodigal son (Luke 15.20); and of the *compassion* which made the Samaritan go to the help of the wounded traveller on the Jericho road (Luke 10.33). In all other cases it is used of Jesus himself.

Jesus was *moved with compassion* when he saw the crowd like sheep without a shepherd (Matt. 9.36; cp. Mark 6.34). He was *moved with compassion* when he saw their hunger and their need when they had followed him out to the desert place (Matt. 14.14; 15.32; Mark 8.2). It is used of Jesus' *compassion* on the leper (Mark 1.41; it is possible that another reading should be preferred in this passage); of his *compassion* on the two blind men (Matt. 20.34); of his *compassion* on the widow at Nain who was going to bury her only son (Luke 7.13); and the appeal of the man with the epileptic son is that Jesus should have *compassion* on him (Mark 9.22).

There are two interesting things about the use of this word. First, it shows us the things in the human situation which moved the heart of Jesus.

(i) Jesus was moved by the *spiritual lostness of the crowd*. They were as sheep without a shepherd. He was not annoyed with their foolishness; he was not angry at their shiftlessness; he was sorry for them. He saw them as a harvest waiting to be gathered for God (Matt. 9.37, 38). The Pharisees said: 'The man who does not know the law is accursed.' They were able to say: 'There is joy in heaven over one sinner who is destroyed.' But in face of man's lostness, even when that lostness was his own fault, Jesus felt nothing but pity. He did not see man as a criminal to be condemned; he saw man as a lost wanderer to be found and brought home. He did not see men as chaff to be burned; he saw them as a harvest to be reaped for God.

(ii) Jesus was moved by the *hunger and the pain of men*. The sight of a crowd of hungry, tired people, the appeal of a blind or a leprous man, moved him to compassion. He never regarded people as a nuisance, but always as people whom he must help. Eusebius (*Ecclesiastical History* 10.4.11) writes of Jesus in words which are either an unconscious or a deliberate quotation from Hippocrates, the founder of Greek medicine. 'He was like some excellent physician, who, in order to cure the sick, examines what is repulsive, handles sores, and reaps pain himself from the sufferings of others.' Jesus never regarded the sufferer with indifference, still less with loathing and disgust. He regarded the sufferer and the needy with a pity which issued in help.

(iii) Jesus was moved by the *sorrow of others*. When he met the funeral procession of the son of the widow of Nain, he was moved by the pathos of the human situation. He was not detached and he was not indifferent; the sorrow of the widow was his own sorrow. In *Sentimental Tommy* Barrie wrote of his hero, who is himself: 'The most conspicuous of his traits was the faculty of stepping into other people's shoes and remaining in them until he became someone else.' The greatness of Jesus was his willingness to enter into the human situation. and to be moved by its poignancy to that compassion which compelled him to help and to heal.

But this word *splagchnizesthai* has a far greater significance than simply the indication that Jesus was moved to the depths of his being by the human situation. The notable thing about this word is that to a Greek its use about anyone who was divine would seem completely and utterly and totally incredible.

According to the Stoics, and they were the highest thinkers of the age, the supreme and essential characteristic of God is *apatheia*. By *apatheia* they did not mean *apathy*. in the sense of indifference. They meant *incapability of feeling*. They argued in this way. If a man can feel either sorrow or joy, it means that someone else can bring sorrow or joy to him. That is to say, it means that someone else can affect him. Now, if someone else can affect him, can alter his feelings, can make him happy or sad, it means that that person has power over him, and is therefore, for the moment at least, greater than he. If God could feel sorrow or joy at anything that happens to man, it would mean that man can affect God, that man has that much power over God; but it is impossible that anyone should have any power over God, for no one can be greater than God; therefore God can have no feeling, he must be essentially without feeling; he must be, in the technical sense of the word, by nature *apathetic*. The Greeks believed in a God who could not feel. To them a divine being who was moved with compassion was incredible.

When Apuleius was writing about the god of Socrates, he said that, according to Plato's thought, 'never God and man can meet. A stone will hear me more easily than Jupiter.' He goes on to say that he does not think so much that the gods are separate and different from us, but that it is quite impossible that our prayers should reach them. 'Not from the care of human affairs, but from contact have I removed them' (*De Deo Socr*. 6.132). If God is God, then he is such that he is essentially incapable of hearing any prayer, or feeling any pity.

When Plutarch was thinking about God, he held that God was quite above having any contact whatsoever with the universe. Any contact of the universe with the divine came through intermediaries, who were the daemons. He said: 'He who involves God in human needs does not spare his majesty, nor does he maintain the dignity and greatness of God's excellence' (Plutarch, *De Def. Orac*. 9, 414 f). As Plutarch saw it, it was impossible for God to be God and to be in the least involved in or affected by human affairs. Once again, to such a thinker it would be beyond belief that God could be moved with compassion.

But the Christian point of view stresses this very pity of

God. God, said Clement of Alexandria, is 'rich in pity'. God is indeed—it is a wonderful picture—all ear and all eye (Clement of Alexandria, *Stromateis* 2.74.4; 7.37.6). He says of the Logos, the Word of God, that though he was essentially and eternally free from passion, 'for our sake he took upon himself our flesh with its capacity for suffering' and 'descended to sensation' (*Stromateis* 5.40.3). To Clement the very essence of the Christian idea of God was that God voluntarily chose to feel for and with men.

The grim thing about pagan ethics was that the Stoics taught that man should seek to make himself like God, and not to care. If a man wanted peace, they argued, he should banish all feeling, all emotion from his mind. Epictetus writes of how we should teach and train ourselves not to care when we lose something. 'This should be our study from morning to night, beginning from the least and frailest things, from an earthen vessel, from a glass. Afterwards, proceed to a suit of clothes, a dog, a horse, an estate; from thence to your self, body, parts of the body, children, wife, brothers' (Epictetus, *Discourses* 4.1.13). Lose anything, see your nearest and dearest die, and say: 'It doesn't matter; I don't care.'

Pagan religious thought believed in a God whose essence was that he was incapable of feeling pity; pagan ethics taught that the aim of life was a life from which all pity and all compassion were totally and finally banished. The idea of a God who could be moved with compassion, and of a life whose motive force was pitying love, must have come to such a world literally like a new revelation.

We think it a commonplace that God is love, and that the Christian life is love. We would do well to remember that we would never have known that without the revelation of Jesus Christ, of whom it is so often and so amazingly said that he was moved with compassion.

XENOS, PAREPIDĒMOS AND
PAROIKOS

THE CHRISTIAN AND THE WORLD

THERE is a group of NT words which have come to be epitomes of the Christian attitude to the world. They all describe a person who is a pilgrim, a sojourner, a stranger and not a permanent resident in a place.

The first of these words is the word *xenos*. In classical Greek *xenos* means a 'stranger' or a 'foreigner'; it is contrasted with *politēs*, a 'citizen' of the country, with *epichōrios*, an 'inhabitant' of the land, and with *endēmos*, a 'native' of the country. It can even mean a 'wanderer' and a 'refugee'.

In the NT it is used of the 'stranger' in the parable to whom help was or was not given (Matt. 25.35, 38, 43, 44). The field which was bought with the blood-money which Judas Iscariot flung back to the priests is to be a burying-ground for 'strangers' (Matt. 27.7). The Athenians were interested in Paul because he preached 'strange' gods (Acts 17.18). The citizens of Athens and the 'strangers' who lived there were fascinated by all things new (Acts 17.21). Before Paul's Gentile converts were converted they were 'strangers' to the covenants of promise (Eph. 2.12), but now they are not 'strangers' any more. Those to whom the Epistle to the Hebrews was written are to beware of 'strange' doctrines (Heb. 13.9). Peter tells his friends not to regard the things that are happening to them as some 'strange' experience (I Pet. 4.12). John contrasts the brethren and the 'strangers' (III John 5). But the passage which gives the word its tone and meaning in Christian thought is the passage in Hebrews where the patriarchs were said to be 'strangers' and pilgrims all their lives (Heb. 11.13). Even so, the Christian is a *xenos*, a stranger in this world.

In the ancient world the 'stranger' had an uncomfortable

time. In the papyri a man writes that he was despised by everyone 'because I am a *xenos*, a stranger'. Another writes home to tell his people: 'Do not be anxious about me because I am away from home, for I am personally acquainted with these places and I am no *xenos*, stranger, here.' Another writes: 'It is better for you to be in your own homes, whatever they may be like, than to be *epi xenēs*, in a strange land.' In the ancient world clubs in which the members met to have a common meal were very common; and those who sat down were divided into *sundeipnoi*, fellow-members, and *xenoi*, outsiders, who are guests only on sufferance and by courtesy. A mercenary soldier who was serving in a foreign army was *xenos*, a stranger (Xenophon, *Anabasis*, 1.1.10). In Sparta the 'stranger' was automatically regarded as a 'barbarian'. *Xenos* and *barbaros* meant one and the same thing (Herodotus, 9.11).

Here then we have the truth that in this world the Christian is always a stranger; in this world he is never at home; he can never regard this world as his permanent residence. And just because of that he will always be liable to be misunderstood; he will always be liable to be looked upon as a strange character, who follows queer ways which are not the ways of other people. So long as the world is the world, the Christian must remain a stranger in it, because his citizenship is in heaven (Phil. 3.20).

The second word which describes the Christian's position in the world is the word *parepidēmos*. In classical Greek *parepidēmos* was the word of a person who had settled temporarily in a place without making it a permanent place of residence. In the NT it is used of the patriarchs, who never had a settled residence, but who were strangers and 'pilgrims' (Heb. 11.13). Peter uses it to describe the Christians who lived in Asia Minor; they were 'strangers' scattered throughout the country; they were exiles from home (I Pet. 1.1). His appeal to his people is that they should abstain from fleshly lusts which attack the soul, because they are strangers and *pilgrims* (I Pet. 2.11).

This word is used in the same way in the Septuagint. When Sarah died Abraham went to the children of Heth to ask for land wherein to bury her. He said: 'I am a stranger and a *sojourner* with you: give me a possession of a burying-place with you, that I may bury my dead' (Gen. 23.4). The Psalmist speaks of himself as a stranger and a sojourner as all his fathers were (Ps. 39.12).

The Greeks who lived at Rome called themselves *parepidēmoi* (*Polybius* 32.22.4). In the papyri a man asks for permission *parepidēmein pros kairon*, to reside temporarily in a place for a certain time; and another man is given permission to stay but he must not *parepidēmein* for more than twenty days; his temporary residence must not exceed that length of time.

The Christian is essentially a temporary resident in this world. He is a person who is essentially on the way. He may be here but his roots are not here, and his permanent home is not here. He is always living as one who is looking beyond. It so happens that this view of life was not uncommon in the great Greeks. Marcus Aurelius (2.17) said: 'Life is a warfare and a sojourn (*parepidēmia*) in a foreign land.' Diogenes Laertius (*Lives of the Philosophers*, 2.3.7) tells of a saying of Anaxagoras: 'He was eminent for wealth and noble birth, and furthermore for magnanimity, in that he gave up his patrimony to his relations. For, when they accused him of neglecting it, he replied: "Why then do you not look after it?" And at last he went into retiremen and engaged in scientific investigation without troubling himself about public affairs. When someone inquired: "Have you no concern in your native land?" gently, he said, "I am greatly concerned with my fatherland," and pointed to the sky.' Epictetus (2.23.36 ff.) draws a picture of life as he sees it: 'Men act like a traveller on the way to his own country, who stops at an excellent inn, and, since the inn pleases him, stays there. Man, you have forgotten your purpose; you were not travelling *to* this but *through* it. "But this is a fine inn." And how many other inns are fine, and how many meadows—yet simply for passing through.' Epictetus saw the world, not as the destination of the journey, but as an inn upon the way.

The word *parepidēmos* describes a man who is passing a temporary sojourn in a place, but who has no permanent residence there. The Christian does not despise the world, but he knows that for him the world is not a permanent residence but only a stage upon the way.

The third word which describes the relationship of the Christian to the world is the noun *paroikos*, with its verb *paroikein*. In classical Greek the word is more usually *metoikos*, and it describes what was known as a 'resident alien'. The resident alien was a man who came to stay in a place without being naturalized. He paid an alien tax; he was a licensed sojourner. He stayed in some place, but he had never given up citizenship of the place to which he truly belonged.

In the NT the word is used several times. God told Abraham that his descendants would 'sojourn' in a strange land (Acts 7.6). Moses was a 'stranger' in the land of Midian (Acts 7.29). On the road to Emmaus the two travellers ask the unrecognized risen Christ if he is only a 'stranger' in Jerusalem because he does not seem to know of the tragedy that has happened (Luke 24.18). When the Gentiles enter the Christian faith they are not 'strangers' to God's promises any more. But once again it is Hebrews and I Peter which give this word its special tone and emphasis and meaning. Once again Hebrews describes the patriarchs as 'sojourners', with no permanent residence (Heb. 11.9); and it is Peter's appeal that his people should keep themselves clean because they were strangers and 'pilgrims' (I Pet. 2.11).

The word *paroikos* occurs often in the Septuagint. Eleven times it translates the Hebrew word *gēr*; the *gēr* was the stranger, the proselyte, the foreigner who was a dweller within the family of Israel. Ten times it translates the word *tōshab*; the *tōshab* was the emigrant sojourning in a strange country, where he is not naturalized.

Thucydides uses the word *metoikos* to describe 'strangers' who have settled in Athens but who have never become citizens (2.13). Herodotus uses it of people in Crete who are settlers there, but not citizens of the country (4.151). It is the word which is regularly used in contrast with *politēs*, the full citizen of a country and with *katoikos*, the man who has his permanent residence there. A Carpathos inscription divides the population into two classes—*politai* and *paroikoi*, citizens and resident aliens. The governor of Priene invites to a festival *politai*, the 'citizens', *paroikoi*, the 'resident aliens', *katoikoi*, those who have their permanent residence in the town, and *xenoi*, the 'strangers' who happen to be there. The ancient world well knew the term *paroikos*; it described a man who lived within a community but whose citizenship was somewhere else.

The words were particularly used of the Jews of the Dispersion. The Jews were said to *paroikein* in Egypt and in Babylon and in the lands outside Palestine to which they went by force or by choice. To the Jew the words described a person who lived within a community and who was yet a stranger within it.

It so happened that this word became specially connected with the Christian and with the Christian Church. The Christian was exactly in this position—he lived in a community, and he undertook all the duties of that community, but his citizenship was in heaven. Clement writes his letter from the Church *paroikousē* (the present participle) at Rome to the Church *paroikousē* at Corinth. Polycarp uses the same way of speaking when he writes to the Church at Philippi. The Church was in these places, but the true home of the Church was not there. Now there comes a very interesting development. The word *paroikos* means a 'resident alien'; the verb *paroikein* meant to stay in a place, but not to be a naturalized citizen of it. So the noun *paroikia* came to mean 'a body of aliens in the midst of any community'; and it is from this word *paroikia* that the English word 'parish' is derived. The Christian community is a body of people who live in this world, but who have never accepted the standards and the methods and the ways of this world. Their standards are the standards of God. They accept the law of the place wherein they dwell, but beyond them and above them, for them there stands the law of God. The Christian is essentially a person whose only real citizenship is citizenship of the Kingdom of God.

The idea of the Christian as a stranger and a pilgrim in the world became so much part of Christian thought that it is worthwhile to consider it a little further.

(i) In the ancient world to be a stranger in a strange place was to be unhappy. It is true that there was respect for the stranger. In Greek religion one of the titles of Zeus was *Zeus Xenios*, 'Zeus, the god of strangers'; and strangers were held to be under the protection of the gods; but none the less there was a certain wretchedness in the lot of the stranger. *The Letter of Aristeas* (249) has it: 'It is a fine thing to live and to die in one's own land; a foreign land brings contempt to the poor, and to the rich it brings suspicion that they have been exiled because of some evil they have done.' Ecclesiasticus (29.22-28) has a famous and wistful passage about the lot of the stranger:

Better the life of the poor under a shelter of logs,
   Than sumptuous fare in the house of strangers.
With little or with much, be contented;
     So wilt thou not have to bear the reproach of thy
      wandering.
An evil life it is to go from house to house,
     And where thou art a stranger thou must not open thy
      mouth.
A stranger thou art in that case, and drinkest contempt;
     And besides this thou wilt have to bear bitter things:
'Come hither, sojourner, from the face of honour,
     My brother is come as my guest, I have need of my house.'
These things are grievous to a man of understanding:
     Upbraiding concerning sojourning, and the reproach of a
     money-lender.

The very fact that the Christian is a stranger and a pilgrim and a sojourner is the proof that comfort is the last thing that he can expect in life, and that an easy popularity is not for him.

(ii) This idea of the Christian as a stranger in the world is deeply rooted in the literature of the early Church. Tertullian wrote: 'The Christian knows that on earth he has a pilgrimage, but that he has his dignity in heaven' (*Apology*, 1). 'Nothing is of any importance to us in this world except to depart from it as quickly as possible' (*Apology*, 41). 'The Christian is a sojourner amongst corruptible things' (*The Letter to Diognetus*, 6.18). 'We have no fatherland on earth' (Clement of Alexandria, *Paedagogus*, 3.8.1). 'We are sojourners, unable to live happily exiled from our fatherland. We seek for a way to help us to end our sorrows and to return to our native country' (Augustine, *Concerning Christian Doctrine*, 2.4). 'We should consider, dearly beloved brethren, we should ever and anon reflect that we have renounced the world, and in the meantime are living here as guests and strangers. Let us greet the day which assigns each of us to our own home, which snatches us hence, and lifts us from the snares of the world, and restores us to Paradise and to the Kingdom. Who that has been placed in foreign lands would not hasten to return to his own country? Who that is hastening to return to his friends would not eagerly desire a prosperous gale, that he might the sooner embrace those dear to him. We regard Paradise as our country' (Cyprian, *Concerning Mortality*, 26).

(iii) At the same time it is to be noted that, although the Christians regarded themselves as strangers and pilgrims and exiles, that did not mean that they divorced themselves from ordinary life and living, and retired into a life of detached and isolated uselessness and inactivity. Tertullian writes: 'We are not like Indian Brahmins or gymnosophists, exiles from ordinary life. We live like you pagans, enjoy the same food, manner of living and dress, and have business relations everywhere' (*Apology*, 42). The greatest of all expressions of this line of thought is in *The Letter to Diognetus*. 'Christians are distinguished from the rest of men neither by country nor by language nor by customs. For nowhere do they dwell in cities of their own; they do not use any strange forms of speech or practise a singular mode of life. . . . While they dwell in both Greek and barbarian cities, each as his lot was cast, and follow the customs of the land in dress and food and other matters of living, they show forth the remarkable and admittedly strange order of their own citizenship. They live in father-lands of their own, but as aliens. They share all things as citizens, and suffer all things as strangers. Every foreign land is their fatherland, and every fatherland a foreign land. . . . They are in the flesh, but they do not live after the flesh. They pass their days on earth, but they have their citizenship in heaven' (op. cit. 5.1-9; H. G. Meecham's translation). It was by living in the world, and not by with-drawing from the world, that the Christians showed their true citizenship.

(iv) The matter may well be summed up in one of the unwritten sayings of Jesus. Dr Alexander Duff, the Scottish missionary, was travelling in India in 1849. He journeyed up the Ganges and in the town of Futehpur-Sikri, which is twenty-four miles west of Agra, he came upon a Mohammedan mosque which is one of the largest mosques in the world. The gateway was one hundred and twenty feet high and wide; and inside the gateway on the right he noticed an inscription in Arabic. It read like this: 'Jesus, on whom be peace, has said: "The world is merely a bridge: ye are to pass over it, and not to build your dwelling upon it." ' We may well believe that that saying did come from the lips of Jesus. To the Christian the world can never be an end and a goal in itself; the Christian is ever a pilgrim who is on the way.

INDEX

of English New Testament Words
with References to The Daily Study Bible

The index is arranged to provide access, through a limited number of English key words, to all the Greek words discussed or mentioned in this book, and to every mention of these words in the seventeen-volume Daily Study Bible. A separate entry has been made for every Greek form. In the case of multiple entries, the distinction between nouns, adjectives, and verbs, or between singular and plural forms, can be clarified by reference to the text.

This index was prepared by Larry K. Drake

Covetousness (*continued*)
Eph. 4:17-24; Col. 3:5-9a; II Peter 2:2, 3, 12-14.
See also Lasciviousness
Crouch, *ptōssein*, 248
DSB: Matt. 5:3

Deceit, *apatē*, 122.
See also Sin
Defraud, *pleonektein*, 233.
DSB: I Cor. 6:9-11.
See also Covetousness
Desire, *epithumein*, 123
Desire, *epithumia*, 122-3.
DSB: Rom. 1:24, 25; 13:8-10; Eph. 2:1-3; Col. 3:5-9a.
See also Sin
Despiteful. See Reproach
Devout, *eusebēs*, 106-8, 111.
See also Godliness
Divers, *poikilos*, 235-7.
DSB: Gal. 4:8-11; I Peter 1:6, 7
Dwell, *enoikein*, 119
Dwell, *oikein*, 119.
See also Sin

Earnest, *arrabōn*, 58-60.
DSB: II Cor. 1:15-22; 5:1-10; Eph. 1:11-14
Effective. See Working
Effectual working. See Working
Embark, *diakinduneuein*, 221
Endurance. See Patience
Energy. See Working

Envy. See Desire
Envy (of the gods), *phthonos theōn*, 126
Equality, *isonomia*, 69.
See also Church
Equip. See Perfect
Eternal, *aiōnios*, 33-41, 150.
DSB: Matt. 18:8, 9; 19:16-22; John 1:4; 3:1-6; 17:1-5; I John 5:11-13.
See also Called
Eternal, *ap' aiōnos*, 33
Eternal, *di' aiōnos*, 33
Eternal, *eis ton aiōna*, 33
Eternal (age), *aiōn*, 33
Everlasting. See Eternal
Example, *hupogrammos*, 138-40. DSB: I Peter 2:18-25
Example, *hupographein*, 139

Faithful, *pistos*, 155. DSB: I Tim. 6:11-16; II Peter 1:3-7; Rev. 13:10; 19:11.
See also Good
Family affection. See Love, *storgē*
Fear, *phobeisthai*, 227.
DSB: Heb. 4:1-10
Fear, *phobos*, 19, 227-32
Fellow-labourer, *sunergos*, 246
Fellowship, *koinōnein*, 173-6
Fellowship, *koinōnia*, 148, 173-6. DSB: I Cor. 16:1-12; Philemon 1-7.
See also Call

CPSIA information can be obtained at www.ICGtesting.com
Printed in the USA
BVOW08s0356151215

430308BV00001B/2/P